What the stars of stage, screen and *Strictly*
are saying about West End Producer's second book

'West End Producer is back. His book is full of all the crucial facts, naughty wit and insider knowledge that every theatregoer needs to have. Hysterically accurate, bitingly savage. Read this before buying your theatre ticket. Fab-u-lous, darling!' **Craig Revel Horwood**

'This book had me snorting prosecco out of my nostrils, dear. Hilarious yet chock full of insider tips – and some stuff we all think about the theatre we know and love, but wouldn't dare say whilst sober. Glorious.' **Meera Syal**

'Sober or drunk, this book is a hilarious, invaluable education into all things theatrical!' **Paul O'Grady**

'Once again, West End Producer has hit upon gold. Deeply insightful and often hilariously accurate, this book could sit proudly on any bedside table, educating and entertaining in equal measure.' **David Harewood**

'Entertaining and funny – I loved it! That's showbiz #dear!' **Kerry Ellis**

'Outrageously funny and disgracefully entertaining, this book had me howling with laughter. Packed full of genuine insider's insight and useful information, shot through with acerbic wit; a genuinely warm-hearted and hilarious take on the theatre world. Essential reading for all theatregoers.' **Paul Chahidi**

'West End Producer is shaping up to be the theatre's version of William Goldman: funny, astute and incisive, slyly twitching aside the curtains of the West End to reveal its most embarrassing secrets. A must for theatre-lovers (and haters), this book might as well have been entitled: *Which Lie Did I Tell, Dear?*' **Joanne Harris**

'I always have problems working out the difference between backstage and front of house, the wings and the flies. Thanks to this very funny book, I have found the solutions to all my theatrical problems.' **Jamie Lloyd**

'West End Producer's new book is exciting, fun and extremely thought-provoking. As we all know, a lot of theatre is much better seen when one is sloshed.' **Christopher Biggins**

'I cannot tell you how much I loved this book. I learnt more about theatre from it than all of my twenty-three years at the RADA. It took my breath away... though that could be my asthma.' **Con O'Neill**

'West End Producer goes to the theatre so you don't have to. But if you find you *do* have to, then this is the book for you. From what sweets to take to leaving discreetly in the interval – this important guide is a vital addition to your theatrical bookshelf.' **Reece Shearsmith**

'WEP does it again! His shrewd observation and deliciously waspish words neatly skewer and illuminate the rarefied world of theatre. I recommend everyone to read the section on what *not* to say to actors and applaud WEP's suggestion of a Theatre Prefect Programme. Theatre may be too dear – but WEP is very dear too.' **Colin Baker**

'A wonderfully witty insight into the world of theatre. Definitely five stars, this book 'tastes' great, so flick-ball change to the bookstore and grab a copy, dear.' **Louise Dearman**

'A hilarious look into all aspects of going to the theatre. Witty, funny, insightful – with enough savvy advice to save you some money as well. And I'm now an official Theatre Prefect! Marvellous, dear.' **Aled Jones**

'Absolutely f***ing hilarious. Funny, acerbic and painfully honest. If you like theatre, you have to buy this book! Six stars (out of five).' **Andy Nyman**

'Very, very funny, dear.' **David Eldridge**

'For *all* theatre fans – forget purchasing souvenir brochures/ programmes on arrival at the theatre to see your favourite show. No! Reading this book should be made compulsory whilst queuing seven deep at the bar during the interval.' **Shane Richie**

'This is a hysterical guide to all things theatre – I actually laughed out loud... not just emoji-ed it. And it's also really informative! Bravo to WEP. What a book!' **Ben Forster**

'Once more into the book, dear friends. A treat for anyone of the theatre, for the theatre or near a theatre. I laughed. I cried. It was as if WEP had written it just for me. Perhaps he did.' **Rufus Hound**

'Funny, informative and more funny. Essential reading for every theatregoer. I laughed out loud.' **Susan Penhaligon**

WEST END PRODUCER

EVERYTHING YOU ALWAYS WANTED TO KNOW ABOUT GOING TO THE THEATRE*

*BUT WERE TOO SLOSHED TO ASK, DEAR

NICK HERN BOOKS
London
www.nickhernbooks.co.uk

A NICK HERN BOOK

Everything You Always Wanted to Know About Going to the Theatre*
first published in Great Britain in 2017
by Nick Hern Books Limited, The Glasshouse,
49a Goldhawk Road, London W12 8QP

Author photo by Matt Crockett (www.mattcrockett.com)
Designed and typeset by Nick Hern Books

Printed and bound in Great Britain by
Ashford Colour Press, Gosport, Hampshire

A CIP catalogue record for this book is available
from the British Library

ISBN 978 1 84842 588 0

MIX
Paper from
responsible sources
FSC
www.fsc.org   FSC® C011748

But Were Too Sloshed to Ask, Dear

For my Lloyd Webber glove puppet, my Jean Valjean teddy and my Miss Saigon *blow-up doll*

Constant companions who always listen, never talk back, and let me drink as much as I want

Contents

One book more!
Another book, another destiny!

Acknowledgements

My dears. Firstly, I must thank *you*: the theatre-lovers who are reading this book, who engage with my articles, respond to my tweets, smile at press nights, and grope me in Soho. I cannot express my gratitude enough. You have kept me writing and producing, always masked, always mocking (in a loving, affectionate sort of way). And for that, my jazz hands are always ready for you, waiting in the wings, ready to be displayed.

To the people who help #keepthesecret, resisting the temptation to unmask me and let everyone see how good looking I actually am. You are the trusted ones who allow me to continue my naughty quest for theatrical escapades and adventures. To Trevor, Matt, Jon, Harvey, Alistair, Tim, Mark, Anne, Linda and those I can't mention: thank you.

To all the actors, performers, creatives, technicians, front-of-house staff, wiggies, crew, and everyone who works in this ridiculous business called 'show'. I admire each and every one of you. You work in an industry that makes no guarantees, is full of ups and downs, and denies the usual advancement of a career ladder. However, the community of theatre, and the spirit of those who dedicate their lives to it is unlike any other. It is a vocation, a playground, a brave and brilliant choice – and I am humbled to play a little role in it. To you all: keep going, keep challenging, and keep creating. You inspire more of us than you know.

A huge thank-you to everyone at Nick Hern Books, who took the plunge by allowing me to bother them with my silly ideas. Again. And especially to Matt Applewhite – my editor, advisor and friend – once again, an immense pleasure to work (and drink) with you. Your patience and humour know no bounds. You have laughed, guided, and whipped me whenever my mind wandered and I started moaning about another bloody awful jukebox musical. Bless you.

And finally, to my dear family. No matter what ridiculous choices I make, and impertinent moods I get in – your constant support, love and counselling keeps me going.

With much love to you all,
WEP
x

Please note: If your name isn't mentioned above, then you failed to give me a decent-enough Christmas present last year. I expect *at least* a £50 Fortnum & Mason voucher. It's your own bloody fault. Put your hand in your pocket next time, dear.

The Audience Announcement

Ladies and gentlemen. Welcome! This book will begin in five minutes. Please make your way to your seats.

Ladies and gentlemen. Good evening. This book will begin in three minutes. I repeat, three minutes. Please make your way to your seats and settle down, or the front-of-house staff will get upset.

Ladies and gentlemen. Tonight's book will begin in two minutes. That's two minutes. Please decant your nasty, overpriced wine into a plastic beaker and find your seat. Otherwise we will force you to watch the latest touring version of *Dirty Dancing*.

Ladies and gentlemen. This book will begin in one minute. I repeat one minute. Go to your seats NOW – or we'll set Elaine Paige on you.

Ladies and gentlemen. The show is about to start. Please can all cameras, phones, recording equipment, pacemakers, lawnmowers and vibrators be turned off. Thank you for your cooperation.

Ladies and gentlemen. This book has now started. If you're late, we have no option but to slap you with the *Complete Works of William Shakespeare* and force you to wait front of house. Then after twenty minutes you'll be ushered into the auditorium, where you'll embarrass yourself and everyone else as you clumsily find your seat. And finally when you get settled you'll realise you have no idea what the hell the show is about anyway. Well, that's your fault for going to see a Stoppard, isn't it, dear?

The Overture

What is Theatre?

A theatre is a place where one group of people go to watch another group of people perform – the audience sit and stare, and the actors stand and shout. Put the onlookers and the talent together (or the 'untalent' if it's the cast of *TOWIE*) and hey presto, you have theatre.

You don't actually need to be in a building called 'a theatre' to create the art form called 'theatre'. As good old Peter Brook said, theatre can take place in any 'empty space', ranging from indoors to outdoors – everything from old warehouses, open park spaces, even the toilets at Waterloo Station. If people are staring and actors are emoting – it's theatre.

Theatre dates back to when Jesus was born – when the first Nativity Play took place for an audience of shepherds, kings, a host of angels, and some extras from *Emmerdale* (sheep). Since that moment, people from across the globe have dedicated their lives to this sacred art form. And its popularity, like Katie Price's lips, gets bigger every year.

Theatres are shrines where people go to escape – to forget the mundanities of life, the miserable weather, and the decline of *The X Factor* – in the hope of experiencing jazz

1

hands, step-ball changes, and sweaty famous people. It is a place where people dress up in their new jumpsuits and pay good money to see their favourite actors pose, dribble, and talk in posh accents (you can occasionally find actors talking in regional accents, but the RSC is trying to eradicate this vulgar practice). It should leave audiences feeling positive, inspired and enlightened, and, unlike so many things in life, there are no adverts, no pause buttons, and no escape once the show has started. Yes, that's right. You are *trapped*, dear.

About This Book

This book should be treated like a theatre trip. Read it any weeknight at 7.30 p.m. for two hours (or three hours if you're a fan of *Les Mis*) – and during the afternoon on Wednesdays/Thursdays and Saturdays for some light matinee studying. You may be particularly eager to prove your theatrical dedication by reading it on a Sunday as well, but if you do it is vital you have Monday off. You don't want to get overexcited and have a premature showgasm.

Whilst my first book reveals everything you need to know about acting (including some things you perhaps don't need to know), this book explores every orifice of the theatre-*going* experience. From booking your tickets to finding the quickest route to the ladies' loos, this indispensible guide will assist you on your quest to watch the hits and avoid the shits, whether you're an unblemished theatrical virgin or a sullied, show-guzzling slut.

My focus is unashamedly on London's West End – I am *West End* Producer, after all (speak to Regional Touring Producer if you want a book from her) – but most of the tips and tricks of the trade can be applied when you visit any theatre, anywhere in the known universe. And probably the unknown universes too, once they're discovered. Theatre is *nothing* if not multiversal.

Each chapter looks at different challenges of going to the theatre. Act One helps you decide what to see and how to see it; Act Two deals with how to get there and what to do when you arrive; Act Three looks at how a show gets made (and how many actors are culled in the process); Act Four deals with the essential matter of how to leave the theatre (in a hurry); and the Act Five finale explores the haunts and hide-aways of London's West End for when you want to venture back.

Sprinkled throughout the book, like hundreds and thousands over a trifle of already-unimaginable delights, there are potted histories of some of my favourite musicals that have attacked and assaulted the stage. You will have heard of most of them, in fact a few of them will have been impossible to miss – but it may be useful to know a little bit more about how they came to be legends of the West End. Did you know, for instance, that *Miss Saigon* was originally going to be called *Miss Blackpool*, but it had to be relocated after Jane McDonald pulled out at the last minute? But I suppose 'The Heat is On in Blackpool' doesn't have the same ring to it, dear.

....

Some are born great, some achieve greatness, and some have greatness when they thrust.

....

ACT ONE: TO GO, OR NOT TO GO?

'...That is the question.
Whether 'tis nobler in the mind to suffer
The slings and arrows of outrageous show lengths,
Or to take arms against such wasted evenings
And by avoiding them, end them.'

I'm not a morning person. I'm not an afternoon person. I'm a 'crawl out of bed at 5 p.m. and go to the theatre' kind of person.

You've decided you want to go to the theatre. Bravo! You won't regret it (I hope – and if you do, don't blame me). But which show, which star, and which seat? With so many shows and dodgy celebs posing up and down the country, the task of choosing what to see and what to miss can be daunting. Fear not! This chapter tells you everything you'll ever need to know about booking your ticket, and more importantly, how to avoid watching *Joseph and the Amazing Technicolor Dreamcoat* ever again.

What to See

One of the most vital things you need to decide before going to a show is what kind of show you want to see. You're going to be parting with several months' worth of salary (or a decade's worth of pocket money if you've got youth on your side), so you want to be sure you'll enjoy it. There is no point going to watch a musical if you actually want to watch a play. Or see Miranda Hart if you want to see Lin-Manuel Miranda. Or go to the Arts Theatre if you want to see something good. It sounds simple, but you'd be surprised at how easy it is to get confused.

The Types of Theatre

So, what types of theatre productions are available for your viewing pleasure? And will you like all of them? Let's have a closer look...

Play – A play with lots of talking, lots of walking, and – depending on the sobriety of the cast – lots of bumping into the furniture. Sometimes called 'straight theatre', which makes no sense at all in a business where most people aren't.

Gray Play – A play that contains actors who can display at least fifty different shades of emotions – and who are rather good at spanking.

XXX Play – A play which has nudity. Or partial nudity. Or a nipple.

Ray – Ray Cooney (of farcical fame); Ray Davies (of The Kinks/*Sunny Afternoon* fame) or just Ray (the name of a bloke sitting in the upper circle).

Musical – A show where there is singing, dancing and acting – sometimes at the same time (only guaranteed if the performer is a Strallen).

Play with Music – A play that has a couple of songs in it. Or some actors humming and squealing for dramatic effect. It's really a regular play with a couple of bars of music added so it can be advertised as having 'live music'.

Actor-Musician Shows – A show with actors who play instruments whilst on stage doing other things at the same time. However, there is always someone in the cast who can't play an instrument at all – this person just blows hard and hopes for the best. These days, the craft of actor-musicianship is a highly trained skill – with actors playing numerous instruments, often tap dancing at the same time

– which is particularly impressive with a double bass. However, at some theatres no instruments are required as the actors simply play with themselves (very popular at the Royal Court Theatre Upstairs).

Dance – A show where there is no talking, no singing, and no acting – just dancers in tight Lycra® jumping up and down to highlight their panty region. As a general rule, the bigger the panty region, the better the performer.

Physical Theatre – A show where actors pretend to be Transformers and contort their bodies into every position possible. Physical-theatre productions involve actors hurling each other around and bending their bodies into impossible positions. Competition to appear in these shows is so intense that actors even resort to having bones removed so they can bend further than newly graduated students from the Laban Centre (otherwise known as the London Academy of Bendily Appendaged Nancies). The very best physical-theatre performers can put their head between their legs and make it disappear up their arse.

Opera – The most expensive theatrical event. It is a well-known fact that the word 'opera' stands for 'Only People Earning Ridiculous Amounts', because these are the only people who can afford to see it. An opera production will have no talking, no dancing and no acting – just a lot of shouting with as much vibrato as possible. This vibrato shouting is performed on a lavish set that has nothing whatsoever to do with the show, upon which the performers wander around, pose, gurn and emote. Often operas are performed in a foreign language – but this will soon be illegal due to Brexit.

Talkie – A play with lots of talking.

Silent – A play with no talking.

Pinter – A play with lots of pauses.

Comedy – A show that is supposed to be funny. But is often not. In which case it is labelled a 'black comedy'.

Tragedy – A play with death, blood, crying and arguments. Easily confused with modern comedies.

Site-specific – A show that takes place in a different kind of venue than a typical theatre. Places like warehouses, nightclubs, graveyards, swimming pools, and Louie Spence's boudoir are very popular.

Performance Art – A show that can be absolutely anything. It is a term directors give to a piece when they have no idea what the hell the show is actually about. It's confusing for the cast, and confusing for the audience. But performance art always gets five stars in reviews – because if art is confusing then it's got to be good, dear.

3D entertainment has been around for years. It's called 'Theatre', dear.

Once you've decided on a type of theatre production, the next step is to choose which specific show you want to see. There are numerous listings websites which will tell you what's on stage currently: WhatsOnStage.com and Official-LondonTheatre.co.uk being two of the best and most comprehensive, with the former having exhaustive coverage of theatre across the whole of the UK. But how to choose between the literally hundreds of shows on offer?

I've always thought it would be quite useful if audience members could have a little look at each show before you decide on which one to commit to. Something like a 'taster' ticket that allows you to wander from side seats in all West End theatres and watch a couple of minutes. This would mean you could watch the famous bits in Les Mis, experience the thrill of Harry Potter playing with his wand, and discover the best moment in Thriller Live (the end). It would also allow you to avoid anything that's playing at the Shaftesbury Theatre altogether. But most people do that anyway.

Of course, you can always get a free sneak peek of shows by viewing their trailers online, or by attending events like West End Live (a yearly celebration of West End shows in Trafalgar Square), or by watching the Royal Variety Performance (if you're really desperate). Show websites are also very useful as they will have production photos, videos and background information about each show. You can even listen to cast recordings or watch filmed versions of the show. But be warned – never judge the theatre production by its silver-screen version. I know many people who were put off watching Les Mis after seeing the film. But everyone knows that was Russell Crowe's fault.

If you're already a fan of a show then obviously that's a good one to see. But if you've not heard of a production, or it's an entirely new piece, then some simple research is required. Google reviews, write a dissertation, consult a fortune-teller and attend some focus groups. And then, most importantly – have a look at the cast list. This is a vital part in your show-hunting decision-making. See if you notice any famous names, or actors you've seen in previous productions – and make sure there are at least five members of the cast who are pretty bloody sexy (difficult in a two-hander). This is the best way to make a decision: go to the show that has the highest number of gorgeous people in it. Then, if the show gets boring, and the actors do too much talking, you can simply stare and drool. After all, you've paid £50 for your ticket; the least you deserve is a semi in the stalls. The number of stalls-semis that occur every night at Wicked is remarkable. People are clearly kinky for green. And flying monkeys.

'Acclaimed' doesn't always mean good. Sometimes it means 'A boring, long, try-hard production that I didn't really understand – but it had lots of impressive words in it.'

Reviews

If you want to know what professional theatregoers think of the shows on offer, then you can search online to read the reviews. Reviews can be very insightful, as they give a good understanding of the show and often include production photos, which is particularly useful if you want to assess the attractiveness of the cast. Never base your theatregoing choices on just one review – dedicate your time to reading thousands. Remember that critics, just like regular audience members, have favourite performers they fancy.

It can be very telling when looking at a show's advertising if all the quotes are from publications or webshites that no one has ever heard of. For example:

'Ruthie was brilliant!' – *ruthiehenshall.biz*

'I loved every minute!' – *westendwilliam.net*

'The songs will stay inside me for ever!' – *musicaltheatredildos.co.uk*

It is also concerning if the reviews quoted are from local publications, and none from the national press – like the *Salford Journal*, *Northern Echo* and *Runcorn Reader's Wives*. This suggests that the locals loved it (the locals always love it), but the nationals thought it was rubbish. You can also make quite astute assumptions if reviewers say things like 'energetic', 'colourful', 'fun' and 'I couldn't wait for it to end'.

Remember that the more stars a show receives, the more free booze the critics were given in the interval. If a show is awarded zero stars then the critic was given nothing to slurp on at all (not even an understudy). If it's one star, the critic was given a small glass of house wine. Two stars, they were also given a bag of nuts. Three stars, they were given a selection of drinks and a Scotch egg. Four stars, they were treated to unlimited drinks and a bag of any salty snack they desired. And five stars means they were given a free bar, three-course meal, complimentary programme, and a backstage tour by the cast member of their choice.

The Types of Star Rating

Aside from the amount of alcohol imbibed, what does a review's number of stars actually mean?

Zero stars (the show is 0–10% good) – This rarely happens, but when it does, you can guarantee that the show is a real stinker. Giving a show zero stars means the reviewer didn't even feel they could award one for sheer effort. A no-star show means you will undoubtedly have more fun staying at home listening to Marti Pellow's musical-theatre CD, which is saying something. Zero stars is like burnt toast – it showed potential, but was ruined by a lack of judgement.

One star (10–25%) – The show is bad. It may have a couple of nice moments and a decent set, but usually your time is better spent reading Elaine Paige's biography. In other words – don't waste your time. Unless it's starring someone you want to sleep with. In which case, go along. They'll be so impressed by your dedication that you'll be awarded a quickie in the stalls. One star is like eating a McDonald's – it leaves you depressed, even though it's called a Happy Meal.

Two stars (25–45%) – The show is okay. But generally try to avoid it. It will have a lot of shouting, some mumbling, and plenty of crass acting (cracting). However, it may still be worth going if there's a celeb in it, because there's nothing as satisfying as watching a famous person being bad. Chandler Bing felt the wrath of two-star reviews in London. Bless. I'm not sure his friends even turned up to watch. Two stars is like eating a sandwich from WH Smith – it's attempting to be M&S, but never will be.

Three stars (45–65%) – The show is average. There's a nice bit of drama in there, and maybe some tuneful singing – but something doesn't quite work. There may even be a couple of really good routines, and some acting that seems on a par with Dot Cotton. Three is the most common number of stars that is awarded. It's when a reviewer doesn't feel they can say the show is actually bad, but doesn't want to say it's that good either. It basically signifies bland. A bit like a goat's cheese pizza – it sounds like a good idea, but isn't.

Four stars (65–85%) – This is a very slick production, with lots of attractive people saying lines in the correct order. The set won't wobble, the actors will be nicely lit, and you'll leave feeling like you haven't wasted your money. But there won't be any nudity, hence the lack of a fifth star. Four stars is like a Sunday roast at a Toby Carvery – it's value for money, with plenty to digest, and you'll invariably go back for seconds.

Five stars (85–100%) – This is a production that not only looks nice, it *tastes* nice as well. It will have a good story, acting so strong that you can hear every word (unless there's a film star in it – in which case mumbling is guaranteed), and a set that moves forwards *and* backwards. It will usually have nudity of some kind – whether this be a chorus of bare chests or a lonely resonating willy (particularly prevalent in productions starring Daniel Radcliffe and a horse). There will be moments when the actors shout, talk, aimlessly walk around, sing, jump, vacantly stare into the audience, ball change, run, spit, cry, and sometimes even do the splits.

(I will never forget Jonathan Pryce memorably doing the splits as Macbeth. He kept getting lower and lower during his 'Tomorrow, and tomorrow, and tomorrow' soliloquy, until finally his bottom reached the floor on 'Signifying nothing'. Heartbreaking.) A five-star show will be comprised of attractive people, a couple of older actors, some unblemished graduates and one person who has been on *Downton Abbey*. And of course it will have lots of dramatic pausing, because everyone knows that good acting is all about good pausing. A five-star show is like eating an à la carte meal freshly prepared by Jamie Oliver, without the slightest aroma of Gordon Ramsay anywhere.

Different critics have different preferences about what makes them roll over and fall asleep or get moist and stand to attention. And the criteria used to decide between zero stars and five varies from reviewer to reviewer. Whereas one may never award that stellar five stars, another may award a full constellation every time they see a new musical – largely because they want to support this genre. It's another reason why you can't solely rely on reviews and star ratings to make your decision. Reading reviews regularly – or online round-ups of reviews – will help you find the critics you agree with and whose opinions you trust, and those who have you reaching for the nearest can of critical insecticide.

Reviews and the ratings system would be a lot easier to understand if shows added together their number of stars and calculated the average – as a poster full of three, four and five stars is terribly confusing. It would be far more useful to be presented with a single star rating: *Matilda* – average star rating 5, *Charlie and the Chocolate Factory* – average star rating 2. Alternatively, every show could just add together the total number of stars it receives and the higher the number, the better the show: *Curious Incident of the Dog in the Night-Time* – 120, *Stephen Ward* – 28. I'll have a word with *The Stage* and see if they can sort it.

We are very lucky in the UK to have some of the best theatre critics in the world – knowledgeable, passionate, engaged, enthusiastic – and reviewing has become an art in its own right. The role of a critic is very important – a host of bad reviews can close a show. But equally, a plethora of good ones can allow a show to run for years. As well as writing reviews, some of our most influential critics have also written specialist books in this field. We have been treated to books on playwriting, theatrical history, actors' biographies, and the correct way to pronounce 'Ralph Fiennes'.

Worryingly, in some quarters, experienced and skilled arts criticism is now threatened with extinction. Several national newspapers have dispensed with their theatre critics, some of whom had been writing for them for years. But why has this happened? It's partly to do with the diminishing value placed on expertise, and partly to do with the expense of employing specialist critics in a newspaper industry desperate to cut its costs (to pay its legal bills).

Additionally, the role of the online critic, the blogger, and the tweeter has risen, meaning that shows get reviewed online, and for free, by hundreds of theatregoers. Check out message boards – where as well as finding out what people are recommending, you can also catch up on the latest theatrical gossip. Theatreboard.co.uk is one of the most popular, with some incredibly knowledgeable (and sometimes beautifully bitchy) regular contributors, and there's also a comprehensive message board on Broadwayworld.com. Get on these sites, log in, and start making theatrical friends. It's a bit like Tinder – swipe left if you like musicals, right if you like plays, and log out if you like Chekhov.

Twitter is also a vital marketing tool for productions – if someone tweets anything positive then it can be used as an instant quote for marketing purposes. Likewise, a negative reaction, sometimes thoughtlessly expressed, can be seen and shared immediately. Overall, though, Twitter is the ultimate democracy: everyone's opinions count, and everyone can be involved in promoting and valuing live theatre (unless your username is @thequentinletts).

But just as important is the professional theatre critic – whose opinions (and ability to write about them) have been honed and crafted over years of experience. If a respected critic endorses a show, it implies it will be of a certain standard. Also, just like almost everyone in the theatre industry, critics don't get paid very much – and they should be admired more for their contribution to the arts. Put simply, the theatre needs critics, just as critics need theatre – they are respected for what they do, and their analysis not only helps sell tickets, but also can help the development of a play. Many regional productions change significantly before they arrive in the West End, with the early 'out-of-town' reviews taken into consideration when shows are reworked and improved for a transfer. Such a shame there was no try-out run for *Viva Forever!*

Some directors say they never read reviews – and that's fair enough. But we producers, the marketing team, and most of the actors do (whether they admit it or not) – and it does have an effect on a show. And this is a truth. If a show is badly reviewed, an audience comes with a preconceived idea. The same applies with brilliant reviews – it all helps aid the experience for audiences. Even a one-star review in *Playboy* will help sell tickets to a certain type of audience member. Just pray you're not sitting next to them.

....

Just received a lovely Father's Day card. But I really wish he wouldn't. Every year I tell Michael Ball I'm not his dad.

....

A Review of Reviewers

Just as there are many different types of theatre, there are also different types of reviewers. There are big ones, small ones, bald ones, hairy ones, male ones, female ones, aroused ones, happy ones, drunk ones, and even ones that gave *Shrek* four stars. Ridiculous.

The Old Pros – These are Britain's longest-serving critics, and are admired for their stamina, intelligence and dedication in sitting through so much rubbish over the years. The old pros are so admired that one of them has even been awarded an OBE by Ma'am, and she only does that to people she *really* likes. These reviewers are seen as being rather reliable, sometimes staid, and fairly traditional in their likes and dislikes. Some of them even lecture at universities, colleges, and late-night drinking dens in Soho.

The Enthusiasts – The enthusiasts are those daring critics who as well as writing about shows also write their own ones. Bravo to any critic who allows his own work to be criticised by the people he has criticised as a critic. The enthusiast is a jolly person, regularly seen around town clasping a glass of vino. They are basically fans with a pen – not the most discerning or critical, but always appreciated and admired for their enthusiasm and encouragement. These critics are also sometimes known as 'Poster Whores' – who like writing nice things so their names appear on all the posters and advertising material.

The Shit-Stirrers – This type of reviewer ruffles a few feathers, with their trenchant politics and penchant for vitriol. Not many theatre people like shit-stirrers, but then again, shit-stirrers don't really like many theatre people. In fact, sometimes it seems they don't like or appreciate the theatre full stop, especially when it's got Arts Council funding.

They certainly don't appear to appreciate theatre's joys, and often don't seem to know what they're talking about. The reviews by shit-stirrers can be so extreme that they've been known to be banned from press nights. They can always get around this by buying their own balcony ticket and reviewing from up there, of course. Naughty naughty, dear.

The Bitter Queens – The bitter queen has been around a bit – doing criticism duties for thirty plus years. That's a lot of shows. The bitter queen finds it hard to be impressed by shows these days, possibly because they're disillusioned by the whole thing, and don't get as much free champagne as they used to. This reviewer avoids people they've criticised by hiding in the gents toilets for several days.

The Mother Hens – Mother hens are big believers in the power of theatre, and are particularly passionate about children's theatre and new work – some mother hens even write children's stories themselves. Hard-working and talented wordsmiths, mother hens can seemingly cover every show, in every theatre, throughout the land – and for years speculation has been rife that there are actually dozens of mother hens out there filing reviews under one or two reviewers' bylines.

The Teddy Bears – These reviewers are cuddly bears, who shuffle along to press nights and get angry if their seats are uncomfortable. The teddy-bear reviewer spends their weekends relaxing at home, writing, and dreaming of reclining theatre seats – or rewatching shows they've already seen a dozen times.

The Angry Young Men (or Women) – These reviewers have very strong ideas about what a show should be. They don't take it on its own terms, and complain about why it's not like a Simon Stephens or Ivo van Hove production. Their reviews are mostly about if a show is cool and edgy (because they like to be thought of as cool and edgy themselves). They write primarily for a younger audience at *Time Out*, *Exeunt*, and various online sites – and can be spotted tweeting and taking interval selfies in their favourite theatre toilets.

Overall, all the professional reviewers offer a brilliantly varied voice for our industry. In fact, they see so many shows that I'm sure none of them get the chance to follow *Strictly Come Dancing*. And that's real dedication. So they all get five stars from me.

Of course, if reading all the reviews seems like too much hard work, just ask your family and friends. You'll soon find out who your favourite auntie is (the one who tells you to avoid the four-hour version of *Gone with the Wind*).

You know a show is not very good when they try to cover it with smoke.

Awards

As well as the reviews, another barometer for whether a show is good, bad or downright ugly is if it's won any awards. There are numerous different ceremonies dedicated to celebrating British theatre – and whilst most of them are good and worthwhile, some are bad and utterly pointless. Most take place during those wintry months of January through to April, so that everyone without coats gets freezing cold and perky nipples on the red carpet.

A Guide to Theatre Awards

Here are the major theatre awards taking place annually in the UK each year. I've also revealed who's most likely to win each award (so hurry down to William Hill now) – and, from my own personal experience (well, my cleaner, Hilda's), how to keep them nice and shiny.

Olivier Awards (olivierawards.com)

The biggest, glitziest night of the British theatre calendar, everyone wants to get their hands on one of these little Larrys. The Oliviers celebrate London theatre, and winning one can change an actor's career nearly as much as if they go on *Celebrity Masterchef*. After 2017, these awards are officially being renamed the Harry Potter Awards.

Who Wins Them

They're voted for by commercial producers and theatre owners (and a handful of members of the public), so no prizes for guessing who goes home with these prizes... (Clue: it's not the public.)

How to Dust Them

It's a bust of Olivier's head, all dolled up like his legendary Henry V – tricky to get your feather duster into all the little crevices of his cape and crown.

Evening Standard Theatre Awards

These glamorous awards, presented by the *Evening Standard* newspaper, celebrate the best celebs who have appeared in theatre productions in London over the past year.

Who Wins Them

Film stars, mates of Evgeny Lebedev, and people who look nice in the *Evening Standard*'s glossy magazine.

How to Dust Them

The trophy is a statuette of a figure sitting on a toilet holding the tragedy and comedy masks – a quick Brasso rub-down will make him shine brightly.

WhatsOnStage Awards (awards.whatsonstage.com)

Voted for by the general public (whether they've actually seen the show or not), these annual 'theatregoers' choice' awards are a fantastic celebration of what's been on stage – and who's popular in any given year.

Who Wins Them

If you've been in *Harry Potter*, *Doctor Who*, *Sherlock* or your name is Tom Hiddleston, make space on your mantelpiece.

How to Dust Them

Very easy – a smooth, wipe-clean Perspex paperweight.

Critics' Circle Theatre Awards (criticscircle.org.uk)

The winners of these awards are selected by the drama section of the Critics' Circle. The Critics' Circle is a bit like the Magic Circle, but whilst the magicians make rabbits disappear, the Critics' Circle can do it to actors.

Who Wins Them

Theatre folk from up and down the country – it's a nice, fair process as the judges vote independently, free of discussion and industry influence. Bravo.

How to Dust Them

The award is a lovely certificate in a black John Lewis frame – so a little polish with some Mr Muscle will do the job nicely.

The Offies (offwestend.com)

The Offies (Off West End Theatre Awards) celebrate independent theatre across London – basically those productions taking place above pubs or in smelly rooms near public toilets. They are hugely important, as they help raise the profile of the creative brilliance that can be found in some of London's off West End and fringe theatres.

Who Wins Them

Performers and creatives who are now skint due to being involved in the profit-share show they've won the award for.

How to Dust Them

The awards are presented in a Twitter ceremony, so everyone's welcome and you don't even need to dress up to attend. The prize-winners also get a certificate, but this time it's in an Ikea frame (due to budget limitations).

Manchester Theatre Awards
(manchestertheatreawards.com)

Formerly the Manchester Evening News Theatre Awards, these wonderful awards, as the name suggests, are for productions in and around the glittering cultural destination that is Manchester. A lovely city, but one I haven't dared visit ever since Liam Gallagher threatened to 'stab me in the fookin' eye' at the first-night party of a tour of *Seven Brides for Seven Brothers*. At least, I think that's what he said – to be honest, I couldn't really understand him, dear.

Who Wins Them

Actors based oop north, actors who can do a convincing northern accent, and actors who have been on *Corrie*.

How to Dust Them

Housed in an attractive presentation box, the trophy is a glass plate on a stand – easy to clean, but also very easy to break. Nothing a bit of superglue can't fix.

UK Theatre Awards (uktheatre.org)

These are the only awards to honour achievements in regional theatre throughout England, Scotland, Wales, Northern Ireland, and Butlins Bognor Regis.

Who Wins Them

Theatre professionals from all areas of the UK who can afford a return rail fare to London to collect their award.

How to Dust Them

A shiny, circular glass award that is best cleaned with a damp cloth and strong wrist movement.

The Stage Awards (thestage.co.uk/awards)

These marvellous awards are presented by *The Stage*, and are presented to all types of theatres and performers around the country: fringe, regional, West End – these awards celebrate them all. *The Stage* also present their Debut Awards to people making their debut in theatre – and are now considering introducing Old Fart Theatre Awards for professionals over the age of sixty-five. Yes please, dears!

Who Wins Them

Theatres, actors and creatives from around the country (as long as they have an annual subscription to *The Stage*). There's also an Unsung Hero Award, a lovely tribute to an individual who has gone 'above and beyond the call of duty in their work in the performing-arts industry'. It's generally awarded to someone who's been doing a thankless role, for no public acclaim, for decades on end, and always brings a genuine tear to my eye. Inspiring.

How to Dust Them

Another attractive glass award, these ones are best cleaned using a dry cloth, a bit of spit, and a gentle rotating motion.

Show Classifications

It can prove difficult to gauge the audience a show is aiming to attract – particularly with some of the mixed messages in advertising. Only recently I was speaking to a family who went to see *The Book of Mormon* believing it was a comedy for kids – but they quickly changed their mind after hearing the fifth swear word being sung. Consequently their youngest daughter now runs around shrieking 'I have maggots in my scrotum' whilst getting ready for school.

Different productions, like any form of entertainment, are suitable for audiences of different ages. Many shows are unsuitable for five-year-olds, just as some are unsuitable for fifty-five-year-olds. No unaccompanied adult should be forced to endure a *Teletubbies* tour, with its cast of well-disguised RADA graduates leaping about in oversized primary-coloured costumes, shouting 'Eh-Oh!' and playing with their Noo-Noo (that's their vacuum-cleaner by the way, dear). Or, if they *do* want to be there, well, then they probably shouldn't be. Instead, to avoid such experiences, theatre should come with appropriate age-ratings, like the well-established code of film classification.

There needs to be more transparency about the target audience, and clues about the content. A very simple system of symbols could work. For example, a play could be identified by a script; a musical with Lloyd Webber's head; an opera with a fat man with his mouth open; and a ballet with a tutu. If the show has elements of all of the above, the symbol could be a fat man in a tutu hitting Lloyd Webber with a script. Who wouldn't pay to see that?

To avoid confusion, certain writers could have their own symbols. A Shakespeare play would be designated with a giant S in a wooden O, Chekhov by a C in a samovar, and Berkoff with a big red J (for 'Jerkoff', dear).

And like the labels on food, theatre would do well to provide an estimation of how many calories are supplied in each theatrical serving. It's a little-known fact that just watching an energetic musical – such as *Footloose*, *Flashdance*, *FootDance* or *Flasher-loose* – will help you burn the fat. And obviously twice as much if you've had to splutter your way up to the balcony.

....

'Fame! I'm gonna live forever, I'm gonna learn how to die (onstage every night).'

....

The Types of Classification

Here's a simple but practical system of classification which could usefully be introduced with immediate effect. You're welcome.

S-U – A Shakespeare play suitable for all – so one that has been adapted to be suitable for children, with no references to Titania having sex with a donkey.

S-15 – A Shakespeare play with some fighting, long speeches, and actors behaving like they're in *Game of Thrones*.

S-18 – An avant-garde Shakespeare production. Normally European, with lots of nudity and sex inserted (in every sense). Or any production of *Titus Andronicus*.

M-U – A musical suitable for all, like *Starlight Express* (although some of the trains in the Bochum production display so much flesh that it's being renamed *Starlight XXXpress*).

M-15 – A musical for ages 15 and over. With a chorus of light sexy titillation and bare-chested chorus boys. Usually found in the most intimate of fringe venues (where if you reach out far enough you can even touch a real-life actor).

M-18 – A musical that has adult content – like *Miss Saigon*, which involves fighting, ping-pong balls, and a big chopper.

P-U – A play suitable for all. Involving lots of embarrassed classically trained actors running around desperately trying to hide their faces underneath big costumes– 'I didn't train for three years to do this, dear.'

P-15 – A play that has bad accents, mild violence, and at least one monologue over ten minutes in length.

P-18 – A play for over-eighteens only. My favourite. With blood, violence, nudity, shouting, drinking, big sound effects, and a massive lighting rig. All of which used to be found at Shakespeare's Globe (until the board put a stop to it because they were all underage).

R (Restricted) – Anything involving Jim Davidson.

'Just as theatre is competitive to work in, it is equally as competitive to watch,' said anyone trying to get tickets for *Hamilton*.

How to Book

Having decided what to see, the next thing to do is to book your tickets – otherwise you face the pain and exhaustion of travelling to the West End only to discover that the show of your choice is sold out and the only thing left is *The Mousetrap*. How disappointing, dear.

It's a sad truth, universally acknowledged, that theatre can be expensive for everyone involved. Believe me, it's expensive to produce with all the colossal costs involved: all those cavernous venues to hire, those sweaty actors on stage to pay, plus those jealous actors working front of house, the priapic musicians and technicians in the dark, the royalties to creatives, and the frocks and the tap shoes, and the confetti cannons, and the crates of Dom, and the posters on the Tube, and VAT at 20%, and, and, and... The list goes on, and I feel a bit faint just thinking about it all. So it's no wonder that it's expensive for the audience to see as well. Or is it?

If I had a pound for every time I'd heard someone say 'Theatre is too blinkin' expensive for me' – well, I'd be able to afford a premium seat at the Piccadilly. The thing is: there are lots of ways to get into theatre for less than you might think, you just don't know about them yet. So trust these tips and you'll be settling down in your seat faster than you can say 'Dame Judi Dench'.

Official Websites

One of the easiest and quickest ways to book your tickets is to use theatre websites. Nowadays there are as many of these as there are shows in Lloyd Webber's back catalogue. A simple way of knowing if a website is legitimate is by checking its spelling. The amount of times I've seen ticket agencies list *The Lion King* as *The Loin King* is really quite worrying (unless of course *The Loin King* is another show entirely – in which case, somebody please send me a ticket). When booking these tickets, always compare the price on a few different sites, and be aware of last-minute fees – like booking fees, which are added for no reason whatsoever, but to make the ticketing company more money.

Several of the booking websites are owned and run by the theatre owners – and these can be a good place to start: Delfont Mackintosh, the Ambassador Theatre Group, Really Useful Theatres and Nimax all have their own. Again, make sure you're on the correct website. For example, when searching for Nimax don't book the Imax, and remember that ATG is not the BFG (although everyone loves a big friendly giant).

Most West End theatres also add a 'restoration fee' onto the ticket price nowadays. If you examine your tickets you will notice this in small print at the bottom. It's usually for a sum of around £1.50 – which initially doesn't sound too much. But with the ticket price, booking fee and service charge (not to mention your travel, accommodation, programme, mer-chandise, interval ice cream and Dom), it can all add up.

The restoration fee is added to ticket prices to generate funds to restore older buildings. Sometimes there is little evidence of where and what this money is being spent on, particularly when the toilets are permanently blocked, the seats cause piles, and the ceilings fall in. Three cheers (and one more for luck), though, for Cameron Mackintosh, who has put the glitter back into London's glittering West End, and beautifully renovated venues such as his Prince of Wales, his Prince Edward and, my own personal favourite, his Prince Albert.

Discount Websites

A browserful of websites now exist that can aid your quest for cheaper or sometimes free theatre tickets, such as Play by Play (playbyplay.co.uk), The Audience Club (theaudienceclub.com), and My Box Office (myboxoffice.biz). These sites require a small annual subscription fee – but the savings you make can be as huge as John Barrowman's ego (and willy).

You pay a yearly fee, and then you'll receive emails whenever tickets become available, which is generally for perform-ances which aren't selling very well – or when it is essential to have a full house. This is particularly the case on press nights, when it's just as important to have a busy, buzzy auditorium as it is to have Amanda Holden wandering around in a revealing frock. It all helps to give the impres-sion that the show is a hit, and not a shit.

Often the tickets will be very last minute – for the same day, or the same week – but it's worth it when you can get £100 seats for 100p. Of course, the downside is that you can't pick and choose whatever show you want – it's all down to what shows are offering the deals – and they're all available on a first-come first-served basis, so you have to be quick.

It can be quite the experience actually picking up your tick-ets from these sellers – it's not as simple as just turning up at a box office, but more like an undercover operation to rival *Mission: Impossible*. After choosing to accept it (i.e. responding to the email and booking your seats), you'll be told to meet someone in a dark alley near the theatre. Your contact will be wearing something obvious – like a luminous Equity badge – and hiding behind a copy of *The Stage*. After saying a password – 'Are you Mr Theatre?' – you'll be given your tickets and ordered never to tell anyone how much you paid (as other people will have paid a lot more). Then, when you turn around again, Mr Theatre will have vanished in a puff of smoke. It's fine, and perfectly safe – but just have your wits about you and know what to expect. Remember that the first rule of Audience Club is: you do not talk about Audience Club...

Other useful sites are From the Box Office (fromtheboxoffice.com) and TodayTix (todaytix.com, also in the form of a swishy app). These sites offer last-minute ticket deals for a host of shows in London and on Broadway – at substantial savings. On TodayTix, the most popular tickets are Rush tickets – starting from £10 – sometimes available in a lottery, which you can enter via the site or app.

Theatre Monkey (theatremonkcy.com) is another excellent site, which, as well as offering tickets, features accurate theatre seating plans – with detailed information about the view you'll get from virtually every seat in the West End. The site's large community of regular users upload their personal experiences, such as:

> 'I just sat in the worst theatre seat *ever*. The view was awful – I couldn't really see the stage at all, and had a job to hear what was being said. The seat was damp, had no cushioning, and zero leg-room. On closer inspection I noticed the seat had a big round hole in the middle. Appalling. Needless to say, I'll never be sitting in seat WC again.'

Ticket Booths

These theatrical little ticket booths are appearing in every bit of spare space in London's Zone One. Only the other day I was minding my own business in Victoria Station's public facilities when a little man popped his head up through the bowl and asked if I wanted some cheap tickets for *Wicked*. A new way of marketing, and quite unhealthy, I'd imagine – but I must say I was so impressed with his nerve that I purchased a pair and gave them to the gentleman in the next cubicle along. I'm nice like that, you see, dear.

When buying from ticket booths, always check that the company is a member of STAR (Society of Ticket Agencies and Retailers) and look for their logo (which, rather obviously, is a star – although I wish it was something more theatrical like Cameron Mackintosh in a *Betty Blue Eyes* T-shirt). If the company is not a member of STAR then there is no guarantee that the ticket is genuine. This also applies when buying tickets online – look for the STAR logo and click on it to verify membership.

Always ask for the face value of the ticket, and if there are any additional fees on top – for example, imagine the face value of the ticket is £58.50; you may be paying the special discounted rate of £49 but with an agency fee of £10 on top you're actually paying more! And think of everything you could do with that extra 50 pence. Pop it in your *War Horse*-shaped moneybox, and in a thousand years' time you'll have saved enough for a ticket to *Elf*.

If a ticket agent refuses to tell you the face value, you should politely decline – they are probably charging you more than the ticket is actually worth, before they've even slapped on their charges. And also always check that you will have a clear view. You don't want to pay £35 for a view of a pillar, unless the show is *Fifty Shades of Grey* starring Russell Grant and Ann Widdecombe.

The most famous discount booth is TKTS, which is based at the clocktower, the only free-standing building in Leicester

Square. This is London's equivalent to the famous TKTS discount booth in Times Square, New York. The half-price ticket booth is owned and run by the Society of London Theatre or 'SOLT' as they're known to friends – although you wouldn't want to pour them all over your chips, dear. Still, more appetising than when they were known as 'SWET' (the Society of West End Theatre).

Theatre tickets can only be purchased from the booth – not online or by phone, but you can check their website (tkts.co.uk) to see what's available on which day and at what price. When going to TKTS be prepared to queue. Always take some reading material with you (like my first book), because, just like Tim Rice's musical, the queue can go on From Here to Eternity.

Day Seats

Day seats are offered by most shows and are particularly good value. However, for a popular production, it means getting up ridiculously early and loitering with theatrical intent for hours. Every morning in London you can spot the biggest hits by the number of fans queuing outside the box office. There are even times when people sleep in front of theatres to get their hands on the hottest tickets. Recent shows to have drawn the overnight buyers include Benedict Cumberbatch in *Hamlet*, Mark Rylance in *Jerusalem*, Nicole Kidman in *Photograph 51*, and The Krankies in *Macbeth*.

Day seats cost around £10–25. They are usually in the first couple of rows of the stalls, which means you will be extremely close and develop a permanent crick in your neck – but this is a small price to pay for cheap theatre.

Discounted Seats

Some of our most-loved theatres regularly offer cheaper ticket options. The National Theatre has its Travelex season offering £15 tickets to many shows, generally in the Olivier auditorium, which can be booked in advance. You have to be quick when the tickets go on sale – but is well worth it when you get to see Jonny Lee Miller writhing around in his show-pants.

The Donmar Warehouse also has similar deals – the latest being their KLAXON tickets. Every Monday at noon, tickets are released for performances two weeks later – at all price bands. The Royal Court offers £10 Monday seats, which are available from 9 a.m. on the day of performance: a real bargain for those who love a bit of artificial deprivation and degradation on Sloane Square.

Many other theatres around the country offer similar discounts and last-minute deals, especially if you're lucky enough to be under the age of 26 or thereabouts. Theatres are rightly eager to nurture their audiences of the future, so most have astonishing discounts available. In fact, the toppest tip of all for getting the cheapest seats is to stay under the age of 26 – *for ever*. A fake NUS card in your wallet, a Hollywood smile, and a forehead full of Botox should do the trick, whatever age you are. Many an actor, naming no names, has also been known to follow this advice.

The best way to get updates on the shows a theatre is presenting, and any discounts available, is by joining the mailing lists of theatres. This ensures that, as well as getting information about tickets, you'll also get emails with photos of actors posing happily and bragging about how their job is much more fun than yours. Pay an annual subscription fee, and you'll also be first in line with priority booking. Take pride by knowing you're beating other members of the public to the hottest tickets – and that even more of your hard-earned cash has gone towards paying for Helen McCrory's herbal cigarettes.

Other Discounts

Kids Week (kidsweek.co.uk) – Kids Week lasts a month (go figure), when children under the age of sixteen can watch certain shows for free when accompanied by an adult paying full price. Not every show partakes in this event as they're not all suitable for youngsters, but there's always a good selection including shows like *Matilda*, *The Lion King*, and numerous plays by Sarah Kane.

Get Into London Theatre (getintolondontheatre.co.uk) – This annual promotion actually allows you to get into a theatre. Yes – you get the chance to get into a real, live theatre! Lucky you. The scheme offers discounted tickets for London shows during the post-Christmas doldrums of January and February, and are available from the TKTS booth and via the Official London Theatre website (officiallondonthe-atre.co.uk). The discounts offered are always very good, although I think a 'Get Wet in London Theatre' promotion would be much more exciting. This is where audience members use water pistols to squirt sweaty actors during hot summer shows, culminating in an Annual West End Wet T-shirt Competition. Marvellous.

Groups – Groups of six people or more usually get a good discount. But obviously, the more people you can bribe to come along, the better. If you're a member of any groups or clubs it may be worth mentioning the idea of a theatre trip. In my experience, ramblers, brass bands, and dogging groups are particularly enthusiastic theatregoers. These groups are always obvious to spot, sitting next to each other, wearing identical jumpers and sporting the same hairstyle. Have a look next time you're going to the theatre. There will be groups of blue-rinse OAPS, clubs of know-it-all drama students, and gaggles of bearded (and non-bearded) gay men. However, you'll never find bearded and non-bearded gay men in the same group. A beard never betrays his boys. That would be blasphemous, dear.

35

Disabled Discount – Most theatres offer a good discount to disabled theatregoers. If you are registered as disabled, you and your carer will be able to make substantial savings.

Returns – If you want to see a show that is usually sold out, you can try and get a return ticket. Go to the box office a couple of hours before the show starts and join the returns queue. These are tickets which are returned to the theatre at the last minute when audience members can't make it due to losing interest, another Southern Rail strike, or because it's the *Bake Off* final. However, these seats will be offered at no extra discount due to the popularity of the show – so it's best to have a few hundred quid in your back pocket just in case.

More Ticketing Tips

A large proportion of people working in box offices are unemployed actors – and it can be worth stroking their egos for discounts. Try saying things like 'I saw you in a play a couple of years ago – you were the best thing in it', 'My friend in the show fancies you, and said I should come to you for tickets' or 'You remind me of a young Patti LuPone.' With a bit of flirting, a nice smile, and a low-cut top you could find yourself getting a nice stalls seat for fifteen quid.

Never think that because you know someone in the cast they'll be able to get you a free ticket – I don't allow my actors to give tickets away willy-nilly, dear. Of course, actors always get a few complimentary tickets, but their agents always steal those (and tell the actors they're bringing a casting director along – when in fact it's a Tinder date). If you're lucky, your cast friends will be able to get you a discounted ticket – say, £35 for £50 seats – but these are often limited to Monday to Thursday performances. Additionally, at every performance, some 'company seats' are reserved for creatives, so even when it is technically sold out, there will be a couple of tickets available in case Andrew Lloyd Webber and Tim Rice want a romantic evening out.

If you have friends in the show, one of the things they can do is ask someone front of house to 'walk you in' (or even better, if you know someone working front of house, just ask them yourself). People who work front of house have much more chance of getting you into a show for free than anyone else. In many ways, the ushers are the most powerful people in a theatre – they decide who goes in, who gets ejected, and who gets whipped for being late.

Another insider's trick is sitting on the sound desk. The sound desk is the big motherboard that is situated at the back of the stalls. You'll have undoubtedly walked past this and felt the sudden urge to move all the settings (particularly after a few glasses of wine in the interval, when you'll be even more tempted to play with the knobs). To sit on the sound desk you'll have to enlist a friend in the show to ask one of the sound technicians. With enough bribery and red wine you could find yourself not only mesmerised by the show, but also by the sound engineer's advanced fingering skills.

You might also consider attending an understudies' performance, though these are generally for friends, family and the resident director only, when all the alternates, understudies, swings and covers get a go at putting on the costumes, and proving they're better than the actual actors.

The expense of theatre tickets drives some people to extreme lengths to save money. There have been adults trying to pay child's prices by wearing school uniforms and walking around on their knees (everyone knew they were adults – but they were given a cheaper ticket for sheer effort). Another valiant effort was by a student so desperate to see a production that she went to the theatre wearing a front-of-house uniform and pretended to work there. However, her uniform was so convincing she was made to work behind the bar – and consequently didn't see any of the show at all. Bless. Luckily for her she earned £30 in tips so used it to see the show the following night. Bravo.

Dance like no one is watching. Because they're not. They're all sitting in the auditorium staring at their phones, dear.

Where to Sit

A theatre has lots of different areas. It has far more than just an outside and an inside. It also has lots of other inside bits inside its inside. A theatre is in many ways like a person. The foyer is the mouth, the stage is the heart, the auditorium is the head, and the stage door is the bottom, as it gently pushes out dirty actors before having a good wipe.

Each area of the auditorium has its own particular qualities, with its own impact on your viewing experience. Let's take a closer look at each section and evaluate your chances of developing deep vein thrombosis.

Stalls

The stalls is the section of auditorium on the ground level closest to the stage, and tends to have a selection of the most expensive and mid-range seats. The first couple of rows are where day seats are located. Although day seats are nice and close, the downside is that all you can see is the top half of the actors; however, it gives a much better view of any nipple-tassel action (frequent in European theatre).

Sitting in the stalls generally gives you a very good view, like you're sitting in business class (or premium economy), with only a slight chance of turbulence if people in the dress circle above start jumping up and down. The central area of the stalls – and increasingly (and infuriatingly) much of the rest of the stalls too – is designated as 'premium seating', an excuse to mark the ticket price up by about a third, in exchange for more ready availability, an unimpeded view, and a 'free' beaker of warm prosecco. It's no coincidence that 'premium seating' is an anagram of 'Smug Matinee Rip-(off)'.

Towards the back of the stalls your view may be slightly obstructed by the overhanging dress circle (particularly common in older theatres), which can cut off your view of the top of the set and make any aerial acrobats appear decapitated. It's for this reason I insist that all my shows are set in bungalows.

The stalls seats are also the ones closest to exits – so these are the places to sit if you want to be first out. If you are particularly keen to make a speedy getaway you can book to sit on the end of a row – meaning you can just get up and leave whenever you want without disturbing anyone. Very useful if the show is bad and the nearby bar is better.

A few productions also offer 'splash seats'. These seats are very popular at the RSC and Matthew Bourne dance shows, where flying bodily fluids are an indication of good work. In fact, there is one little old lady who always books the splash seats so she can collect acting spit and sweat – which she bottles and sells on eBay. Apparently one bottle of genuine Ian McKellen spittle reached the staggering price of £250. Not bad for a couple of dribbles of drama, dear.

On Broadway, the stalls section is called the 'orchestra' – as it's the area of seats closest to the orchestra pit. Because of this, it's very popular with people who like to watch musicians getting drunk throughout a show. If you are very lucky, you may even be able to touch a real-life conductor as they're waving their little stick around.

Dress Circle

The next level up is the dress circle – and many consider it to contain the best seats in the house, with plenty of leg room and an excellent view of the entire breadth and depth of a stage. Specifically, I always recommend that people sit in the circle when watching a musical as it gives a 'bird eye's view' – perfect for seeing all those loose-limbed dancers in all their tightly drilled configurations. As a bonus, you will enjoy a unique feeling of superiority because you won't have to see or share any space with the cheap people in the balcony above, and are in the perfect spot to look down and throw sweets at the people below in the stalls.

This area is sometimes called the royal circle because traditionally the Queen and King's boxes were on this level – where they park their posh posteriors and wave at their subjects. It is called the mezzanine in Broadway theatres after the Italian word for 'middle' – despite often being the top level of seating in those theatres. Ah, America.

The dress-circle bar is the most showbiz of theatre bars – sometimes with an outside balcony where you can look down at the world whilst pretending to be the Queen of Theatreland, though there are actually many queens of Theatreland (usually found posing on the balcony and gazing down Old Compton Street at the appropriately named Prince Edward). During the interval you will have quick and easy access to this bar, allowing you to find your pre-ordered Dom Pérignon in comfort, and scoff your special edition 'Sea Salt with a Hint of David Tennant' ice cream.

Upper Circle

The upper circle is like the dress circle, but higher up and for poorer people.

Balcony

The balcony (or the gods) is where you will generally find the cheapest seats. It's the place where most people have their first experience in a theatre, usually watching Dame

Christopher Biggins' Widow Twankey playing kiss chase with Aladdin. The average ticket price in the gods is around a quarter of the price of more expensive seats, but of course you have to be aware of the obstacles.

If you suffer from vertigo or altitude sickness – and you don't want to risk deep vein thrombosis – then this section is not for you. The balcony is very high, so high in fact that it may be necessary to tranquilise people to make their ascent more tolerable. Another downside of being so high is that the actors look tiny. You can resolve this by renting some theatre binoculars fixed to the seat in front – which as well as allowing you to zoom in are perfect to help you peek at attractive audience members and plan who you're going to seduce at the interval.

Watching teeny blobs on stage might not sound entertaining – but it really does have its advantages. One fun thing to do is to imagine that you're actually watching a big Hollywood star – that little-known actor stage right can become Brad Pitt, and the actress running off in the opposite direction can be Angelina Jolie. Anybody you want! It's extraordinary how much more exciting *Hamlet* is when Johnny Depp is giving his Ophelia.

A common side effect of sitting in the upper levels is neck and back pain. You will find yourself hunched and leaning forward in these seats, doing all you can to give yourself a better view. But who cares about permanent neck damage if you only paid a tenner for your ticket? It's all about priorities.

There is an annoying safety rail running along the front of the upper levels in every auditorium – and wherever you sit you'll find it right in the centre of your view. However, it's there for health and safety reasons (to stop the peasants in the gods falling onto the posh patrons below). So please don't attempt any clever gymnastics, or try to poke your head through for a closer view. You could get stuck and be forced to spend the rest of your days watching *Mamma Mia!* Horrifying.

It is common that the entrance to the gods is at the side of the theatre – where it can take a full hour to climb the thousands of steps to get to your seat (Rapunzel was never locked in a tower, she was simply trapped in the balcony at Her Majesty's). The reason for this separate entrance is because when Cameron Mackintosh designed the West End he didn't want the poor people mingling with the important ones.

If you have the time and inclination, sometimes you can be clever and get your cheap ticket upgraded. When a show has not sold well, the front-of-house manager will close the upper levels and move everyone down into the dress circle or stalls. It's a waste of resources having staff working on a level that has only one man and a bag of nuts. Also, it is far nicer for the actors to perform to two fuller levels, than having audience members littered around three or four. So you could be moved into a £65 seat for the bargain price of £20.

The best nights to attempt this upgrade trick are early in the week – Monday and Tuesday especially. But there are several ways to check if a show is 'quiet': one is by calling the box office and enquiring; and the other is by using online booking services. This way you will see a plan of the auditorium – which lets you select your seat and see how many other seats are available. If there are lots of seats left then you should book in the upper circle and keep your fingers crossed. Then, when you arrive at the theatre, you will hopefully be moved into a more expensive section.

Another crafty little trick is to survey the auditorium before the show starts and look for empty seats. If you spot some vacant ones in the stalls or dress circle, remember where they are and at the interval double check to see if they're still free. If so, quickly gather your things, and surreptitiously head downstairs. Then, just as the bells for the second half ring, head straight to the empty seats and sit. If you are unlucky and an usher tells you to move, or asks to see your ticket you should pretend you can't understand and put on a ridiculous European accent: 'I do not comprende. Theatre.

Auf Wiedersehen. Brexit. Yes? Michael Balls. He good at sing.' Eventually the staff will just give up and leave you to it.

Restricted View

A restricted-view ticket means that your view of the stage will be limited. This could be because your seat is on the side, your seat has a pillar in front of it, or your seat is actually on the roof – where the only thing visible is the couple copulating in the flats opposite. As a general rule, if you have bad eyesight, vertigo, or actually want to see what the hell is going on, don't purchase a restricted-view ticket.

One advantage of these seats is that they are, on the whole, cheaper. But never pay more than £25 for the privilege of only seeing a bit of the stage. I know theatre is all about the whole experience and atmosphere, and part of that is simply being there – but it really does make the whole thing less appealing if all you can see is the glowing shine off Patrick Stewart's head, dear.

If you are willing to risk a restricted-view seat then do your research and have a good look at seating plans prior to booking tickets. Some venue websites have photographs of the view from each area of the auditorium. If a website doesn't offer this, you can call the box office directly and ask what they think. However, if you take this approach make sure that a) the box-office assistant has been in the auditorium before, b) the box-office assistant is not on work experience, and c) that you haven't actually called your local swimming baths instead.

Boxes

Boxes are traditionally the place where you sit to be seen, since you will be very noticeable to the rest of the audience. When sitting in a box you tend to be very close to the stage, which is a good thing – but because boxes are on the sides of the auditorium, your view can be obstructed by at least a third. If the play is boring, then you can distract the rest of the audience by putting on a play of your own. Do a little dumb show, display your jazz hands, take some Punch and Judy puppets along – and before long, the audience will become more engaged with your performance than the one on stage.

When sitting in a box it is essential you always remember that you are very visible. I have witnessed many a kinky couple getting carried away – a theatre box is not a hotel bedroom. I recall one pair suddenly disappearing onto the floor, only to reappear three minutes later looking red-faced and dishevelled. Perhaps they were playing Hide and Seek, or maybe they felt the urge to do some mid-show push-ups. Anyhow, whatever they were doing, it was lovely to see Charles and Camilla enjoying themselves.

One of the biggest advantages of the box is that you can leave easily without having to disturb anyone. This makes it a particular favourite for people with a weak bladder, or people who like going to the bar for refills. The main reason I adore sitting in a box is because the chairs aren't screwed to the ground so you can move them around and sit where you want (particularly handy if the show is rubbish – just move your chair to the back, open your iPad, and watch *Love Island* instead).

Standing

Some theatres also offer standing tickets. These are pretty self-explanatory, and allow the audience member to stand at the back of the auditorium at designated locations. However, there are strict rules about how to stand. You are not permitted to lean, slouch, kneel, hop, jump, stretch or breathe. All your ticket allows you to do is stand perfectly still and face forward. If at any point you attempt an illegal lean or crouch, you will be swiftly attacked by the front-of-house manger with a lasso and be thrown into the public bins outside.

Standing tickets usually only go on sale when the rest of the house is sold out. This prevents cheapskates, bargain hunters or students buying these tickets when we producers want the proper seats sold instead. But if you are waiting to see a long-running, successful show – with 'Standing Room Only' – then chances are you will be able to squeeze in. One place where standing space is always available is Shakespeare's Globe in Bankside, where tickets to stand in the yard are just £5; great value to see some Shakespearean-scale spitting and soliloquising up-close.

If you are considering getting a standing ticket, be very careful about what show you decide to see. Never stand and watch something that is more than three hours long. It is not good for anyone, and can result in paralysis, varicose veins, and an unnatural urge to star jump. I have witnessed many eager audience members lose a leg due to overambitious standing. Always plan ahead – do plenty of deep lunging before the show starts, and wear your most comfortable shoes. (I'd wear my *Les Mis* slippers – they're comfy, hairy and have a 'one day more' guarantee. My casting director would prefer his six-inch stilettos.)

Finally, whilst we're on the subject of different areas of an auditorium – I've always found it interesting that critics are given the best seats in the house on press nights. It would be a more honest and balanced review if they were seated around the theatre – some in the stalls, some in the upper circle, and some in restricted-view seats, which is what most of the general public can afford anyway. If this doesn't happen (which I doubt it will – no producer would put Billington in the balcony), then it should state on all reviews where the critic has been sitting and how much that ticket would have cost.

Actors – please wear appropriate sunblock. We don't want the boys on the barricade looking like they should be in *Mamma Mia!*, dear.

When to Go

Previews

Previews are a period of performances that happen before a show officially 'opens' on the press night. They are usually less expensive than normal ticket prices (and jolly well should be!), as at that stage the show is still being rehearsed. They are an important part of a production's development, allowing the cast and creative team to work on a show with the added benefit of having an audience's reaction. During this period, a show can change immensely – with lines altered, songs added, scenes removed, and actors killed. In some cases, things are changed drastically. I recall one production where an actor was playing a castrato, and during previews the director made the actor have his testicles removed to ensure the show was truthful. A painful procedure, yes, but some actors are prepared to go that extra mile to 'suffer for their art'. As a consequence of this small sacrifice the show was a resounding success – and Joe Pasquale has had a thriving career ever since.

The length of preview periods can vary significantly depending on the size and location of a venue. If a play is opening in a regional theatre, the preview period is usually a few days.

If it's a nursery schools' tour of *Trainspotting* there won't be any preview period. And if it's a West End show the preview period can last for up to four years. It all depends on how perfect we producers want the show to be (and how much money we don't mind losing on cheaper tickets). An acquaintance of mine got confused only last week and thought that *The Mousetrap* was still in previews – mainly because of the wobbly sets, under-rehearsed actors, and tatty mouse costume.

Preview performances are very popular – obviously because they are cheaper, but also because of the hype surrounding them. And of course, the first preview performance is particularly packed. This is the first public showing – and the cast, creative team and people working backstage all get incredibly excited and find it hard to hide their stage-semis.

Preview performances are also a very good time to go and spot the director in the audience, and offer your own notes. Directors love it when audience members tell them what they think, and definitely won't hit you if you give constructive feedback. But always remember to do this in a positive tone – perfect when delivering notes like 'It's great, really funny', but be extra positive when saying 'That was really slow and boring. It needs more gags.'

Of course, there are downsides to previews – you could end up watching a show that is very, very long. Many productions start off being a lot longer – and it is the preview period when we get our scissors out and decide who and what to cut. It is a well-known fact that *Les Mis* was sixteen hours long when it first opened. Now they've got it down to just over three (or five depending on how overindulgent the current Jean Valjean is). And who can forget Trevor Nunn's musical version of *Gone with the Wind* in 2008? I've tried, but it still haunts me. That production actually lasted four days in previews, but by the opening night they'd got it down to just over two.

Preview performances are also when most of the technical problems occur. It's not unusual for sets to get stuck, microphones to be faulty, and costumes to be unfinished (rather lucky if the show stars Kerry Ellis, not so lucky if you're watching Kerry Katona). Over the years I've witnessed many a problem at preview performances, and in honesty most of them have been far more entertaining than the shows themselves...

Preview Problems

The great glass elevator – which was meant to be the climactic highlight in *Charlie and the Chocolate Factory* – had many awkward stops during its first few flights and caused several previews to be cancelled. There were reports of the elevator getting stuck as it was flying over the audience – at which point the stage manager came on stage, apologised, and the crew had to pull it back down manually. However, most people said it made it more fun (well, let's be honest, anything would have made that show more fun).

Cameron Mackintosh's Drury Lane production of *Oliver!* had a spectacular set with big pieces of scenery flying in and out throughout. However, they would sometimes get stuck, and not move down properly, the worst offender being Fagin's Den. This clunky piece would be flown in from the fly-tower above, but often during its descent would hit other bits of set, and consequently wouldn't hang properly on the section below. So the show would have to stop – and all before Mr Bean (Rowan Atkinson) had made his first entrance. Of course, because there were so many children involved in the production, safety had to be paramount (adult actors are more expendable) – and the first two performances were cancelled. They say never work with children or animals – well, dear Cameron loves defying rules – so in addition to over 150 kids (different groups of kids for different shows), and flatulent bull dogs, he made matters even more challenging by employing numerous temperamental comedians.

A 2007 'musical' version of *The Lord of the Rings* also played at Drury Lane – with one of the most expensive sets in theatre history. The show cost around £12.5 million – if only more of that budget had been spent on the score... It was a multitiered, mechanical set that elevated with various sections moving around. Obviously the health and safety implications of such a show were a nightmare. During one performance, an actor got caught in the machinery of one of the revolves and broke his leg. Audience members could hear screams of 'My leg, my leg!' – but of course didn't know if it was part of the show. However, fellow performers rushed to help the actor, and the performance was quickly cancelled. Luckily the actor's leg healed well and he is back being the brilliant dancer he was before – but it could have been a lot worse. The forty-five-foot stage had three revolves and seventeen lifts – so chances for accidents were high. That's why I always insist on spending as little as possible on sets – they cost too much money, and always get in the way.

Famously, everything went wrong with *Spider-Man: Turn Off the Dark* on Broadway in 2010. Costing a reported $75 million, it had numerous bad accidents, near-deaths, a preview period of 182 performances (I'm not even exaggerating), a sacked director, bad reviews, and an unhappy Bono. Money doesn't buy you happiness. And it certainly doesn't buy you a happy show.

I'm excited about the new Lloyd Webber show, *Dunkirk: The Musical*. An all-skating, all-singing, semi-nude musical. Starring Arlene Phillips as Harry Styles.

Press Nights

If you are fortunate enough to go to a show's press night, the chances are you will find a photo of yourself on a random website the following day, usually holding a glass of wine and a handful of Twiglets, standing gormlessly behind Nigel Havers. So it is essential you look good on such occasions.

Press nights exist to publicise a show. Everyone involved is hoping the show will be well reviewed with lots of juicy four- and five-star reviews. They're also about people commenting on Twitter and Facebook – nowadays word of mouth really is just as powerful as any form of paid promotion. Just look at *The Book of Mormon* – where a whole advertising campaign was based on comments the general public made on Twitter. When feedback is coming directly from the paying audience it is easier to trust and believe what you are reading, unless they're raving about *Aladdin*.

If you want to attend a press night, and know someone involved in the show, contact them early and ask if they have any allocated tickets. If you're sleeping with them they may even get you a free ticket (and if you're not, then start). Otherwise, book as early as you can. Press nights traditionally begin earlier – usually at 7 p.m. instead of 7.30 – so reviewers can write their overnight reviews. But more importantly, it's so that everyone has more time at the first-night party. And let's be honest, that's the real reason why people go to press nights anyway.

Some press nights consist of a bag of salted nuts and a free pint at the local Wetherspoons. Others, however, are the most showbiz nights in the calendar – in a central London venue overflowing with unlimited champagne, canapés, live music and special guests. Some producers even lay on an 'after-press-night-party' party, which occurs at a secret location when all other guests have left. These are more intimate affairs, and consist of cast members, directors, Rupert Everett, and boys with six-packs going over their audition technique.

If a show has transferred to the West End and already received good reviews at its first venue, sometimes there will be a 'gala night'. This has all the pomp(osity) and circumstance of a press night, without any critics writing another review – thereby avoiding the risk they'll give it a worse rating second time around. That way we can drop the act and skip straight to the Dom.

Long-running Shows

It is generally best to see a long-running show as early on in the run as possible – when the cast are still giving fresh performances. After six months in a show, an actor's enthusiasm is replaced by a desire to get through the thing as quickly and vacantly as possible (so they have more time to pose and drink in Soho). Performing in a long-running show is tough – as actors have to do the same thing, in the same position, with the same people, eight times a week (or fourteen times during the Christmas season). There is a presumption that actors have much more variety and fun than a 'normal' person has in their job – but this is entirely false. In an office job there are at least different targets, different projects, new clients – whereas in a long-running production there is no variety at all. Actors have to do the same thing in the same way night after night after night.

Long-running shows do, though, have cast changes every year – where zactors (zombie actors) are led off and culled in a room and replaced by new, enthusiastic, younger ones. These new casts are good to watch, as they bring a new energy and spark to tired, dusty productions. But it can also be worth watching the final few weeks of a remaining cast – when they all suddenly start performing energetically again. A cast's final night can be particularly emotional, with actors crying, screaming, and combusting downstage centre during the curtain call.

Days of the Week

The best night to watch a show, when the audience are up for it and actors remember all their lines, is a Friday. This is the end of the working week for the audience, who come in excited about their weekend ahead. Saturday nights are usually full of hen parties and people who actually want to be at home watching Ant and Dec. Sunday shows, although they sell quite well, have an atmosphere of theatrical depression. And wet Thursday matinees tend to be slow, depressed, and performed by understudies and swings.

Shows on a Monday and Tuesday evening are the performances where you can get the best deals, as they don't sell as well as the rest of the week. And of the two, Monday nights are usually better shows – as the actors are nice and relaxed after a day away from their resident director.

Muck-up Matinees

There is a naughty tradition in the industry where actors and stage crew get carried away on their final matinee in a show – which is usually the last Saturday. This show is rather hedonistically called the 'muck-up matinee'. The name speaks for itself.

This is the performance where actors feel they have full permission to mess around – by wearing different costumes, saying wrong lines, using different accents, and trying to make each other corpse (the theatrical term for laughing on stage – and called this because if an actor is spotted doing so, the director will quickly turn them into an actual corpse). However, the actors are not actually allowed to do any of this at all. There is no Equity rule that states: 'On the final matinee you have permission to muck about in front of the paying public.' But as it's the end of the contract, and management can't sack anyone at this late stage, actors ignore all warnings and do everything in their power to be as annoying as Katie Hopkins.

The problem is that many audience members will have paid a lot of money to watch the show, and won't want or expect actors to be messing around. I, of course, don't condone this outlandish behaviour at all – especially when I hear of props being replaced by rubber chickens, actors bowing in just their show-pants, and the most outrageous display of male anatomy during 'Edelweiss' you can imagine.

The worst case of naughtiness I ever witnessed was in a play involving copious amounts of alcohol. The set was littered with prop bottles of fake booze. But on the final matinee they were replaced by real bottles of the strong stuff. Needless to say, halfway through Act One the drunken acting on stage got very realistic indeed. It got so bad that one of the actors spent the entire second half confidently walking off-stage to vomit in the wings. Hats off to him, he carried on with the show – but it did look rather peculiar when every ten minutes he staggered off stage right. I imagine the audience presumed it was a clever bit of staging. But of course it wasn't – the actor was just following the most important rule of theatre: the show must go on... whether you're retching in the wings or not, dear.

The Cinema

It is now very popular to watch live theatre in the cinema. The National Theatre has been the pioneer of this with NT Live – where productions are broadcast live to cinemas around the world. These have proved so successful that other commercial and subsidised theatres have followed suit. You can also download shows from Digital Theatre, who have a whole library of productions available (digitaltheatre.com).

There are arguments for and against these broadcasts. Some say that watching a theatre production on screen is a poor indicator of what the show is actually like – and it's true that there's nothing quite like seeing something live. But by watching theatre in a cinema, or in the comfort of your own home, it makes the whole event more affordable. As a bonus, if you watch a production online you can skip through all the boring bits (and have as many intervals as you like).

Experiencing a production on film also gives a totally different viewpoint. Whereas in a theatre you can sometimes barely see the actors, and audibility can be an issue, on screen you are treated to close-ups, perfect volume, and the ability to see every facial expression (Botox-willing). Some performances have been so popular that there are now repeated showings called 'encore' screenings. The production of Benedict Cumberbatch and Jonny Lee Miller in *Frankenstein* has had lots of these encores – audiences just can't get enough of them and their little frankfurters.

There is a worry that broadcasting live performances can take away people's desire to watch them in a theatre, therefore taking money away from it. This is potentially an issue in the regions – where smaller venues, who used to book rural or touring theatre companies for a night or two, now prefer to show the cheaper, easier and more popular live screenings from London. I look forward to the day when smaller or regional theatre companies also get the chance to have their work broadcast across the UK – besides, their work is just as important as any in the West End.

Overall I find the rise of the broadcast, downloadable or streamed theatre productions a cause for celebration. Often by seeing a film or listening to an album, even reading a book – it makes you want to go and see a live event even more. You have a connection, and an understanding of what is happening, giving you a thirst to experience it live. The NT Live screenings don't seem to have affected ticket sales at the National Theatre itself, where most of their shows usually sell out anyway (well, the good ones at least) – and the extra revenue from cinema sales is invaluable income for venues and producers. These live broadcasts make shows accessible to those who wouldn't otherwise have the opportunity to see them; they allow companies, creatives and actors to share their work with a different, more diverse type of viewer; and all this brings a vital new audience into the theatre.

But remember: just because theatre is being filmed and released in this way it doesn't give anyone else permission to whip out their mobile and record the show next time they're in a theatre. This will result in theatre rage of the most violent kind. And more on that later, dear...

....

Get busy living. Or get busy pretending you're living by uploading photos to all of your social-media feeds, dear.

....

THE PHANTOM OF THE OPERA

History – In 1984, Andrew Lloyd Webber was missing romance in his life after Tim Rice had walked out (after a creative tiff over who was eating all the Hobnobs) – so he was eager to write a romantic piece to win back his long-term collaborator. He called Cameron Mackintosh to help, and they organised a date night to watch both of the original *Phantom of the Opera* films (the 1925 Lon Chaney and 1943 Claude Rains versions), but soon realised it was going to be difficult to make the idea work as a musical. So, after a couple of gallons of Babycham, they put the idea on hold and watched *Footloose*. However, not long after, Lloyd Webber was in New York and found a copy of the Gaston Leroux's novel from early twentieth-century Paris, *Le Fantôme de l'Opéra*, which inspired him to begin developing the show.

After a few months of sitting at a grand piano and figuring out the chord of C Major, Lloyd Webber started writing the music, and in 1985 a preview of the first act was performed in Lloyd Webber's house (a modest three-bedroom semi in Sydmonton). In this staging, Colm Wilkinson played the Phantom and Sarah Brightman, Lloyd Webber's then wife, played Christine. It contained lyrics by Richard Stilgoe that were later changed when Charles Hart, an unknown twenty-five-year-old lyricist came on board: 'Think of Me' was originally called 'What Has Time Done to Me', and 'Notes' was 'Papers'. The mask in this workshop production also covered the actor's entire face (perfect if employing an ugly actor – an ugtor), but due to it making the actor sound like Darth Vader they replaced it with the now famous half-face mask.

The musical opened at Her Majesty's Theatre in the West End in 1986, produced by Mackintosh, directed by the Broadway legend Hal Price, with Michael Crawford playing the Phantom and Sarah Brightman playing Christine. The amazing set by Maria Björnson has lots of stairs, gold, candles, smoke, an underground gondola and an elephant – but is most famous for a chandelier which plummets (or rather plods) towards the audience just before the interval. (Oops, sorry I forgot to say 'spoiler', dear.) Don't sit in the centre stalls if you're tall.

The show was an instant success and transferred to Broadway in 1988. The rest is history. Literally. It won the Olivier and Tony Awards for Best Musical, and at the time of writing, it has run for over thirty years in the West End and is the longest-running show in Broadway history. Lloyd Webber is the most successful British composer of musicals. And Charles Hart has worked for a couple of days on a handful of shows – but after the success of *Phantom*, he didn't even need to bother doing that.

Plot – A man wears a mask, spends his time in solitude playing with his organ (don't we all, dear?), and stalks a beautiful opera singer. She feels stuck between her boyfriend and a severe case of Stockholm syndrome.

Characters – Opera singers, ballet dancers, theatre managers, and a disfigured man who likes wearing a mask to the theatre (weirdo).

Best-known actors to have played the Phantom – Michael Crawford, John Owen Jones, Gerard Butler and Ramin Karimloo.

Most likely to play the Phantom in the future – Michael Barrymore, Michael Caine, Michael Keaton and Mikhail Gorbachev.

Best-known actresses to have played Christine – Sarah Brightman, Sarah Lawrence, Sierra Boggess, Sara Jean Ford, Samantha Hill and Sofia Escobar.

Most likely to play Christine in the future – Any actress whose name begins with an 'S'.

Best-known songs – 'The Music of the Night'; 'Phantom of the Opera' (the shrieky one); 'All I Ask of You'; 'Angel of Music' (the other shrieky one); 'Masquerade'; 'Wishing You Were Somehow Here Again'.

Rejected songs – 'Get Away from Me, You Weirdo'; 'Do You Actually Own the Freehold of This Underground Lair? If Not, I'll Have You Evicted'; 'It Worked for Beauty and the Beast'; 'Would You Like to Play on My Organ?'

WICKED

History – Based on Gregory Maguire's novel – itself a witty, alternative history of the events leading up to the classic book and musical, *The Wizard of Oz* – *Wicked: The Untold Story of the Witches of Oz*, to give it its full title, features songs by Stephen Schwartz with a book by Winnie Holzman. After tryouts in San Francisco, *Wicked* premiered on Broadway in 2003 to enormous acclaim and fan-girl appreciation, going on to win three Tony Awards and Six Drama Desk Awards. The production flew across the Atlantic on a broomstick in 2006 where it has been playing at the Apollo Victoria, a barn of a venue only slightly smaller than Victoria Station just next door. Shrek is not involved in this production, thank God.

Plot – Essentially, a witch who is different (green) gets bullied, tries to help others, and everyone hates her for it. Typical.

Characters – Elphaba (a green witch), Glinda (a white witch, friend of green), Fiyero (a man with a six pack who fancies green), and the Jolly Green Giant.

Best-known actresses to have played Elphaba – Adele Dazeem, Louise Dearman, Kerry Ellis and Rachel Tucker.

Most likely to play Elphaba in the future – Mazelle Zareem, Allswell Mazeem and Hareem Greenbean.

Best-known songs – 'Defying Gravity'; 'The Wizard and I'; 'Popular'; 'I'm Not That Girl'; 'Dancing Through Life'; 'As Long As You're Mine'; 'For Good'.

Rejected songs – 'I'm Not the Incredible Hulk, Thank You Very Much'; 'I Don't Have My Flying Licence Yet'; 'Eat All Your Greens, Kids, and You Too Could Grow Up to Look Like a Cucumber'.

CATS

History – Andrew Lloyd Webber used to love reading about cats when he was young, and until the age of thirty enjoyed nothing more than snuggling in bed and looking at photos of felines. He decided to set one of favourite books – *Old Possum's Book of Practical Cats*, an anthology of poetry by T. S. Eliot – to music, and then did what he usually does, and put on a little concert for some friends and family at his Sydmonton home, to see what they'd think of it, and if they could help him invent a plot. Luckily, Eliot's widow, Valerie, was staying in a nearby Travelodge that night so she was invited over to see the showcase. She loved the songs so much that she allowed Lloyd Webber to produce a full-length musical based on the catty poems. But, as is often the case when permission is granted for existing text to be used in a show, there were conditions – in this instance, the Eliot estate stated that no new script could be added, and only the original poems could be used – hence the reason why the show doesn't actually have a story.

Cameron Mackintosh came on board as producer, Trevor Nunn as director, Gillian Lynne as choreographer, and lots of famous actors as the moggies. But in early rehearsals, the actors had no idea about what they were meant to be doing. Clawing at the furniture didn't seem to be quite enough for a whole show. Hearing of this plight, Valerie Eliot showed Lloyd Webber an unpublished segment from her husband's poems, describing Grizabella the glamour cat. This segment was only eight lines long – but it brought the production team a cat with an 'intensely recognisable character, with powerful human resonances, while introducing the themes of mortality, and the past, which occur repeatedly in the major poems' (I've no idea what this actually means, but Sir Trev said it, so it must mean something).

Using Grizabella as a central focus, the team were able to give the show a (sort-of) storyline, with another Eliot poem – 'Rhapsody on a Windy Night' – adapted by Nunn to become the show's big number: 'Memory'. Judi Dench was originally cast as La Griz – but in rehearsals ruptured her Achilles tendon after having a particularly violent furball lodged at the back of her throat. The role was taken over – rather like Radio 2 on a Sunday afternoon – by Elaine Paige. When the show opened at the New London Theatre in 1981, the scoffers' and the mockers' smiles were wiped off their faces. It was a triumph, ran for twenty-one years in London (before several revivals), and transferred all around the world. 'Now and forever' indeed.

Plot – It's about some cats. Specifically, some cats called the Jellicles who partake in a dance-off to see who is allowed to come back to life and eat a final bowl of Whiskas.

Characters – Cats.

Best-known performers to have played a cat – Dancers who look good in Lycra®. Or who used to look good in Lycra®. Or can remember the original choreography. Or who Gillian Lynne likes. These have included Elaine Paige, Brian Blessed, Paul Nicholas, Bonnie Langford, Wayne Sleep, Nicole Scherzinger, Beverley Knight and Leona Lewis.

Most likely to play a cat in the future – Kat-herine Jenkins, Denise Van Meowten, Macavity Culkin, Neil Catrick Harris, and Ed (Fur) Balls

Best-known songs – 'Memory'; 'The Rum Tum Tugger'; 'Macavity'; 'The Jellicle Ball'; 'Skimbleshanks'; 'The Journey to the Heaviside Layer'.

Rejected songs – 'God, I Have Another Furball'; 'Anyone Got Some Tuna?'; 'If I Can't Find the Litter Tray (I'm Going to Pee in the Stalls)'.

ACT TWO: GOING...

'Oh, that this too, too sullied show would melt,
Thaw, and resolve itself into a dew,
Or that the everlasting had not fixed
His canon against discount tickets...'

Partners may leave you. Directors may scold you.
Agents may hurt you. But theatre will always love
you, dear.

You've decided what you want to see, you've booked your tickets, and you've memorised the original cast recording so you can sing along (silently in your head, please). This chapter features all my top tips for making sure that your trip to the theatre goes as smoothly as Craig Revel Horwood's nose.

Who to Take

A theatre trip is a very intimate and personal experience. Once the lights go down it is just you and the performers – the rest merely melts away. Or most of it does. The things that never melt away, however much you might wish it, are the people sitting next to you.

As an audience member you can only control *who* you are going with – you can't control the other audience members sitting around you. And this can be a problem. Particularly if they're not regular indulgers in personal hygiene, and have a habit of unwrapping crisp and sweet packets (and never offer you one. How rude, dear). Whenever I go to the theatre I dread sitting next to a sweaty Susan or stinking Steve of an evening, whose pungent aroma upstages even the greatest of acting. But what can be done about this nasal nightmare?

Well... I'm hoping that in the future when choosing theatre seats, you will also be able to find out crucial facts about the people who have already booked. For example: who they are, their age, where they live, what they do, what they look like, and, crucially, when they last bathed. This extra information would make the whole theatrical experience even more fulfilling, allowing you to sit with the people you choose. Furthermore, a rating system for audience members – like an Uber rating – would let you report back on those who have either made or marred your evening:

> '★ ★ ★ ★ Gloria to my right was lovely. She let me look at her programme and woke me up for all the good bits.'

> '★ ★ Fred was sitting on my left, but it was rather awkward. He put his hand on my leg and squeezed during all the scary scenes. I wouldn't have minded, but we were watching *Mamma Mia!*'

It's that time of the year. Luggage is packed, dresses are hung, thighs are slapped, and Buttons is a pervert. It's panto time, dear.

The Types of Audiences

We've all been to the theatre and groaned with despair when sitting next to someone who noisily wafts their programme, takes their shoes and socks off, and updates their Twitter status ('I'm at the theatre, getting kultured' or 'Watching @lindsaylohan trying to act. #LOL'). Sadly, sometimes there is no escaping these annoying people – it is something which you simply have to put up with.

Over the years there have been reports of all sorts of behaviour in the auditorium – ranging from people talking loudly about how bad the show is, answering their phones and having full-volume conversations, to a couple actually having sex in the stalls, which was quite extraordinary to watch. Most theatre seats don't have enough room for legs, let alone enough for intercourse. Theatre attracts all sorts of people – and it all depends on the type of show as to what kind of audience members you can expect.

There are many different types of audience – the snorers, the laughers, the fans, the actors, the tourists, and the people who actually thought they were going to the cinema. If the show you are watching is boring or bad, it is rather fun to have a look around to see if you can spot these different audience types. And if you are feeling brave, see if you can decide which one you are yourself. And be honest. Nobody is judging you, dear. Well, only several hundred other people in the audience.

The Fans

Fans are very easy to recognise. They wander around the theatre in their show T-shirt, hugging the programme, clutching the soundtrack, and wearing an outfit that is meant to resemble a character from the show (ranging from small accessories like cat's ears to full train outfits with roller skates attached to every limb). These kinds of audience members are obviously very popular in the theatre industry, as they spend their hard-earned money in our buildings, seeing a production time and time (and time and time) again – and they are passionate, vocal supporters of the show.

They sometimes convene in a group outside the theatre posing for photos, discussing the cast, and peeking through windows in the hope of seeing actors in their show-pants. Generally, fans are lovely and incredibly passionate people who have found a special connection with a show – and their support is important to its success. Sometimes, however, they begin to think of the production as their own property.

This is where it can get a little difficult – as they openly offer their advice and criticism to performers, particularly those in long-running shows. You will occasionally overhear them saying things like: 'He's not as good as the one that's just left', 'He's a bit wooden' or 'She sings like SuBo' (sometimes their assessments are spot on). It gets even worse when they offer feedback to actors post-show: 'I think you're good, but the actress before you did this... and it was much better', 'You were great, but you're not going to keep doing it like that, are you?' They will then follow their remarks with a request for a lingering kiss. As a result, some fans have been slapped, spat on and dismembered by annoyed actors. One cardinal rule of theatre is *never* give an actor any criticism or advice (even if you're a fellow actor) – particularly straight after a show. That is the time when an actor is on an adrenalin high and wants everyone to tell them how good they are, even if they're not.

The Obsessives

Like fans, but with an evil stare and voodoo doll of their favourite actor.

The 'Just Landed' Tourists

These people are very easy to spot as they will either be asleep, speaking in a funny accent, or wearing a 'Make Theatre Great Again' cap (American tourists only). The 'just landed' audience members will literally have just got off a flight but, in an effort to cram as much into their holiday as possible, will force themselves to see a show. Which is a complete waste of time as they'll fall asleep within the first five minutes, only to wake up at the curtain call and applaud enthusiastically. All so they can excitedly update their Facebook status with: 'We've already watched a West End show!!!'

The Snorers

These people, usually male, don't want to be at the theatre at all. They've been dragged along by their better halves on a cultural visit to see something arty – when in actual fact they want to be at home watching *Match of the Day* and not Darren Day. But that's perfectly understandable.

The most annoying thing about snorers is the volume at which they choose to do it – alerting everyone to their dreaming at the most quiet of stage moments. 'I Dreamed a Dream' is not meant literally, dear. It's just as bad when the snoring is quiet – as they wake up, forget where they are, and scream wildly (I frequently do this when watching an Ibsen).

However, I do understand how easy it is to fall asleep in theatres – they can be very comfortable places, especially after a couple of bottles of Dom. When you're comfy in your seat and the lights go down, an auditorium can become a big theatrical bedroom – dark, warm, with the scent of stale sex (particularly prevalent on the fringe).

The best thing to do upon hearing a snorer is to throw something. Maltesers are perfectly sized and fly across the air brilliantly. You get 90 theatre points for every sweet you manage to get into the snorer's mouth. (See page 104 for how to win maximum theatre points and become one of my Theatre Prefects.) Some snorers are so sleepy, however, that this technique doesn't make a jot of difference – in which case you have to revert to extreme measures and throw something heavier. Like a brick.

The Critics

Critics are the ones dressed in old suits and dusty shirts, often confused for the homeless tramp sitting outside – in fact sometimes they *are* the tramp (they don't get paid as much as they used to). These species will usually be found on a press night, eagerly scribbling away in their notebooks – where it looks like they're recording well-observed thoughts about the show when in fact they're drawing cartoons of the actors.

Sometimes you may even find critics making an appearance before press night – which they're not supposed to do – particularly if it's a Shakespeare starring Benedict Cabbagepatch. But these are the rebellious ones who are not following protocol, and their early reviewing causes widespread theatre rioting of the most dramatic kind. First critics' commandment is: Thou Shalt Never Upset Producers. Especially Sonia Friedman.

The Kiddies

Now I'm a big advocate of children going to the theatre. They are, after all, the future, and will be the ones supporting the arts when I'm in my theatrical grave. So we should do as much as we can to allow youngsters to experience the thrill of live performance. However, sometimes when going to a show, the last thing you want is to be surrounded by these little darlings. So plan ahead. If you want to avoid the sound of children screaming in the aisles then you should avoid theatre during school holidays. Also, it is useful to find out when there will be a school's performance – which you can easily do by calling the box office. A school's performance is when the whole auditorium is filled with coachloads of children, apart from the unfortunate couple who have been seated slap bang in the middle of them. Because the children are on day release they get so excited that it becomes virtually impossible to hear what the actors are saying. Of course it all depends on the age of the child as to how noisy they will be – the worst run around with their bags of Haribo and cartons of Um Bongo, falling over, crying and babbling like they're characters from *In the Night Garden*. But then we were all eighteen year-old A-level students once, dear.

Obviously the type of show you are watching will depend if children are in the audience. If you're going to a modern gritty play at the Royal Court there won't be many there – apart possibly from a coachload from Walthamstow who will be grittier than anyone in the play anyway. If attending a play that is on the school's syllabus, or a musical like *Oliver!* or *Matilda*, then of course you will be surrounded by thousands of the little cherubs – both on *and* offstage. So if you have a child allergy, like Mr Bumble or Miss Trunchbull, avoid these productions at all costs.

The Hen Parties

At some shows you may find yourself sitting near a hen party. Now there's nothing wrong with ladies enjoying themselves before one of them is led to the guillotine of marriage, but there are far better venues for this ritual than a dark theatre. However, saying that, some shows are aimed at this sort of audience – and involve male torsos, erotic dancing, and puppetry of the genitals. It really is remarkable what the RSC is doing to make Shakespeare more accessible.

If you want to avoid the cackling sounds of overexcited ladies then you might want to miss shows like *Mamma Mia!, Girls Night Out* and anything starring Duncan from Blue. You will easily be able to spot the hen parties by the combination of headdresses, feather boas, matching T-shirts, and wobbly models of Jean Valjean's penis (at the end of the day it's another day longer, dear).

The Good Timers

These people go to the theatre with the sole intention of enjoying themselves. They've usually paid upwards of £50 for their ticket, and therefore will do *anything* they can to make it feel like they've got their fifty pounds of theatrical flesh. Typically, these people laugh at everything, ostentatiously sniffle at the sad bits, and ovate wildly at the curtain call – all in a vain attempt to prove to themselves and everyone else that they're having a great time (even when they're not). These determined audience members are very easy to spot – and hear – as they'll guffaw loudly at every opportunity, taking their cue from other people's genuine laughter.

The Gays

Where would theatre be without gay men? Gay men work in theatre, watch theatre, make theatre – gay men *are* theatre, dear. Even people like Laurence Olivier, who wasn't actually gay, ended up being a little bit gay.

Gay men are easily recognisable at the theatre. They will be well groomed and very comfortable in their theatrical surroundings. They will either be sitting on their own studying the programme and remembering when they first saw the play as a child, or will be in a big group of friends loudly discussing all aspects of the show and the latest season of gay plays to be produced at the King's Head. You can always spot gay men sipping something sweet in the interval, and chatting about the first time they saw Hugh Jackman in *Oklahomo*.

The Romantics

There are always a couple of horny people on their first date at a show, which puzzles me. Theatre dates don't allow much talking, limited drinking time, and only one twenty-minute interval for fornication. But I suppose at least it limits the number of awkward silences – and the darkness can be good for brave first-date fumbling.

You can easily spot the different types of couples by the way they behave with each other:

- First-date couples spend the show exchanging shy glances with each other.
- Couples in a new relationship can't keep their hands off each other.
- Newlyweds are deliriously happy, but so drunk they can't keep it up.
- And couples who have been in a relationship for five years or more haven't got anything to say to each other. So theatre is perfect for them.

Sometimes the romantics become so confused that they think the theatre is actually a hotel room, and spend the entire show partaking in their own private performance (which can be particularly awkward if you're sitting next to them, or particularly exciting if you're a pervert). Only recently there was a couple in the front row at *Women on the Verge of a Nervous Breakdown* at the Playhouse, where actors Tamsin Greig and Haydn Gwynne had to ask ushers to stop the couple playing with each other. Now it wouldn't have been so bad – but they were doing it mid-performance. They could have at least waited until the end, dear.

The Creative Team, Understudies and Swings

There will always be a member of the creative team in the audience. The director, resident director, associate director, casting director, fight director, children's director, director's boyfriend – the list goes on. These are the people that walk into the auditorium just before the shows starts, smile insincerely at people working front of house, and march to their designated seat. You will then see them leave just before the interval – so they can get backstage in time to discipline actors who have forgotten lines – and will re-enter the auditorium the second before the second half begins. During the curtain call they will either clap enthusiastically, or shake their head and begin taking off their belt for whipping purposes.

You may also spot some young people wearing tight denim, baseball hats, trainers, and carrying around a large folder – these people will be the swings or understudies. These are the talented individuals who have to learn and rehearse numerous roles, so that if actors are off they can step in and allow the show to go on. Swings and understudies always have a look of fear on their faces, as they pray they don't get asked to suddenly play a part they've never done before. They often go unnoticed by the public, but in truth they deserve as much, if not more, recognition than anyone else in the company. To the theatre world, swings are the fourth emergency service.

Sometimes you will spot swings deftly scribbling notes onto their script, as they frantically record any new moves that are happening on stage. Also, you can often spot members of the actual cast sitting in the auditorium having a 'show watch' – which is their opportunity to watch the show. This is particularly prevalent in long-running West End productions, where the actors also understudy a role as well as playing their normal part. It can be alarming looking at your programme and spotting an actor sitting next to you whom you expected to see on stage. But very handy for getting those mid-show autographs.

The Actors

These extravagant specimens will be smartly dressed in tight attire, or casually flaunting the 'I've just come from rehearsals' look (jogging bottoms and a Pineapple Studios T-shirt). They will have managed to blag a cheap ticket by sweet-talking the box-office manager, or by chatting up a cast member the previous evening.

People who work in theatre will always walk into an auditorium and see someone they know. It's a small world – and there's no smaller world than the one of entertainment. They will shimmy into the dress circle with their cravat and chinos and instantly spot a fellow actor. They will embrace and chat loudly about what they are currently rehearsing, involving words like 'darling', 'recall', 'change agent', 'Billie Piper', 'profit-share' and 'dear'. If they're particularly keen they may even whip out a script and point at their lines (but only if they've got lots of them). After that, they will laugh politely, hug again, pat each other on the bottom and return to their designated partners. This ritualistic pattern will continue until they've told everyone about their guest lead on *Holby*. These same actors will whisper comments throughout the show, always ending with 'It should have been me!'

The Friends of the Actors

These people are only at the theatre because they know someone in the cast. Maybe they feel obliged to be there, for fear of upsetting their friend, but really they are glorying in the fact that they know a 'real actor'. You will be able to recognise this audience member instantly as they shout loudly about knowing their friend in the show, and laugh inappropriately whenever they are on stage. During the curtain call they whoop and stand up for their friend, then quickly sit down again when anyone else is taking their bow. It can be awkward watching these people when they go to stage door after the show, only to have their actor 'friend' walk straight past them as they don't remember them. Turns out they only met once when they were kids on a caravanning holiday in Llandudno.

The Heavy Drinkers

You can spot these people in the local Wetherspoons before, during and after a show. They find a stiff drink is the only thing that gets them through such a harrowing thing as being at a theatre. Which is really quite worrying – particularly as most of them are the cast.

The Normal People in an Audience

Not very often.

Last night £1000 was stolen from a West End theatre. Thieves took four tubs of ice cream, three bags of sweets, and a handful of souvenir brochures.

What to Wear

We live in an age of Twitter, Snapchat, Instagram and Facebook – where you can get snapped by the paparazzi at any moment and your photo uploaded onto the internet within seconds. And this means dressing correctly at all times – you don't want that photo of you resembling a giant marshmallow going viral, do you, dear?

There is a constant pressure to wear the right things at all events – which can be very confusing when going to different types of productions. You obviously want to look nice and feel good – but there also has to be a practicality about what items you choose to hide your body (or not hide your body, if watching *Mrs Henderson Presents*, *Calendar Girls*, *The Girls* or The Chippendales). Many people see theatre as a treat – and use it as an excuse to dress up for the occasion. It adds to the excitement, and makes the whole experience more glamorous – which should be encouraged. There's nothing as off-putting as sitting next to someone who is wearing a stained jacket, ripped shirt and has an odour of urine – but I suppose everyone has to sit next to a director at some point.

The first thing you have to do before putting on your posh frock and heels is to know what kind of venue you are attending. There really is little point wearing the latest miniskirt from Topshop if you're going to a village hall to see a two-man play about a prime minister and his pet pig. Of course, if you're going to your local theatre then you should definitely wear something nice. Chances are you will bump into someone you know – so wearing a nice crop-top is bound to get the neighbours talking, particularly if you're a man.

Producers have been known to encourage the audience to dress up: for Mark Rylance and Louis Jenkins' play *Nice Fish*, a limited number of free tickets were made available to audience members who came dressed as fishermen or the catch of the day (stinking of fish was optional – though most went all out).

Your Perfect Theatre Wardrobe

Here is my essential guide to the different types of clothing I recommend for some specific types of productions and varieties of venues. Follow it religiously and you're guaranteed to be wearing the perfect attire for your theatrical adventure, dear.

Local Arts Venues/Church Halls

Wear lots of layers to keep you warm, as often these venues don't have heating of any kind. Take a hot water bottle, heated blanket, and large hairy partner to get your body temperature up at the interval.

Open-Air Theatres

I recommend taking two different options if you're going to be sitting outside. You need some nice shorts and a T-shirt for those beautiful balmy summer days when you're working on your tan. And you'll also need a woolly jumper, waterproofs and thermal vest in case the heavens open, leaving you a wet, dribbling mess by the curtain call (and nobody likes being a wet, dribbling mess at that time of night – unless you've been out in Soho, of course). Enduring all weather conditions is part of the thrill of open-air theatre –

if you like battling the elements and watching actors getting drenched then this is for you.

The National Theatre

When attending the National Theatre you should imagine you are back in the Cub Scouts or Girl Guides, and 'Be Prepared' for every eventuality – because chances are, you will get lost. The National Theatre is a labyrinth of theatricality; not only has it got three auditoria (the Olivier, the Lyttelton and the Dorfman – formerly the Cottesloe), it has restaurants, coffee shops, toilets, a souvenir shop (formerly a bookshop), a box office, an educational centre, and a lovely statue of Julian Clary outside.

The National (or 'The Nash', as it is called by people who want to work there) is rather beautiful inside, in stark contrast to its exterior appearance of an NCP car park. It is a place where drama is found, egos are trapped, and youngsters are lost (only to emerge ten years later as Rory Kinnear). It is always advisable to plan ahead when visiting. Be sure to know what auditorium you are visiting, what time the show starts, and where the nearest toilets are. The first time I went I got so confused I ended up walking on stage during a particularly emotional scene in *Hamlet* – it was all rather alarming, particularly when Daniel Day Lewis ran at me with a prop dagger.

So as well as taking a map, a flashlight, breadcrumbs to mark your route on the floor, and a compass, you should wear something lovely and fluorescent – this way your friends can find you when you inevitably get lost searching for the loos.

Shakespeare's Globe

Take waterproofs, to protect you from all that Shakespearean spitting. Or if you really want to be authentic, wear tights, a ruff, stockings, codpiece, doublet, breeches, cloak, hat and corset – and then whenever you feel so inclined you can just wander on stage. Do it with confidence and the rest of the audience will presume you are part of the production (whilst the rest of the actors stare at you and shit themselves).

Studio Theatres

Lots of bigger theatres have a second space where smaller, more intimate productions are staged. These kinds of venues are compact, condensed and cosy. There will often be limited leg room due to theatres cramming in as many seats as possible, and you will be sitting on hard plastic chairs. So I advise wearing at least three pairs of pants or take your own cushion for added bottom comfort (bumfort).

Often at these kinds of venues you will be sitting opposite other members of the audience – either in traverse (with the audience on either side), or in the round. This can be wonderful, but also horrendous. If the acting is bad, you have the added pleasure of looking at your fellow audience members and spotting who you want to chat up during the interval. I have even witnessed audience members playing Wink Murder across the stage.

Press Nights

If you chance upon a press night, wear your nicest frock, biggest heels, and brightest lipstick. Press nights are all about being seen – so avoid anything that makes you get lost in the crowd. If you fancy getting your mugshot on

WhatsOnStage.com or in *The Stage* (and who doesn't?), walk down the carpet with confidence and purpose. Look like you belong there, stare at the cameras, and push celebrities out of the way. This is your moment to shine, don't let anyone stop you (though if you see security heading in your direction, drop your pose, abandon your heels, and leg it, dear).

Pantomimes

Pantomimes are wonderful events, and I'm a big fan of anything that involves men wearing dresses – but it is simply impossible to avoid children and their infections at a panto (unless you're going to one starring Jim Davidson, but then it's best to avoid them altogether). Be prepared, and wear everything that can help your fight against airborne germs and half-sucked sweets. Personally, I favour a latex mask.

Immersive Theatre

There are many companies that specialise in immersive shows. This form of entertainment goes by many different names: immersive theatre, site-specific theatre, interactive theatre, close-up theatre, promenade theatre, and sweaty theatre. These kinds of shows don't have a designated seating area, as the performance happens everywhere – above you, below you, in front of you, and sometimes, inside you (if you are lucky). They can be very liberating experiences – and defy the old stuffy traditions of theatre to give the audience something new.

Some immersive shows even require you to wear a mask before entering, so that you become totally anonymous – giving you a sense of freedom to explore the show yourself, at your own time, feeling no obligation to stay tied down with your partner. A mask truly is a liberating thing. The venues for these kinds of shows vary significantly – from abandoned warehouses in East London, to old theatres, circus spaces, parks and dark alleyways.

There was even a touring show that was performed in people's living rooms, where the event turned the audience's house into a theatre – a thrilling idea. Nowadays, though, I won't allow any actor to perform in my house. The last time that happened, Brian Blessed broke two vases, squashed my niece, refused to shout 'Gordon's alive!', and ran off with a bumper pack of Penguins.

When going to immersive theatre, always avoid wearing your nicest outfit – it will inevitably get covered in sweat, water, tears and acting fluid.

Opera

Wear your nicest suit or poshest M&S frock. Opera can be an amazing spectacle, with delicious voices and emotional performances. If you've never been to an opera it can be quite overwhelming – and your ears may need protecting from all the tuneful warbling. So as well as dressing to kill, you should also take some earplugs to prevent your eardrums from exploding.

We've decided not to give A-level results today to students who want to act. They need to get used to not getting an answer, dear.

What to Take

As well as *wearing* the right things, you also need to be sure to *take* the right things. You don't want to get comfy only to realise you haven't bought your Jean Valjean teddy with you. So, what things should you always remember to take to the theatre?

Your Essential Theatre Kit List

Sweets – Emergency sweets are essential. If the show is slow, the acting stodgy, and the theatre uncomfortable, you can always rely on Jelly Babies to lift your spirits.

Glasses – If you are sitting a long way from the stage then take your spectacles. And make sure they are the right ones (Ray-Bans aren't much use in a darkened theatre, dear).

Money – You may have already taken out a loan to pay for your ticket, but you'll need more than that to get through a theatrical spectacular. You might want a programme or souvenir brochure, though personally I wouldn't bother as you can get all the info online these days. The only exception I'd make is in purchasing a 'programme-text', where the script of the play and the programme double-up in one beautifully produced, attractively designed, durable, affordable book, so that you can re-enact your favourite speeches on the Tube home and make yourself look clever when your friends look at your bookshelves. (NB. My publisher forced me to put this bit in.)

You will also need money for a car park, if you're driving, and some for your interval alcohol, if you're not driving. And of course if you've bought children along, you'll also need extra pennies to invest in show merchandise. Little darlings love wasting mum and dad's money on useless gifts – especially those plastic flashing lights at pantomimes that get waved around for two minutes and then break. Show merchandise can range from CD soundtracks, T-shirts, scripts and caps – to more unusual items, like inflatable Andrew Lloyd Webber dolls (life size, and very popular with the over-sixties).

Ticket – This piece of paper is your entry pass to performance heaven (Stephen Sondheim) or performance hell (*Stephen Ward*). It is the currency of the theatre world. If you don't have your ticket, you will be refused entry and asked to leave without so much as a 'Thank you and goodbye.' If the show doesn't have reserved seating you should arrive promptly so that you can proudly claim the best seats in the house – only to be told to move along to the end of the row. If you have the option, it is advisable to print your ticket at home, or collect it early from the theatre to avoid the last-minute stampede at the box office.

Slippers – For cosiness reasons.

Earplugs – For blocking out any singing that's a bit shitty (shinging).

Nuts – For eating. And throwing at bad actors (bactors).

Tissue Paper/Handkerchief – You don't want to be trapped in the middle of a show and need to blow your nose, only to realise you have nothing to blow it on – so an emergency hankie is an essential item for such occasions. They are also useful if you get particularly emotional during a show and need to wipe away tears – recommended when watching *Blood Brothers*, *Les Misérables* or *Puppetry of the Penis*.

Water – Everyone who works in theatre knows the importance of a constant supply of water. Indeed, it is an

Equity rule that actors must carry a bottle of H2o with them at all times. As an audience member, you should also partake in this pastime – because, as we all know, hydration is key. Theatres can be hot places, with all those lights, fellow audience members, and actors emoting everywhere – it is important to have something to cool you down. Stripping into your panties is another alternative, but please avoid doing this, as it distracts the actors.

Booster Seat – Essential if you are short. Or if you have a child with you. Or if you want to annoy the person sitting in the row behind.

Condoms – Essential for single people, those going on a date, and audience members sitting in a box.

A Copy of the Script or Vocal Score – Not essential, but it can be fun if you are sitting in the first couple of rows. Nothing makes actors more nervous than seeing someone in the audience following the script or score as they perform – it makes them feel that they have to be as precise as possible. Keep an eye on actors if you ever do this – it is marvellous fun, dear.

What Not to Take

There is a common and perfectly understandable practice in theatre nowadays where security will check your luggage, hand baggage, plastic bags, Tupperware, coat pockets, and even down the front of your trousers (if you're lucky). Small hand luggage should be permitted into the auditorium; larger items are to be checked in at the cloakroom, along with your cloak, before curtain-up/take-off.

You should avoid taking too much luggage to the theatre, as I hear that some venue owners are thinking about introducing an excess baggage fee. Obviously it is understood that if going to see any show over three hours, you might need to take a suitcase – as you may want to change your outfit in the interval, or slip into pyjamas if it gets past your bedtime.

The use of photographic or recording equipment of any kind is, of course, strictly prohibited, mainly because actors don't want their performance appearing all over YouTube before they're 'ready for their close-up'. So leave your telescopic lenses and tripods at home, please.

Many theatres will also not allow alcohol to be brought into the building – purely so audiences have to buy it from the extortionate theatre bar. However, if you want to smuggle some in, you can either hide it in your bag, decant it into a water bottle, or insert a selection of miniatures into your bottom. Whichever sounds more appealing. Anything on (or in) your person that looks like a weapon will be confiscated, so avoid turning up with one of those new musical-theatre sex toys (the 'Elphaba' green dildo is particularly easy to spot).

Due to new healthy food regulations the song 'A Spoonful of Sugar' has been renamed 'A Spoonful of Low-Calorie Sweetener', dear.

What to Eat (and Not to Eat)

'Ladies and gentlemen, may we remind you to turn off your mobile phones and electronic devices. And may we also take this opportunity to invite you to open all crisp, sweet, and food wrappers now. Thank you.' Cue a cacophony of rustling, opening, crunching and crinkling – and then the sound of silence, hopefully.

The issue of food in a theatre is a delicate one. Many per-formers feel it should be banned from theatres altogether, and indeed Imelda Staunton succeeded – it is now illegal to eat anything within a fifty-metre radius of her.

For now, you are allowed to take sweets and snacks into most theatres, but anything that could be considered a three-course meal will be frowned upon. Recently a young couple arrived at the theatre with a portion of fish and chips – and I had no alternative but to ban them after they refused to give me a chip. If you're going to bring smelly food into the auditorium, at least let me have a mouthful, dear.

Nonetheless, I think it would be foolish to enforce an out-right ban on everything – it's a matter of being clearer on what is acceptable. Just be considerate. Noise, unless com-ing from the stage, invariably frustrates and annoys other audience members and actors. It takes the focus away from the drama on stage, and brings everyone back to reality when they hear the crunching of crisps, the snapping of Kit Kats, and the salty smell of skipjack tuna. If you open a packet of Jelly Babies ensure it's a bumper bag so the rest of your row can partake. And never take anything that smells more pungent than a chorus boy's jockstrap.

It is also essential that any food you decide to take is opened before the show has started. There is nothing worse than hearing someone opening a can of baked beans halfway through a rousing rendition of 'Some Enchanted Evening'. So by 'open', I mean *fully* opened and resting in your lap. This means your hand won't rustle the packet every thirty seconds, and also allows Doris in the next seat along to help herself.

As well as being considerate when opening food wrappers, you should also take the same care with the volume of your mastication (i.e. your chomping and chewing). A noisy eater can distract from even the loudest acting. In the theatre there is a tradition of sucking – it is how actors get jobs, singers lubricate vocal folds, and directors get talent out of performers. The same applies to audience members – if you have something to eat, suck it. You'll appreciate it more and the pleasure will last a lot longer. Suck and swallow. One of the most trusted of theatrical traditions.

Your Ideal Theatre Menu

Luckily for you, dear reader, my crack team of theatre-etiquette scientists have performed noise-pollution tests on some of the most common products used for snacking purposes. I can report that the following treats have been certified as acceptable for a theatre trip – as long as all packets have been opened in advance of curtain-up.

Pringles (or any other crisp/potato-based snack in a tube) – Far less noisy than regular packets. However, keep the lid off the tube until the interval or the end of the show, since continual popping of the lid can become tiresome, unless you do it in time with the music. But, as you know – once you pop, you can't stop (the beat).

Chocolates – Fine to take to the theatre (unwrapped), since they are easy to eat and silently melt in the mouth. However, avoid taking them on hot days as they will turn into a slimy brown mess all over your new outfit. As for chocolate bars and biscuits, try soft ones like **Snickers**, **Mars Bars**, **Turkish Delight** and **Jaffa Cakes** – unwrapped in advance. A **Bounty** will allow you to taste paradise in two halves – before and after the interval. And **Maltesers** are little chocolate balls of joy; better to suck than to crunch, though.

Chewing gum – Permitted. But please refrain from sticking it under your seat or to the person in front.

Sweeties like **Fruit Gums** and **Pastilles** are ideal. As is **Haribo** – but avoid those super sour ones, as they have a tendency to make people scream 'Eurgh', 'God, that's disgusting' and 'My tastebuds are melting.'

Popcorn – Fine, as long as it's in a box which is opened before the show. And it's not a disgustingly flavoured, artisanal popcorn, which doesn't have the word 'anal' in it for nothing.

Cans and bottles – Fine, as long as the cans and bottles are opened before the show, and are plastic. Sadly, Dom Pérignon doesn't yet come in plastic bottles, but I'm working on it...

Ice cream – Quiet to open, quiet to lick – it's simply the best quiet treat for the theatre. In fact, ice cream was actually invented to be the perfect theatrical food.

Nuts – My favourite.

And here's a list of absolute no-nos. If I see you eating any of these, I really can't be held responsible for my actions – suffice it to say, it will make Sweeney Todd look like a Care Bear.

Foil-wrapped crisps.

Individually wrapped sweets.

Big Macs, **KFC**, **kebabs**, **chips**, **Burger King**, **Domino's** and **takeaways** – because all of these are too smelly, even if you drown them with Febreze beforehand. And **YO! Sushi** – because it's overpriced and mediocre.

A picnic – There's just no room, unless you're sitting in a box or at an open-air production. Then go for it, dear.

Crunchie – Too crunchy.

Flake – Too flaky.

Biscuits – Too biscuity.

And finally, no **Easter Eggs** – apart from Easter weekend when some shows have relaxed egg-eating performances.

How to Get There

Sometimes going to the theatre can be very confusing, even before arriving at the venue. You can get off at the wrong Tube station, forget to wear your show-pants, leave your tickets at home, or go to the cinema by mistake. Once I waltzed into the wrong theatre and watched the first half of *Lord of the Dance* when was I meant to be watching something better. Of course, mistakes like this are rare outside of London – it's very difficult to go to the wrong theatre in somewhere like Lyme Regis – as there's only one. The truth is, London has nearly as many theatres as it does people, so the opportunity for error is particularly high.

So plan ahead. Theatre is a serious spectator sport, and you don't want to waste essential drinking time by going to the wrong one. Some theatres are very easily confused because their names are so similar – it's easy for the uninitiated to confuse the Lyric Theatre, Lyric Hammersmith and Hammersmith Apollo; or the Royal National Theatre, the Royal Court Theatre, Theatre Royal Drury Lane and Theatre Royal Haymarket. Don't confuse the Apollo Victoria with the Apollo or the Victoria Palace, which is also different from the Palace, The Other Palace, Buckingham Palace, Victoria Station and Victoria's Secret. And please don't go to Cambridge to find the Cambridge Theatre, or end up in Chicago to see *Chicago*.

With a little research, plenty of gin and reading Act Five of this book, your quest will be resolved in no time. The best apps and websites to plan your theatre journey are the Transport for London (TfL) Journey Planner (tfl.gov.uk/plan-a-journey), City Mapper (citymapper.com), Google Maps (maps.google.co.uk), and Trainline (thetrain-line.com). These will present you with the quickest routes to your destination, and include options for every mode of available transport: trains, buses, by foot, by bike, on the Tube, and – on City Mapper – Teleporter (genuinely).

Travelling on the London Underground is painful, and can result in the undesirable loss of your money, confidence and virginity. You will invariably sit next to someone who is a stranger to deodorant – and may even have someone attempt to talk to you. In London, if a stranger tries to make any kind of verbal communication then they are classed as a first-class weirdo, even if they're asking for medical assistance. People in London don't communicate with other people – particularly on public transport. You should also avoid smiling at people, just assume a steady, vacant gaze at all times. It is an unwritten law of commuting in our dear capital.

However, if you get really lost, then look for people wearing jogging bottoms, a baseball cap, a hoodie emblazoned with the name of a show, and holding a water bottle – these will undoubtedly be actors who will happily help you find a theatre (particularly if you're trying to find the one where they're performing). Alternatively, then just pop into the first theatre you find and ask staff to direct you. Most theatres and ticket booths will also give you a free little map of Theatreland – at no extra cost (which is a wonderful thing to give your auntie for Christmas). It's not so useful if you're trying to find a fringe or off West End venue, though. The uncharitable would say that's your fault for booking to see a show there. I say: just get a bloody iPhone, dear.

The forty-odd West End theatres can be found in Theatreland, an area stretching across much of the City of Westminster in the centre of London, generally considered to cover from Oxford Street in the north to the Strand in the south, and Regent Street in the west to Kingsway in the east. The name 'Theatreland' always amuses me. It sounds like a dramatic amusement park. And I suppose in a way it is. Except you have to pay for every ride. And each ride can cost up to £100.

How to Find Your Seat

Having successfully located the correct theatre, your next challenge awaits! The auditorium is a dimly lit maze, with rows upon rows of seats – and now your aim is to find the one where you will be resting your derrière for the duration of the evening.

Sometimes you will turn up to what you believe is the right area of the auditorium – only to be directed to a different part. For example, you may find yourself heading into the dress circle, only to be rugby-tackled to the ground and told to use a different entrance. Some bigger theatres will have different entrance areas for each section of the auditorium – South Terminal, Area A, Gangway 4, Row F, Seat 12, etc. – and this will be printed on your ticket.

Even when you've actually managed to make your way into the right area, your task has barely begun. Then you have to identify the correct seats – which can be terribly confusing, especially if you don't know the alphabet. The rows are labelled in alphabetical order from the front to the rear of the auditorium (though some theatres omit rows I and O, because these letters look too much like the numbers 1 and 0 to stupid people), and are generally marked by tiny little letters found on the last seat, or floor of each row. Sometimes these letters are so small that it can be hard to identify which row is which. If this is the case, you have to use your alphabet skills to start from the front and work your way backwards.

However, saying that, sometimes it is not that straightforward – as rows towards the front may have been removed to allow for a bigger set or an orchestra pit, or simply so that the producers don't have to pay the actors as much (there are different grades of theatres, and one way we producers can pay actors less is by taking seats out to make it a smaller-grade theatre). In this case, the row at the front may not be A at all; it may actually be row E. Conversely, shows not requiring a big set/orchestra pit can have extra seats inserted at the front, so that the rows start AA, BB, CC and so on, before reverting to the alphabet that *Sesame Street* taught us.

When you do manage to find your row then all you need to do is find your seat. This is always made more complicated by the sea of people already sitting down. You can pretty much guarantee that your seats will be in the middle, and in your way are lots of sullen-looking audience members dribbling into their programmes. Things get even more complicated if you find someone else in your seat – where you either have the option of turfing them out with physical force, or sitting on them until they get the point.

Top Tips for Finding Your Seat

- Arrive early. Really early. Claim your seat just as the house opens, and sit for half an hour memorising the programme and laughing at your fellow audience members as they hunt for the correct row.

- If the row behind yours has fewer people in their seats, consider walking down this row and climbing over into your own seat. However, don't try this if you're wearing a miniskirt; unless you're an exhibitionist – in which case, do.

- Consider purchasing seats at the end of a row, or a private box. This makes life a lot easier.

- Shout 'Can everybody move, please!' at the top of your voice. This will wake people up, and they'll also feel intimidated, so consequently will do anything to cooperate.

- Pole vault across people to get to your seat. It saves you having to ask everyone to move, and looks mightily impressive.

- Walk in at the last minute, as there won't be as many people cluttering up the aisles. Only attempt if you have a high tolerance for being tutted at.

- Take rope, helmet and climbing equipment and abseil down into your stalls seat from the dress circle (or the balcony if you are Bear Grylls).

- Do the opposite of everyone else, and don't ask people to stand – ask them to remain seated and lift their legs. Then simply get on all fours and crawl to your designated seat. This is fun, gives you a boot-camp-style workout, and a lovely view of everyone's show-pants, dear.

Arriving Late

You are a good, well-behaved, discerning individual with excellent taste – which is why you are reading this book. But there is an undesirable species in the world who refuse to take their role in society seriously. They spend all of their time getting ready, changing and re-changing – or instead simply don't even bother and go straight to the pub. Upon reaching their desired destination, they will begin moaning, panting and vomiting on front-of-house staff who won't let them in until an 'appropriate moment'. I am, of course, talking about the latecomer.

Latecomers have a terrible habit of not only ruining the theatrical experience for themselves – they are also terrifically qualified in mucking it up for the other 1,500 audience members (or eight audience members if watching a fringe show). In fact, often at smaller venues, latecomers are not allowed in at all – as getting to their seats would involve walking over the stage – and a random audience member trying to find their seat is generally far more interesting than the play itself.

If you are late for a show – don't be! – you will not usually be allowed straight to your seat. The front-of-house staff will place you in a holding area just outside the gentlemen's toilets where there will be a TV monitor showing a live link of the stage. One bonus of being a latecomer is that whilst you're watching this monitor outside you can decide if the show looks rubbish. If it does, you can politely leave and go to the pub next door, and thank the god of theatre that you don't have to sit through three hours of dreary, posh shouting.

Whilst waiting, you also have the chance to mingle with other latecomers – where you can all moan about not being allowed in after you've paid £50 a ticket ('That's at least 50p a minute. So if you let me in ten minutes late that's a fiver's worth of drama I've missed').

At the 'appropriate moment' you will be led carefully into the auditorium by the tiptoeing usher. Your duty at this point is to be as silent as possible – particularly when working your way into the middle of a row (latecomers always have seats in the middle, it's the law). In the past I have seen spectacular displays of upstaging from latecomers, ranging from falling over, spilling drinks on OAPs, sitting on and suffocating small children, and refusing to go to their seat by repeatedly stating 'We don't want to distract anyone' which distracts everyone – until finally an usher threatens to swap their ticket for the eight-hour Greek tragedy that's on at the Almeida.

If you ever find yourself being led discreetly to your seat, just follow the usher who should direct you as quickly and efficiently as they can. However, often the usher will make the situation a lot worse by shining a torch as they lead you down the aisle – and then point it at your seat – thus making everyone in the auditorium, including the actors, see you. When this happens, work your way to your seat mouthing the word 'Sorry' to everyone you clamber over. If the journey is taking a particularly long time you may even want to apologise to the actors (especially if they've stopped mid-speech to stare). Once at your seat, sit still, don't fidget, and look forward. You must then focus on the action, even though you'll have no idea what's going on. Or simply fall asleep.

The other option is to ask the usher to sit you somewhere less distracting – maybe there are some empty seats towards the back. These seats will perhaps not be as good as the ones you've paid for – however, you will only have to stay in them for the first half, and then at the interval you can find your real seats without upsetting everyone who is better than you and turned up on time.

Now Andrew Lloyd Webber has given up his peerage, can I have it? 'Lord WEP of Shaftesbury Avenue' has a certain ring to it, dear.

Front-of-House Staff
(of Front-of-Horse Staff if watching *War Horse*)

When going to the theatre you will undoubtedly come into contact with the people who check your tickets, show you to your seat, sell you programmes and ice creams, and spank you if you use your mobile mid-performance. They will be wearing a shirt, black trousers, and a hideously fashioned waistcoat – which makes them resemble the cartoon penguins in the *Mary Poppins* film. These people are, of course, the front-of-house staff or ushers (unless you've wandered into London Zoo, in which case, they are actually penguins).

Front-of-house staff are generally out-of-work actors or students training to be actors. They spend most of their time trying not to lose any stock or give the wrong change, because inevitably if they make a mistake it will be taken from their pay packet by monstrous managers venting their frustrations about their own impotent lives.

The pay is pretty poor – usually around £30 a show – and with eight shows a week that's a grand total of £240 (which in London allows you to live in a shed and suck on a lettuce leaf). But for actors there are obvious perks. Most of the performances are in the evenings, so they are free to audition, read Stanislavsky and practise doing the splits all day long. And drama students can work in the evenings after spending the day pretending to be a tree.

Some actors like working in a theatre when they're not acting because it allows them to be around like-minded people, and find out what's going on in terms of castings, upcoming productions and Bill Kenwright's money-saving skills. However, other actors hate working front of house – they inevitably end up selling programmes to directors, agents and casting directors they've met. And there can be nothing worse than sitting through a show, eight times a week, on an uncomfortable jump seat at the back of the theatre, when you know the show back to front, and could do it better than some of the muppets in the cast.

Sometimes the front-of-house staff are volunteers. When this is the case, the balance suddenly changes, as they are doing a favour – so the monstrous managers aren't quite as monstrous. The ushers may even be treated to the odd complimentary ice cream. Voluntary front-of-house staff are becoming particularly prevalent in off West End and regional theatres – where their continued free support is one of the reasons that allows these theatres to continue operating. They are an important part of the theatre community, and without them even more theatres would be facing closure. So thank you and bravo to you all.

Everyone should be nice to anyone working front of house. It's not their fault that the ticket agent double-booked your seats, or that their manager didn't order enough mint-choc-chip ice cream. They're not responsible for that dramatic offering floating in the gentlemen's toilet (well, they might be), and you can't blame them if Sheridan Smith is not performing. They are just standing there in their hideous waistcoat trying to make your theatrical experience go as smoothly as possible.

And that's an important point to make: everyone is as important as everyone else in the theatre. If no one worked backstage, the set wouldn't work; if there were no actors, there'd just be an empty space; and if there were no front-of-house staff, there would be no audience. Theatre really is a team effort – it is, in many ways, like that term that so many actors hate: an 'ensemble'. To make a show takes a whole ensemble of people, each one as essential as the rest. Though, of course, the producer is a little bit more essential than everyone else, dear.

Recently I was at the London Palladium when I recognised the young chap selling me a programme. I'd seen him in a production a month earlier at the same theatre, playing one of the leading roles. But now, this same talented performer was working front of house in exactly the same theatre, tearing the tickets. I had a little chat with him, and he told me that working front of house is 'just a job – and I love this theatre. When I started I felt a little embarrassed, but then realised that it works for me – and just because I've been a working actor doesn't mean I've saved much money. A guy's got to live...'

So you never know who could be selling your interval ice cream – it could even be Claire Sweeney – wouldn't that be fun?

Acting is a profession that allows you to do the thing you love. If the thing you love is telesales, dear.

Understudies

One of the main reasons people go to the theatre, apart from the ice cream in the interval, is to see celebrities. It's a sad truth, but our obsession with celebs – and who they've been playing Twister in bed with – is at an all-time high. To get more bums on seats and even begin to balance the books in the West End, we producers know that there simply must be a well-known face in a show. Indeed, the only time 'bums on seats' doesn't rely on celebs is if the show is a long-running musical, if it's been written by Lin-Manuel Miranda, or if it's a sequel about Harry and his ginger lover Ron. So you can imagine the frenzied wailing, gnashing of teeth and moans of despair if this said celeb is 'indisposed' ('got a tickly throat') or 'otherwise engaged' ('sloshed and incapable') – and that's just me. You should have seen the infamous 2001 Drury Lane Riots which broke out in the stalls when the announcement came over the tannoy (at virtually every performance) that: 'Due to the indisposition of Martine McCutcheon, the role of Eliza tonight will be played by Pam St. Clement...' I could have wept all night, dear.

When people have sold a kidney to afford a ticket it is understandable why they get annoyed if the celeb they wanted to see is not on. My advice: don't pay that much for a ticket if you're only going to see a celeb. You should also have a desire to see the production. Unfortunately, in theatre there is no way of guaranteeing the person you want to see will actually be on. Contrary to popular belief, famous people are not special or superhuman – they also have shows off due to illness, holidays, or pulling a sickie to go to the National TV Awards. However, if you do arrive and your favourite star is off, some theatres will be happy to swap your tickets for another performance. Check at the box office before the show starts.

So, what is the best thing to do if you really want to ensure a celebrity is going to be performing? A show's website should list when leading actors won't be appearing, because of planned holidays and other commitments (no one can predict when they'll be too sick or sloshed to appear, though). There are still some big shows and musicals that don't do this – as they are afraid that tickets will suffer on these days – but it should be commonplace for shows to be as transparent as possible with the paying public. Another way of finding out is by enquiring when booking tickets. This can be done by calling the theatre's box office, or by going one step further and calling the stage door. (They'll hate me for writing this – stage-door keepers hate getting too many phone calls. It prevents them from playing on their Xbox.) Of course, with Twitter, it is even possible to contact actors directly. Send them a message and ask when their holiday dates are, and keep an eye on their Twitter feed about illnesses and days they can't be bothered to go on.

As well as listing when leading performers are off – I see no reason why show websites shouldn't list the holiday dates for the entire cast. Every performer in a company becomes a semi-celeb these days, thanks to social-media platforms, and there may be a member of the ensemble who has a big following in Uruguay. Their fans would be very disappointed ('muy decepcionado') if they travelled all the way to London to hear them sing their one line in *Phantom*, only to hear it being sung by Cyril their understudy.

However, if you do turn up and the celeb you were hoping to see is not performing, I urge you to stay and give the under-study a chance. Understudies are often just as good as the regular actors (and sometimes better), with new energy and enthusiasm that the regular performer may have lost. There is nothing worse for an understudy than excitedly walking on stage, only to hear an auditorium full of tuts and sighs as they open their mouth for that first line. Don't sigh. Rejoice – because you could be witnessing the birth of a star, dear.

I'm going to install seats in theatres that give electric shocks to people who play with their phones mid-performance, dear.

How to Behave

Gone are the days when theatres would solely be full of genteel, old ladies watching matinees of *The Sound of Music*. Now we have shows about men in six-inch kinky boots, productions about boys playing with their wands, and musicals where puppets have an addiction to porn (the latest Sooty Show was particularly racy). Theatre has moved with the times, and is just as likely to cause controversy as it is to cause drowsiness. And with this has come the birth of theatre rage.

Theatre rage is something that has become as common as Natalie Cassidy returning to *EastEnders*. It is the middle-class version of football hooliganism, road rage and cage fighting – all rolled into one slightly nicer-spoken ball of mild violence. And it can begin before you've even arrived at the theatre.

It's impossible to walk through Leicester Square without spying excited theatregoers in a scramble for tickets – particularly around the TKTS half-price ticket booth. People stand for hours, days, even years, to get their hands on the tickets they desire. Sometimes, however, after all the hours of shivering in the cold, tickets for the show they want become unavailable – and this is where the frustration begins.

Tell-tale signs of a brewing theatre-rage incident are the angry displaying of jazz hands, aggressive ball-changing, and a noticeable absence of words like 'love', 'darling' and 'dear'. Full-scale rioting is common on Saturday mornings when people are told that *Phantom* is sold out and the only tickets left are for *Evita*. Think boxing is violent? You should see angry OAPs who can't get tickets for *Carousel*.

It's not much better once you arrive at the theatre. Several hundred strangers expected to sit politely and quietly in the dark for a few hours is not an environment conducive to good manners. If anything, bad behaviour is becoming more and more rife, as people pay more money to go to the theatre, and then expect to behave however they want. But when you've paid good money to be there too, don't you have a right to enjoy the production in peace, when all about you are losing their heads? Read on for my essential tips on how to be a good audience member – and what we're going to do (yes, me and you – together) to eliminate the naughty ones once and for all...

The Ten Golden Rules of Good Audience Etiquette

Going to the theatre is not just about watching the show and having a good time. It's also about being on your best behaviour and not standing out for the wrong reasons. The following list will help even the most inexperienced theatregoer look like a seasoned pro.

1. Never use your mobile phone after the show has started. Put it on silent or turn it off; a vibrating phone is still an audible one (same applies to vibrators). Even if you think you're being discreet as you send a text or check Tinder, the glow of your phone will surround you with a guilty halo – which doesn't make you look angelic, it makes you look like an ignorant prat.

2. Keep noise to a minimum. This includes coughing, rustling, opening crisp packets, belching, farting and breathing.

3. Only laugh when others laugh. Even if you don't understand what they're laughing about. No one likes a random giggler. (Take note, Biggins.)

4. Try not to be overly tall. If you are, you should shuffle around the theatre on your knees, and only sit on the back row.

5. Avoid owning Brian May hair – unless you are prepared to comb the middle of it down so the person behind you can see.

6. Don't be too smelly. And if you are, conceal it with roses around your neck, lavender in your ears, and potpourri in your pants.

7. Avoid speaking or whispering when actors are emoting – though if they're doing a long, boring speech it is encouraged. And never join in with any singing, unless it's the megamix at the end.

8. Only go to the toilets before the show and in the interval. It is far more respectful to the actors and fellow audience members if you just wet yourself.

9. Never be late. Unless you've been reliably informed that the first half-hour is rubbish. In which case, go and get sloshed. It will make everything more tolerable.

10. Don't indulge in acts of a sexual nature. Even in the interval. Because, as we all know, the interval is *not* the intercourse.

I have a dream that one day this nation will rise up, and live out the true meaning of theatrical etiquette. All people are created equal – actors, audiences, even understudies – and the time is now to show respect for all. But until every living theatregoer has read this book (merely a matter of time), don't be surprised to see several of these rules being disregarded by selfish individuals. It's sadly not unusual to see a few being broken at every performance you attend – or all ten if you're watching *Jersey Boys*.

Practically the most popular thread on the message board Theatreboard.co.uk is 'Bad Behaviour at a Show' where you can weep and wince at tales of people trying to clamber onto the stage, starting fights in the bar, answering their phones, coughing, singing, vomiting, barking like a dog... Oh, I do wish Lesley Garrett would learn how to behave.

Here are some ideas about what you can do to combat any anti-social behaviour amongst your fellow patrons:

- Speak to the front-of-house staff and mention it politely.

- Confront the offender in the loos.

- Stare at them aggressively followed with a sharp 'Do you mind?'

- Resort to your own theatre rage, and hit them with your programme/handbag/cattle prod.

- Direct them to the naughty step (outside the theatre manager's office).

- Post about it afterwards on a message board (therapeutic at least).

- Sigh, tut, do nothing, and get even more annoyed because you didn't do anything (the most common reaction).

- Or alternatively, report them to a Theatre Prefect...

The Theatre Prefect Programme

If you've ever wanted to channel your own theatre rage into something positive, and help rid the theatre of pesky audience members – your chance is now!

The Theatre Prefect Programme is my new initiative – and it is more essential than ever. With a growing trend of annoying, rude and immature audience members, Theatre Prefects will become the guardians of the auditorium, on patrol throughout a performance, armed with batons, tasers and signed copies of Kristin Chenoweth's headshot. One day soon, they will have permission to turf guilty audience members out of their seats and ban them from the rest of the performance – or, in the case of persistent offenders, from theatre for life.

My Theatre Prefects are genuine theatre-lovers who feel the time to put a stop to disruptive audience members is *now*. Applications to join the programme are now open; to acquire your Prefect's status and badge, simply tweet me your stories (@westendproducer), using the hashtag #theatreprefect, stating how you have earned your theatre points (see the table below) – and with photographic evidence, where possible. My PA will review your application and, if you pass muster, obtain your address and send you an official 'West End Producer's Theatre Prefect' badge. Wearing one of these to the theatre will alert everyone of your importance, and in time will ensure *everyone* is on their best behaviour.

Theatre Points

Earning theatre points and becoming a Theatre Prefect are the best ways of disciplining problem patrons and unwanted audience members (and of relieving boredom in overlong shows).

The more theatre points you earn – the higher chance you stand of becoming one of my Theatre Prefects. If you tell someone to be quiet you earn 20 points; waking up a snorer gets you 30. And if you accumulate lots of points and prove yourself to be an indispensable guardian of theatrical etiquette, you might be made Theatre Head Girl or Boy. Here's how to start scoring:

- Pointing and laughing at latecomers.   10 points
- Telling people to be quiet.   20 points
- Waking up snorers.   30 points
- Turning off someone else's mobile phone.   40 points
- Throwing someone else's mobile onto the floor and stamping on it if it rings.   50 points
- Turfing out drunks.   60 points
- Taping shut the mouth of an incessant talker.   70 points
- Spraying smelly audience members with Febreze.   80 points
- Throwing Maltesers into a snorer's mouth.   90 points
- Rescuing a fellow audience member if the theatre ceiling starts to fall on their head.   100 points

Disclaimer: Obviously, some of the above should only be attempted if you feel it is safe to do so. I would advise observing from afar, and if you feel you can ask someone to be quiet or to switch their phone off without them getting violent, then your Theatre Prefect status is guaranteed. West End Producer does not accept any responsibility for any drama, on stage or off, whilst earning your theatre points.

Once you have been formally confirmed as a Theatre Prefect, you should consider yourself my official representative in any auditorium you find yourself in – and empowered accordingly. All venue managers and ushers will give you their full support in carrying out your essential duties. The actors, the audience, the staff: everyone is relying on you to ensure the evening's entertainment runs smoothly. Wear your badge with pride, and be sure to encourage others to enrol.

If you are not yet a Theatre Prefect, but see one on duty, then please support them in their vital work. If they are advancing down the row to seize and eject an overly noisy chewer, then treat them as you would an ambulance with its siren on: indicate, and flatten yourself against your seat until they're safely past. Don't be offended if you're subjected to a random frisking mid-performance – if your phone is safely off, you'll have nothing to fear. And if a Theatre Prefect looks parched at the interval, then offer them your drink to sustain them through their second-act commitments. Ask not what a Theatre Prefect can do for you, but what you can do for a Theatre Prefect.

Let's change theatre together for the good. Because united we can all 'Make Theatre Great Again', dear.

OLIVER!

History – *Oliver!* is based on a Charles Dickens novel (serialised from 1837–39) or a Christmas Day episode of *EastEnders* (serialised since 1985), I forget which. It was written by Lionel Bart, who couldn't write music so just sung his melodies into a tape recorder, and let someone else sort it out; not to be confused with Lionel Blair, who knows how to do everything.

Premiering in the West End in 1960, *Oliver!* has become one of the most beloved of all British musicals. It has been revived numerous times and was made into a wonderful Oscar-winning film by the director Carol Reed (whose nephew Oliver played Bill Sykes). It is a staple of schools and youth theatres throughout the world, as long as Cameron Mackintosh will let them have the performance rights. It is the very definition of a 'misspent youth' if someone was not in a production of it during their childhood.

Plot – Oliver Twist is a young orphan boy who runs away to London. He ends up living with lots of other boys and a bearded man who hasn't passed his DBS check. He soon befriends a lady called Nancy who is in a violent relationship with a man named Bill, and they spend most of their time in a pub shouting at each other. Eventually, Oliver is reunited with his real mother's father, and they all live happily ever after (apart from Nancy, who is battered to death by Bill).

Oliver! is basically *Les Mis* – but sanitised for younger audiences. There are lots of similarities: Oliver steals a handkerchief, Valjean steals a loaf of bread. Both shows feature a thief – Fagin and Thénardier. Oliver is sold, Cosette is sold. They both have a rousing songs in public houses – 'Oom-Pah-Pah' and 'Master of the House'. 'Bring Him Home' is a song with a three-word title, as is 'Who Will Buy?' (try singing the lyrics of one to the tune of the other). And both were originally written in a foreign language – *Les Misérables* in French; and *Oliver!* in Cockney. Uncanny, eh?

Characters – Oliver (kid), Artful Dodger (kid), Fagin (man), Bill Sykes (man), Nancy (woman), Bullseye (dog).

Best-known actors to have played Fagin – Ron Moody, Rowan Atkinson, Russ Abbot, Robert Lindsay, Roy Hudd – basically any actor who has a name beginning with 'R'.

Most likely to play Fagin in the future – Roy Walker, Ryan Gosling, Rod Stewart, Russell Brand, Rupert Grint, Robert Downey Jr., Ricky Martin and Robert De Niro.

Best-known actors to have played Oliver – Children from Sylvia Young Theatre School, who then grew up and discovered that the glamorous world of theatre can be pretty shit when you're older than sixteen.

Most likely to play Oliver in the future – Children from Sylvia Young Theatre School, who *will* grow up and discover that the glamorous world of theatre can be pretty shit when you're older than sixteen.

Best-known songs – 'Food Glorious Food'; 'Oliver!'; 'Where is Love?'; 'Consider Yourself'; 'Pick a Pocket or Two' (our government's anthem); 'I'd Do Anything'; 'Be Back Soon'; 'As Long as He Needs Me'; 'Who Will Buy?'; 'It's a Fine Life'; 'Oom-Pah-Pah'; 'Reviewing the Situation'… Basically, all of them, except 'It's Your Funeral'.

Rejected songs – 'Nude Glorious Nude'; 'Buy One Boy, Get One Free'; 'Stealing is an Honest Business'; 'Asking for "More" Lands You in Deep Shit'; 'I Knew I Shouldn't 'ave Trusted That Old Man Who Lives with All 'em Boys'.

THE LION KING

History – *The Lion King* is one of Disney's finest films, released in 1994, and basically retelling the story of *Hamlet* but with a happy ending (not *that* sort of happy ending). It has songs with lyrics by Sir Timothy Miles Bindon Rice, and music by Sir Elton Hercules John: officially the most remarkable middle names in the business, after James Kimberley Corden, Billie Paul Piper, and Ralph Nathaniel Twisleton-Wykeham-Fiennes (though Elton actually chose his middle name; his real one is Kenneth).

The film was so successful that Disney Theatrical Productions wanted to make more money out of it, and turned to visionary director Julie Taymor to create the African Pride Lands on stage with some wonderful puppetry. The show opened in Minneapolis in 1997, before moving to Broadway later that year, and the West End in 1999. Since then, *The Lion King* has taken more money at the box office than any other stage show or cinema release: more than £3.8 billion in ticket sales alone – not including merchandise, cast recordings, or revenues from the film. Clearly 'Hakuna Matata' doesn't only mean 'No worries'; it also means 'Loadsamoney'.

Plot – A lion cub is made to feel responsible for his father's death (though it's actually the fault of his evil uncle and a stupid herd of wildebeesties), so he runs away and gets insurance from a meerkat. The meerkat's best friend is a warthog, and between them they show the lion cub the secret of life – jumping up and down while shouting ridiculous words. The cub grows up, goes back to his family, kills his uncle, becomes king, and marries a lioness. All narrated by Sir David Attenborough. Sadly there are no donkeys in *The Lion King*. I love donkeys.

Characters – Simba, Scar, Mufasa, Nala, Timon, Pumbaa, Chumbawamba.

Best-known performers to have played a lion – James Earl Jones, Jeremy Irons, Matthew Broderick, Bert Lahr (who played the cowardly one in *The Wizard of Oz*).

Most likely to play a lion in the future – Any actor who can carry a giant lion mask around on their head (it's a bonus if they can roar in tune).

Best-known songs – 'Circle of Life'; 'Hakuna Matata'; 'Can You Feel the Love Tonight?'; 'I Just Can't Wait to be King' (Prince Charles's favourite); 'Shadowland'.

Rejected songs – 'Dodecahedron of Life'; 'God, This Puppet is Heavy – I Need Physio'; 'Warthogs Have the Most Fun'; 'Never Trust Anyone Called Scar'; 'They Didn't Have to Wear Heavy Masks in *Cats*, Did They?'

LES MISÉRABLES

History – *Les Misérables* (often shortened to *Les Mis* – or *The Glums*) is not a musical chronicling the life of Les Dennis (although I'd pay good money to see that), but is based on the novel *Les Misérables* by Victor Hugo. It is not set in the French Revolution, as many people think – but against the backdrop of the June Rebellion of 1832, which was a small Parisian uprising forty-three years after the French Revolution.

Les Mis was written by Alain Boublil and Claude-Michel Schönberg, originally released as a concept album in French, and then produced at the Palais des Sports in Paris in 1980, where it ran for three months. Cut to a few years later, and Cameron Mackintosh was sipping champagne when the French album crossed his desk. His eyes flashed up with franc signs (this was before the euro, remember?) and he soon enlisted friend Herbert Kretzmer to translate it into English (the only useful French words Cameron knew were 'Moët' and 'Chandon').

Mackintosh also realised it needed some 'proper good acting' in it, so he went to the Royal Shakespeare Company and asked them to co-produce the musical. His *Cats* collaborator Trevor Nunn took on directing duties, with John Caird as co-director (or 'bloke who agrees with Trevor and makes the tea'), and an original cast led by Colm Wilkinson as Jean Valjean, Alun Armstrong as Thénardier, Roger Allam as Javert,

Michael Ball as Marius, Frances Ruffelle as Eponine, and Patti 'Scourge of the Mobile' LuPhone as Fantine. Originally the production lasted over four hours, but after judicious cutting and quicker conducting they got it down to about three.

Les Misérables opened at the Barbican in 1985 (then the London base of the RSC) – to widely negative reviews. 'A witless and synthetic entertainment,' moaned the *Observer*; 'A lurid Victorian melodrama,' grumbled the *Sunday Telegraph*. Mysteriously, those critics were never heard of again... Meanwhile, due to word of mouth and the public disregarding the reviews, demand for the show was overwhelming, and it started selling out, transferring to the Palace Theatre in December 1984, then down the road to the Queen's in 2004. It is now the world's longest-running musical with productions all over the world, a version for schools to perform, about three-dozen different cast recordings, anniversary concerts in vast stadia, and even a film starring Wolverine (see below). Dear Cameron well and truly had the last laugh.

Plot – Essentially, a man steals some bread and has a game of chase with another man who is holding a truncheon. Everyone dies.

Characters (all said in a French accent) – Jean Valjean, Javert, Thénardier, Madam Thénardier, Eponine, Cosette, Fantine, Marius, and a load of other people who do some stuff but no one really knows what they're called.

Best-known actors to have played Valjean – Hugh Jackman, Colm Wilkinson, Alfie Boe, Ramin Karimloo, John Owen Jones.

Most likely to play Valjean in the future – Any actor who can grow a decent beard and sing high enough to make 'Bring Him Home' sound nice eight times a week.

Best-known songs – 'At the End of the Day'; 'I Dreamed a Dream'; 'Castle on a Cloud'; 'Master of the House'; 'Stars'; 'Do You Hear the People Sing?'; 'One Day More'; 'On My Own'; 'Bring Him Home'; 'Empty Chairs at Empty Tables'.

Rejected songs – 'Where's My Bread?'; 'Come Catch Me, You Big Idiot – I Can Run Faster Than You'; 'I'm a Whore and You Know It'; Act One closer: 'Three Hours More'; 'God, It's Dark on This Stage'; 'Hate to Say It, But I Think We're All Going to Die'; 'Yes, I Was Right, We're All Dead'.

Les Mis **on film** – Despite being co-produced by Cameron Mackintosh, the 2012 film of *Les Mis* is actually very different to the stage production. It tells the story of Wolverine trying to escape from Gladiator – before getting distracted by Catwoman and looking after her kitten. Wolverine then buys said kittens from Ali G, and they go to Disneyland Paris for a bit. Catwoman's baby, being looked after by Wolverine, grows up to look like she'd be more comfortable singing ABBA on a Greek island, and falls in love with Stephen Hawking. Stephen Hawking and his friends get into an argument with some extras from *Beauty and the Beast* – and they all get shot, apart from Stephen who confuses them all by wearing a dress. He then goes home, Gladiator jumps off a bridge, Wolverine dies of old age, and Stephen and the girl from Greece snog. The End.

ACT THREE:
...GOING

'Is this a show I see before me,
The acting toward my face? Come, let me watch thee.
I hear thee not, and yet I see thee still.'

It's not what you know. It's not who you know. It's *how* and *why* you know them.

You're in your seat, and you know where the emergency exits are (at the front and back of the auditorium, and out of the window of the leading actor's dressing room). You've done your pre-show trip to the loo (your pre-wee), and opened your bottle of fizzy pop and salted snacks. You are ready to behave as an impeccable audience member: to sit back, relax and enjoy the performance as the house lights go down.

But just how is the theatrical magic you're about to witness made? This chapter doesn't set out to ruin the unique thrill of live performance, but to lift the curtain on some of the secrets of what has gone into creating theatrical legends, and who all those people wearing blacks actually are. If you already work in the theatre, you will (hopefully) know all of this already, so you can read this chapter nodding along sagely and feeling smug.

My first book, *Everything You Always Wanted to Know About Acting (But Were Afraid to Ask, Dear)* – with the catchy acronym 'EYAWTKAA(BWATA,D)' – goes into more detail about every step of putting on and being in a show (auditioning, rehearsing, performing, touring...), so make sure you buy and read a copy of that as well. And if you already have a copy, buy another and give it to your nearest and dearest. It will be their favourite Christmas present of the year.

Who's Who in Theatre

To begin with, let's explore exactly what everyone involved in the theatre industry actually does. From the master carpenter to the person who cleans the musical director's baton – everyone has their special function and role in the creation of a theatrical spectacular.

Some jobs in theatre – whether on stage or off – are never really discussed or diagnosed, so their actual role in a production is misunderstood by members of the public (or 'muggles' as they are known). How many times have you wondered what a DSM is, what a swing does, and if a wardrobe mistress is actually a whip-carrying dominatrix? Well, wonder no more, my dears – next time you buy a programme you will know exactly who everyone is, what they do, and who they do it with.

The Producer

The most important people in the business, dear. These are the people who put the show on, maybe had the idea, fight for it to happen, get investors involved, buy Hobnobs for the cast, and try to make some money. They are actively involved in all aspects of a production, including approving a cast, the creatives, and getting their favourite director on board. They are experts in getting on the good side of people – whether that be to bribe a writer so they can have the rights to their work, or promising celebs that they will have fun shouting lines into the dark eight times a week. A producer has to be very good with money – including their own money, other people's money, and money they haven't even got yet.

Producers also have to be brave and take chances. It is well known that Cameron Mackintosh had to be an au pair in Paris for three years to finance *Les Misérables*, and that Lloyd Webber had to get on all fours and purr for two months to secure the rights to *Cats*. Some producers also write books and articles, and spend a large proportion of their lives downing free alcohol at press nights. It's a hard job, but somebody has to do it, dear.

Many of the UK's most respected, prolific and wealthiest theatre producers are listed below – alongside anagrams of their illustrious names (for a bit of fun). As someone once said, 'Anagrams never lie', but looking at this list, they must have been lying. Surely?

Cameron Mackintosh – Hmm, a Canniest Crook

Sonia Friedman – Is On Fine Drama

Nica Burns – Runs in Cab

Andrew Lloyd Webber – Barely Blown Wedder

André Ptaszynski – Zaniést, Dry Spank

Bill Kenwright – Wrinkle Blight

Michael Codron – Chemical Donor

Thelma Holt – Lethal Moth

Howard Panter – Orphaned Wart

Mark Goucher – Grouch Maker

Caro Newling – Canine Growl

Sally Greene – Yes, Allergen

Edward Snape – Spawned, Dear

Kenny Wax – Wenny Kax (When 'e Cacks)

David Ian – Diva and I

David Babani – Diva and a Bib

Matthew Byam Shaw – 'Twat Shame' by Wham!

Dafydd Rogers and David Pugh – Far Drugged, Vapid and Shoddy

Jamie Hendry – Hired My Jean

Danielle Tarento – Talented or Alien?

West End Producer – Screwed-up Rodent

And that's quite enough of that, dear.

The Playwright/Writer/Composer

These talented wordsmiths wrote the thing. They had the arduous task of sitting in front of a blank computer screen or piece of paper, putting some words together, and hoping for the best. Highly skilled in the art of joined-up handwriting.

The Director

A director is in charge of the artistic vision of the entire show – deciding things like where it is set, what accents should be used, and whether to cast David Hasselhoff as King Lear. In rehearsals, they tell the actors where to stand and how to say their lines.

These days a respected director can influence ticket sales just as much as a famous actor. That's why people want to work for directors like Marianne Elliott, Richard Eyre, RuNo (Rufus Norris), Sammy Mendes, Josie (Duchess of) Rourke, and Rupert Gooldenballs. Trevor Nunn used to be on this list, but was quickly taken off after his fatal *Fatal Attraction*. It's all about being well known – and directors are becoming just as famous as the actors they are shouting at. They are masters of saying things that sound impressive, but actually mean nothing at all – for example, 'Don't drop the ball', 'Keep everything fresh' and 'Let the acting be organic.'

The best advice I've ever heard a director give to an actor: 'Be fast, be funny, and fuck off.' If every performer adhered to these rules we'd always get the last train home, dear.

The RD (Resident Director – or Ropey Director)

This person often used to be an actor, but couldn't hack the bad pay, endless auditioning, lack of independence, and feeling of no self-worth. So they become a resident director instead – and ended up feeling exactly the same.

Resident directors stay with a show once it has opened, attempting to keep it as fresh and good as it was on opening night – if it *was* fresh and good on opening night. If it was old and tired then they have to keep it that way. The resident director's job is tricky because if they change anything or add their own ideas then they get severely beaten up by the original director.

The AD (Associate Director – or Another bloody Director)

Shows often have more directors than they do performers. The associate director works with the cast when the actual director isn't available – but associates never know what they're talking about, so everyone just smiles politely and plays with their phones instead.

The Assistant Director

Tea-maker.

The MD (Musical Director – or Musical Dictator)

Musical directors are in charge of the band (or backing track if the show is *Dirty Dancing*). They also teach and inform the actors on how to sing the songs, when to sing loudly and softly, and when to *shut up*. In rehearsals they spend their time sitting at a keyboard, fingering all the notes, and using various methods of torture on actors who are flat. During performances they stand in the orchestra pit and wave their rod around in the hope that the instrumentalists will follow, but rarely do.

The Assistant Musical Director

The Assistant MD waves the musical director's rod around when they can't be bothered.

When reading music it is essential to remember that sharps are not hashtags, dear.

The Fight Director

A fight director is required on two occasions. Firstly, to choreograph fights in the show; and secondly, to split up backstage fights between the cast. There is a conventional idea that an acting company gets on wonderfully and that everyone is best friends. Sadly, this is not always the case. More often than not, there is a diva in the company who tickles, teases and taunts everyone else – which can result in all sorts of violence. People's costumes can be switched, lines cut, directors castrated, and actors humiliated. However, if a fight director is backstage when such events occur, you can be sure that the leading actor's face won't be harmed in these company scraps. ('My face is my fortune – don't touch it. I've spent thousands on Botox, darling.')

The Voice Coach

Voice coaches teach actors how to open their mouths properly so that the audience can hear what they're saying – which is a lot harder than it sounds (especially if you're talking about Hollywood stars making their stage debuts). Some voice coaches also help actors with accents, working with them to make sure that their Brummie isn't crummy, their Geordie isn't tawdry, and their RP doesn't sound like they've got Boris Johnson's plums in their mouth.

The Casting Director

Casting directors are the gatekeepers of the theatre world – organising, planning and marshalling the whole audition process. They decide which actors get invited to audition, and which ones get instructed to stay at home and suck their thumb.

The Designer

The designer will work closely with the director to design the entire 'look' of a show, principally the set. Especially talented ones can design the costumes as well. The designers are the ones who can save a show – if the actors are rubbish and the script is bad, it's amazing what a good set can do. If a set is used in the correct way it can distract even the most experienced critic from all the bad acting. After all, you can't polish a turd, but you *can* roll it in glitter. It really is remarkable how many shows have been saved by the clever placement of glitter, dear.

The Lighting Designer

The lighting designer decides which actors are lit and which are not. Actors insult them at their peril.

The Sound Designer

Sound designers carry responsibility for everything that the audience hears. They also decide what the audience doesn't hear, by setting the actors' microphones to 'mute'.

The Costume Designer

The costume designer creates the 'look' of every character: what shoes are worn (not necessary in physical theatre which is always performed barefoot), how hair is styled, if wigs are used, how make-up is applied, and if plastic surgery is required. They work closely with the set designer to make sure both of their visions compliment each other – an easier task if it's one and the same person. Actors have to be extra nice to costume designers – as they're the ones who can make them look like a giant chicken for the next six months.

You can't hide bad acting. But you can give it a better costume, dear.

The Choreographer

Choreographers conceive, create and teach the performers all the dance routines, and crucially decide how many jazz hands are going to be used. The better the choreographer, the more plentiful their use of jazz hands. As the great Bob

Fosse said, 'Choreography is writing on your feet', and as Wayne Sleep said, 'Jazz hands, jazz hands, splits, step-ball change, spin, don't fall over, smile, jazz hands!'

The Dance Captain

The captain of the dance ship. And the dance ship is something that lives at the bottom of Craig Revel Horwood's garden and contains every dance move ever invented (according to Craig's agent).

A dance captain, as well as being in the cast of a show, has the responsibility of ensuring the dance numbers stay up to scratch. As soon as a show opens, the choreographer will disappear to Mykonos – leaving the show in the capable hands of the dance captain. Dance captains can then call extra rehearsals if splits are looking sloppy and pirouettes pathetic. They are dominating professionals who wear as little as possible – usually trainers, nipple tassels, and pink hot pants. Brilliant if your dance captain is a Strallen. Not so brilliant if it's a Keith Chegwin.

The Assistant Dance Captain

The assistant dance captain is a constant form of support – just like a human sports bra. The assistant dance captain's main job is to run the company warm-up when the dance captain can't be bothered.

The Actors

See all 223 pages of my previous book, dear.

The Understudies

Understudies step up to the mark and play a role if another actor is ill. There are different types of understudies: onstage and offstage. An onstage understudy will also play a small role in the show, as well as understudying a leading role. And an offstage understudy will do nothing in the show, but will be in the theatre in case an actor is taken ill. Offstage understudying can be a harrowing task – sitting alone in a dressing room, watching re-runs of *Last of the Summer Wine*, whilst being simultaneously desperate and terrified of being asked to go on stage.

There is a wonderful theatrical anecdote about an old actor, who had been understudying in *The Mousetrap* for a number of years. One day she arrived at the theatre and the company manager ran up to her shouting, 'You're on! You're on! The leading actress has been taken ill with a bad case of food poisoning. It's your big moment, my dear!' The understudy, rather taken aback, said, 'Oh, that's marvellous! I'll just go and get my make-up bag from the car'… and was never heard from again. Apparently, even though she had been an understudy in the production for years, she hadn't learnt her lines yet – so she went back to her car, got in, and drove off. Bless.

The Swings

Swings have the unenviable task (or enviable if you're a masochist) of covering multiple roles in a show. They won't be in the show every night, but will always be in the theatre on standby in case an actor is ill or has a mid-show breakdown – in which instance they go on and play the role.

Swings are some of the most talented people working in theatre – they spend all their time learning four or five different roles (so they can swing between them) – and have to be ready at a moment's notice to step into another actor's shoes. It is a difficult task, and one that deserves far more appreciation and understanding. A regular actor in a show will get weeks to rehearse – whilst swings only get a few hours, after which they're thrown on stage with the encouraging words: 'Don't fuck it up.'

The Alternates

Sometimes a lead actor will need to take off a couple of performances each week to recover, rest their voice, and catch up on Netflix – and on these occasions, their role is covered by their alternate.

It is important that a leading actor gets this chance to rest, especially if they have a physically draining or exhausting singing role (like the 3rd Monkey in *Wicked* or the helicopter in *Miss Saigon*). There is nothing worse than watching an actor with a sore throat croak their way through a performance. Not nice for the actor, not nice for the audience, and not nice for the understudy (who should actually be doing the job).

Many years ago, an esteemed actress playing Grizabella in *Cats* had such a bad throat that she had to revert to different lyrics when singing 'Memory':

> 'Nodules,
> Not a sound from my vocals.
> Has my voice lost its memory?
> It was powerful then.
> Oh, the high notes –
> A shriek, a screech, a moan, and a groan.
> Someone give me
> Their last Vocalzone.'

Some actors take their voice preservation very seriously indeed – giving up alcohol and coffee for the duration of a run, and inhaling vapourised steam as if it was a precious commodity. Others go on 'voice rest', where they don't speak for lengthy periods. Voice rest is one the best ways of fixing a sore throat, and also an excellent way to avoid talking to your partner for a few days.

The Emergency Cover

An emergency cover is on standby in case all the other understudies are not available. They are just like a surgeon on call – at any given moment they may have to drop their child, get into scrubs, and leg it to theatre. Often, emergency covers aren't even in the show; they will have left a few years ago – but, because they previously played the role, are ready to step in if needed.

In extreme circumstances, actors on emergency cover have even had to leave their current show to go and cover a role in another production. There have been matinee performances when the actor playing the Phantom has been told that he's required to play Jean Valjean that evening.

There will usually also be an emergency cover in the existing cast – who will have had a couple of quick rehearsals so that they can get through the show. However, as they are an emergency cover, and only used in extreme circumstances, when no one else is available, this actor will not look right at all. I'll never forget the time Warwick Davis had to play the Phantom. He was far too short but performed a haunting rendition of 'Music of My Height'.

The best understudy is an understudy who the audience doesn't know is an understudy.

The Musicians

Put a lot of musicians together and – voilà! – you have an orchestra (one that smells of a brewery). Traditionally, musicians spend the performance hidden in the orchestra pit playing with their instruments. However, sometimes they are actually allowed to be visible on stage, but only when they are particularly good-looking. Musicians rehearse with the musical director separately from the cast, and meet the company during the first sing-through (the sitzprobe). You can always spot musicians pre-show as they'll be assembled outside the closest pub, dressed in tuxedos, and downing as many pints as possible before they have to stagger into the theatre and play the overture.

The GM (General Manager – or Genetically Modified)

General managers are a producer's bootlicker, backslapper and spy on the ground, supervising the show from a financial and business perspective once it is up and running. They are both someone to rely on, and someone to blame. I love them.

The CM (Company Manager – or Certifiable Monster)

A company manager has the unenviable task of looking after everyone in the company, and operates as the go-between for the cast, crew and management. Living in a broom cupboard in the theatre, they are in charge of important logistical tasks like payroll, absences, warnings and whippings (when the chorus misbehave). They have to be very diplomatic, dealing with precious performers on a daily basis – and spend most of their time answering the phone to actors calling in sick after a night out.

Everyone in a theatre is scared of the company manager – mainly because they don't want to end up on the show report. A show report is produced every evening after a performance and lists practical aspects of the show – like running times, changes to the cast, the size of the audience, and who's been overacting again. If naughty behaviour is reported, a senior member of the management may pay a visit to discipline the guilty party.

Here is an example of a show report:

Show Report	
Company	Dramarama Theatre Company
Show	*Snow White and the Eight Dwarves: A Study of Polygamy*
Venue	Reigate Village Hall
Date	23/11/17
Company Manager	Huw Janus
DSM (On the Book)	Samantha Janus
About the Show	
Start Time	Scheduled: 7.30 p.m. Actual: 7.38 p.m. (Due to Mr Barnes realising he was wearing his Act 2 costume. Mr Barnes had another of his 'nights out' last night.)
Interval Time	9.35 p.m. – 9.57 p.m.
End Time	11.19 p.m.
Running Time	Act One: 1 hour 57 mins Act Two: 1 hour 44 mins Total Running Time: 3 hours 41 mins

Performance Notes	Mr Barnes skipped back to the beginning halfway through Act One, and the rest of the cast followed. Consequently, the audience were treated to the first half-hour again. Hence, tonight's show was rather long. Mrs Turner dried in Scene 3, during her 'I've got eight lovers, but they're all bruvvers' speech. She totally forgot the names and called Grumpy 'Stumpy'. This was the main cause of the fight in the green room: 'I'm not Stumpy, I'm Grumpy, you old hag.' The doorbell sound effect stopped working, so Mr Peters offered the sound with his own voice. A valiant effort – and appreciated by the company. Although it did sound like a constipated Dalek. Mr Elliot noted that ten real cakes were consumed in Act Two as oppose to the usual two. Upon questioning, Ms James said she felt her character was 'particularly hungry tonight'. I reminded her that the budget only affords us two per show.
Technical Notes	LX Cue 16 was late because Derek was texting his ex.
Other Notes	Derek got into an argument with his ex and left the LX box during Scene Change 8 – before he'd brought the lights back up. So most of the scene was performed in the dark. It worked rather well, though. And lots of the audience commented on what a clever bit of direction it was. Perhaps keep this? It's the best feedback we've ever had.

About the Audience	
Audience Size	30, including Mr Lionheart, the director.
Audience Response	15 people left in the interval – which is much better than last night. So, all in all, a positive atmosphere backstage.

The SM (*Stage Manager – or Stoic Messiah*)

Stage managers run the show. With the help of their team, they ensure that everything to do with the production is ready and working. You can always spot people who work backstage by their top-to-toe black clothing. They wear 'blacks' so the audience don't spot them during scene changes when they move sets and strike actors.

Stage managers can be found in the pub closest to the theatre after a show until chucking-out time – where you'll see them huddled in the corner downing Special Brew and munching scampi fries.

The DSM (*Deputy Stage Manager – or Deputy Stoic Messiah*)

DSMs have the most important job in the theatre business. They decide when it is tea break. They are generally in the wings throughout the show and 'on the book' (a script marked up with all the technical cues). From this position, they 'call' the show – reading out numbers and pressing little buttons which cue the lights, the sound effects, and the fly floor (the area high above the stage from where backdrops, large set pieces and lazy actors are lowered).

'In every job that must be done, there is an element of fun' – apart from the technical rehearsal. There's nothing fun about them.

The ASM (*Assistant Stage Manager – or Absurdly Suppressed Minion*)

Assistant stage managers are yet another member of the stage-management team, but play the role of 'general dogsbody'. They are employed to do anything and everything to anything and everyone – just like a runner on a film or gimp in a sex show. ASMs have been made to cut actors' toenails, hold buckets under bottoms, and warm the leading man's balls during hazardous weather conditions (Equity guidelines state that no actor is allowed on stage if their balls are less than five degrees celsius). The assistant stage manager also gets the blame if anything goes wrong; it's part of their job description:

> 'Clause 34.5: If any accidents occur during the tenure of your employment, even if you are blameless, you will be held directly responsible.'

Assistant stage managers are also required to set the show props. Now this sounds like an easy job but it can be tortuous – especially if the show is 'proppy'. Next time you see a production with lots of pointless props littered around Bonnie Langford spare a thought for the poor ASM.

The Wardrobe Mistress

The wardrobe mistress (and her department) is in charge of the costumes for a show. They make sure that costumes still look good after years – sometimes decades – of use by countless perspiring actors, and they alter costumes if actors have been eating too many pies. In a long-running show, the wardrobe mistress oversees the fitting of costumes on all new actors – adjusting outfits, providing show-pants/socks/ lingerie, and teaching actors how to tie their shoelaces properly.

The Wig Department

Those who work in the wig department (the 'wiggies') spend their time backstage in solitary confinement looking after the cast's hairpieces. Big West End productions can have as many as eight full-time wiggies, since there may be thousands of wigs, with spare ones in case of problems (like lice or mice infestation). The wig department dress wigs daily, making sure they look perfect for each show. They are also on hand during performances – fitting wigs on actors, stopping them wearing the wrong ones, ensuring hair is styled correctly, and providing free haircuts (and actors love a freebie).

In some productions, the wiggies also have to provide merkins for when discreet areas of the body are visible. For example, it is essential Elphaba has a merkin during 'Defying Gravity' – if you're ever in the first few rows you can't miss all those bright green pubes, dear.

The Master Carpenter

The head of the stage department, and in charge of staff working on the show, the master carpenter maintains the theatre building and productions that are resident there or visiting. This includes helping with performances, making sure the set is working, repairing props, and fixing broken actors.

The Technicians and Operators

These creatures of the night wear blacks (in and out of the theatre), don't say much, and spend the performance skulking in corners, moving pieces of set about, and playing with their knobs. Having said that, the production wouldn't run without them. They're every bit as important a part of the theatrical magic as the actors. But don't tell the actors I said that – or the technicians for that matter (they'll only want another bloody raise).

The Stage-door Keeper

Sits at the stage door and permits entry to the theatre. They allow in actors, technicians and creatives, and ward off fans, obsessives and drama students. You can leave gifts for actors with the stage-door keeper – but avoid leaving cakes, chocolates and alcohol, as these will never reach their desired destination. They will just reach the stage-door keeper's mouth.

The Production Timeline

Shows don't just come together with a click of the fingers (more's the pity). They can take months or years to reach the stage – or minutes, in the case of a Theatre-in-Education tour.

To understand how a show comes together, here's a concise timeline of the key hoops through which every production must jump. In a full production schedule, every last moment needs to be rigorously planned to allow enough time for each aspect of the show: rehearsals, performances, gin drinking...

Production Timeline	
Casting	The arduous task of finding actors who can say the lines, stand in the right place, and most importantly – fit into the costume. This process usually takes a few weeks, but can be considerably longer if Simon Russell Beale isn't available.
Rehearsals	Traditionally four weeks, but can be a lot less or a lot longer depending on where the show is being performed. A regional panto gets two days; National Theatre productions get six months; or a play at the RSC – four years.
Technical Rehearsal	The technical rehearsal is for the technical team. This is when lights, sound, set and costumes are added to the production. It is during this long process that actors question their career choice and regret not working in admin.
Dress Rehearsal	When the production is performed in full show conditions – with costumes, make-up, lights, sound, and, on rare occasions, acting.
Previews	Performances to the public, but at a cheaper rate as the show is still being worked on. Invariably previews are where actors dry, directors cry, and producers get high.
The Run	The performance period. Ranging from a day to decades (some elderly actors have been touring in *Blood Brothers* since they were children).
Unemployment	The time directly after a run. Some actors try to make this sound more exciting by calling it 'Funemployment' – but this initial enthusiasm quickly disappears after they realise they haven't saved any money from their Equity-minimum touring wage. This period tends to last a couple of months, unless the actor is lucky and has a job lined up, in which case they are known as 'jammy gits'.

Sometimes a production has an R&D (research and development) period long before rehearsals begin. This is where the writer, director, producer and actors say the script out loud and run around the rehearsal room for a bit. This is often followed by a workshop – where the show is worked on for a week – followed by a 'friends and family' showing. The audience are then invited to give comments about the show whilst drinking free wine and eating sausage rolls.

Rehearsals: Where the actors are given a line reading, get told where to stand, jump into bed with each other, and catch an STD (Suspicious Typecasting in a Drama), dear.

How Actors Act

We've all been to see a show and wondered how the actors managed to achieve the seemingly impossible. But, of course, there are lots of ways that actors 'cheat' in theatre – and in this section, I'm going to play a metaphorical Dorothy Gale, drawing back the curtain to reveal that actors are mere mortals too (and the Wizard of Oz is actually just a little, wizened man from Nebraska).

Acting is all about putting on a façade, about lying convincingly, and knowing the best way of wearing a tight jockstrap without grimacing. And actors go to extreme lengths to fool the audience that they actually know what they're doing – when in reality they rarely do. An actor's nightmare is that they will one day be 'found out' that they're making it all up – but of course they are. And that is the joy of acting. It is all about make-believe, playing and pretending.

This fantasy façade is also evident in the very buildings where shows are staged. Next time you step into a theatre – whether it's a small Victorian music hall or a majestic old playhouse owned by ATG (Any Theatre Going) – explore the front-of-house area and notice how many of the beautiful features are actually 'acting'. Tall, marble pillars, in particular, are often as hollow and wooden as the acting happening on stage. Plush curtains are made from the excess material from Cameron Mackintosh's boudoir (that's why they're garish and pink); the 'antique' fittings were purchased from Ikea, and the ornate ceilings in the style of Michelangelo were actually stencilled by Mikey on work experience.

How Actors Remember All Those Lines

People often wonder how actors manage to learn all their lines. The truth is that it can be very difficult and frustrating, particularly if the actors don't like the dialogue they're learning (making it virtually impossible for actors in *Hollyoaks*). With time and practice, actors will learn a technique that works for them. Some use the old tried-and-tested 'parrot fashion' method, where they say the lines over and over again for years on end until they've learnt them. Others record the script and listen to it constantly, playing it whilst they sleep, when they're running, even during copulation (some actors find this guards against premature excitement) – anything and everything until it's fully committed to memory. Others literally sleep on top of the script, or with it under their pillow, and allow the words to absorb into their body.

Some, however, simply cannot grasp any line-learning method, so spend their entire time trying to think of alternatives – and clever ways in which to cheat. Some resort to writing lines on various body parts – when you see actors looking at their hands and gesticulating wildly they are simply reading them. Others hide 'cheat sheets' behind props and on the set – sticking relevant passages behind sofas, tables, and on fellow cast members' backs. However, some actors never master the sacred art of line-learning at all so just make the whole thing up.

There is always an interesting atmosphere backstage when an actor forgets their lines. Normally, the offending actor will run offstage and proclaim, 'Oh God, I'm so sorry. I just froze.' This is where other actors and members of the company are contracted to say, 'It's fine – no one noticed a thing' – when in fact every single one of them noticed the actor had started reciting his shopping list instead. This must never be admitted to the guilty actor, though, otherwise they are prone to fits of doubt, fear and trepidation – and the company may be forced to put the understudy on. In fact, if anyone ever does anything wrong on stage, the rest of the company are legally obliged to say, 'No one would have noticed a thing.' It is one of the biggest lies in the business.

If an actor forgets what to say and can't improvise, then they ask for a prompt, normally by calling out 'Line!' – however, some shout, 'Yes', 'Please' or 'Shit, what's my fucking line, dear?' For this technique to be effective it relies on the stage manager to be actively following the script – which can be tricky, particularly if they're asleep. I knew a lovely stage manager who was touring with a four-hour production of *Jane Eyre*. One of the leading actors had never learnt his lines properly, and always got confused at the beginning of the second half. The stage manager used this to her full advantage, and whenever the guilty actor called for a 'line', she took huge delight in shouting out entirely the wrong line from the end of the play – which made the production an hour and a half shorter, resulting in a much better show, happier actors, and a lot more drinking time.

Most actors don't like admitting they've forgotten a line and will try everything they can just to carry on and hope that no one notices. The keen theatregoer will spot when such incidents occur – but to the untrained eye it can be difficult. A big giveaway is an extensive use of pauses – and I don't mean a couple of seconds, I'm talking about those kinds of pauses where the actor wanders around the stage for ten minutes before sitting down and holding his head in his hands – followed by loud sighs and moans until finally the god of theatre flies above him and drops the line into his head. Some people may confuse this for brilliant acting, but it is not. In fact, it is not even acting at all. It is the dark art of 'walking around and hoping that no one notices I don't know what the hell I'm doing'. Which, on second thoughts, sums up acting perfectly.

Depending on the production, actors can resort to other methods to hide their forgetful moments. If you spot actors doing any of the below when performing in a specific show then you can be sure they don't know what their next line is.

- *Comedy* – The actor will start laughing manically, do a stand-up routine, and tell some end-of-pier jokes until another actor runs on and saves the day.

- *Shakespeare* – The actor will look around with purpose, fiddle with their sword, and whisper 'de dum de dum de dum de dum de dum' as quietly as possible.

- *Greek Tragedy* – The actor will wail loudly and hug a fellow actor until they remember their line (this has been known to go on for hours, and is applicable to any tragedy).

- *Musical* – The performer will do some free-style dance moves, making them as close to the style of the rest of the show as possible. This will inevitably end in them doing the splits, leaping offstage, and then ball-changing back on after checking the script.

- *Bertolt Brecht* – The actor will look out into the audience in a confrontational way, eyeball the entire audience, and wait.

- *Anton Chekhov* – The actor will look wistfully out into the middle distance and say something about longing for 'a brighter future', until the line comes back to them.

- *Harold Pinter* – The actor will say 'fuck' and do an extra-long pause.

- *Tom Stoppard* – The actor will spout some gibberish about quantum physics, the Russian Revolution or Nietzsche that makes even less sense than usual, though no one will notice the difference.

- *Caryl Churchill* – The actor will keep repeating the same word or phrase over and over again, going back to the beginning of the scene, and doing something 'formally interesting' until they're back on track.

- *Any Preview Performance* – The actor will come out of character and shout, 'Bugger it. What's my line, love?'

Some actors don't even help their colleagues if they notice they're stuck – they much prefer to stand back and watch the actor suffering for their art. It can be brilliant to watch – and is yet another reason why watching live theatre is so thrilling. Anything can happen. And there is nothing as exciting as witnessing a well-known actor having a breakdown in front of our eyes. For some actors, stage fright hinders their performance, often resulting in them forgetting their lines. There have been many cases of well-known actors becoming so scared of going onto stage that they simply haven't. This usually comes down to a fear of failing, especially with the added pressure of expectation placed on them. Many techniques like hypnosis, meditation and alcoholism help combat this affliction.

Some of our most experienced actors (who shall remain nameless) have a far more effective technique when forgetting lines: they simply walk off stage. This makes it look like they haven't forgotten anything at all – and that it's the actor left fumbling on stage who has made the mistake. Naughty.

In certain instances, older actors have been known to use hidden earpieces to remember their lines. This means that they never actually have to remember anything – they just repeat what is being said to them through the earpiece.

However, it does take a fair amount of trust from the actor to do this – if the person reading the lines doesn't like them, they could say whatever they want, or indeed nothing at all. This use of earpieces is reserved for actors who are well known and forgetful, as we producers generally expect that normal actors will do everything properly. Of course, it could be argued that using an earpiece means the actor *isn't* doing their job properly – but if it allows certain grand dames to carry on performing then who cares?

In a musical it can be very awkward if an actor forgets what they are singing – as improvising song lyrics is especially hard: 'Somewhere over the rainbow... God I'm high. There's a lamb that I heard of, a witch cycling in the sky.' Actors must also accept that a musical director will never wait for them to remember the lyrics – they will simply plough on with the music. A good way of seeing when an actor has forgotten lyrics is to watch the conductor – whenever anything goes wrong the conductor will shake their head in disgust, or voice the words 'Bring Barrowman back' under their breath. On occasion, a conductor may even throw his baton at the offending actor and walk off, leaving the orchestra to carry on alone. It is a well-known fact that some musical directors are not supportive in the slightest during an actor's time of need – however, if anyone in the orchestra goes wrong, the conductor will smile and giggle like he's looking after a high-school band.

'No actors were harmed in the making of this production' – said no one, ever.

How Actors Know Where to Stand

If you find yourself sitting in the dress circle, upper circle or (heaven forbid) the balcony, you will notice many different-coloured bits of tape on the stage. This isn't because the stage crew couldn't be bothered to clean it – they are actually markers so that the set and props are put in the right places. Keep an eye on where furniture and props are set, and you'll notice that it's always on these marks – to ensure that the scene on stage is happening in the right place (and avoids something called 'acting in the dark' – where an entire scene is not lit – very popular at the Almeida).

These marks can also show where an actor needs to stand, hence the term 'hitting your mark'. All the marks are in different colours as the different set pieces go on specific coloured marks – each colour representing a different scene. Of course, with all these hundreds of marks it can become confusing for everyone at the beginning of a run. That's why in preview performances sets can be put in entirely the wrong place, and actors can forget which mark to stand on so hopscotch across all of them. This is the only reason *The Curious Incident of the Dog in the Night-Time* is such a physical show. During previews, the leading actor couldn't remember which mark he was supposed to stand on, so started jumping madly across them all. The director loved it, and the brilliant, Olivier Award-winning show was born, dear.

In some productions, particularly big musicals, the stage can be divided into little squares, and actors are told which ones to stand on throughout the show. This is all well and good, and can save precious rehearsal time – but becomes very annoying for the actor who is forced to be more concerned about what square they're standing on as opposed to their acting performance. It is a prime example of when creativity for the performer doesn't exist and they simply become pawns on a chessboard. Still, better than being an out-of-place prawn on a cheeseboard.

How Actors Change Their Costumes So Quickly

Actors are masters of the quick change – we've all seen those shows when an actor walks behind a piece of scenery only to appear from the other side in a completely different costume. A miracle to watch, and wondrous to think where their used jockstraps have ended up. Backstage in a theatre, as well as a collection of old, unemployed actors, lives the endangered species called the 'dresser'. These remarkable mammals spend their life dressing and undressing actors. Now, I imagine a lot of people think what a joyous job that must be – undressing their favourite actor into their smalls, then helping them into their next item of clothing – but the job is by no means as glamorous as it sounds. In fact, it can be bloody awful. Dressers don't get to undress any actor they desire – it is all down to the wardrobe mistress to decide who is dressing whom. Actors also look forward to discovering who will be dressing them – and pray they get a beautiful, blonde bombshell, or a solid, six-packed stud.

A dresser is highly skilled in whipping an actor's clothes off and then speedily throwing them into their next costume (usually during the show, but sometimes out of working hours too). It requires a lot of skill, and the timing has to be incredibly precise – any slight delay can result in a performer baring more than their soul on stage. In musicals and highly physical shows, the dresser not only has to dress and undress – they also have the added obstacles of sweat and odour. A dresser will begin their job an hour before actors enter the building – unless they've been summoned to do ironing duty. Ironing costumes and shirts is a laborious task – particularly when shows have hundreds of things that need ironing out (including actors' egos). It is not unusual for an enthusiastic, young wannabe to tell their family about a new dressing job before suddenly disappearing off the face of the Earth – as they get lost in a constant cycle of washing, ironing, drying and dressing.

When the dresser arrives in a theatre, they gather up all the costumes for their designated actors. They then carry them to the appropriate quick-change area or dressing room (which is rather exhausting in those West End theatres that are ten storeys high) and lay them all out in the correct order. If costumes aren't laid out in the right order the actor will put on entirely the wrong costume for entirely the wrong scene. Putting on costumes for an actor is just like following a Sat Nav when driving a car. Actors will just follow the order of the costumes, and put on whatever the dresser gives them without checking – which can have tremendous results. Who can forget the time that Miss Hannigan in *Annie* was dressed to look like Craig Revel Horwood? Horrifying, dear.

If you ever have the inclination to become a dresser, it is essential you can cope with dramatic skid marks, showbiz sweat, theatrical nipples, and dancers' cheesy feet. It can be a very daunting task indeed. A dresser also becomes an actor's counsellor – it's amazing the things someone will share with you when they're standing in front of you in their pants.

How Actors Know When to Walk On Stage

If you've ever been backstage in a theatre you will notice how dark it is – especially in the wings at the sides of the stage. These are the 'holding areas' for actors – and can be very interesting places to observe. It is marvellous to witness how actors behave in the wings – some wait for hours before their entrance, thinking about their character, doing erratic tongue twisters, and practising their lines – so that they walk on stage with purpose, confidence and a vague idea of what they're meant to be doing. Others, however, simply stand and flirt with anything and everything they can spot, often becoming so enraptured by this little dating ritual that they forget to go on.

This is where another little cheat device comes in handy: cue lights. These are little lights that flash green when an actor is meant to go on stage. It makes an actor's life a lot easier as they don't actually have to listen to the show, they can just hang around touching their toes until the green light flashes instructing them to 'GO ACT!' Easy-peasy, dear. The only problem comes when actors start thinking all green lights are cue lights, and begin randomly bursting into song and reciting Shakespeare at traffic lights. Marvellously entertaining, but also incredibly dangerous when you can't drive because there's an actor in the middle of the road going through the choreography from 'All That Jazz'.

How Actors Follow the Orchestra

When you walk into an auditorium before a musical extravaganza, notice the little televisions hanging from the front of the dress circle just above the stalls. These screens will show a live link of the conductor, allowing actors to sing with their heads up, knowing when to start singing and keeping in time, and not spend their entire performance staring down into the orchestra pit (we don't just want to see the top of Michael Crawford's head, do we, dear?).

These screens are also useful for when actors are missing their favourite television programmes. Take a glance next time you're watching a musical – the monitor could be showing whatever TV show the leading actor wants to watch. So, that moment when Javert is gazing across the audience singing 'Stars', he's actually catching up on *Strictly*.

Often in big musicals, although the performers are singing live, they are also being helped by a backing track – which is called a 'click track'. A click track has been previously recorded and plays underneath the actors singing live on stage, to give the song a 'fuller' sound. Click tracks aren't used as a solo voice, they are comprised of many voices used to boost the 'chorus' sound. Although it sounds like an awful cheat, it actually makes a lot of sense – particularly in shows that have a lot of high-energy hoofing. When actors jump around, pouting, it's only natural that they'll be out of breath, so the sound department boosts the voices by playing this click track. Of course, it means that the singing isn't all performed live, but I don't think it matters. Everyone performing in front of you will also be singing live, but the sound is just enhanced by the pre-recordings – and if it makes the performance sound better/in tune, who cares?

The only problem comes when you get a performer who can't actually sing the show every night, so mimes their song to a backing track, or can't reach the high notes any more – so the sound department plays a recording during these sections. This really is a cheat too far. However, these people are pretty easy to spot, as they will invariably be bad at lip-synching – and look about as convincing as Cheryl Cole/Fernandez-Versini/Tweedy/Payne/Baker.

How Actors Can Be Heard

Yet another useful trick that helps actors are head mics, otherwise known as radio mics. These little, flesh-coloured microphones can be spotted dangling discreetly (or sometimes not so discreetly) beneath an actor's wig, or if they are of the hairless variety it will protrude around their ear. They are essential in big musicals, as an actor's normal voice could never compete with the sound of an orchestra (or two-piece band on a Bill Kenwright tour). If an actor is feeling delicate then the sound engineer can increase the volume of their mic – giving the poorly little darling a chance to recover.

One of the overlooked geniuses of Theatreland is the sound engineer, who operates these mics, night after night. They stand (well, slouch) at the back of the auditorium behind an enormous control panel, positioned here so they hear the sound much as the audience will. They are in charge of all the microphones in the building: the radio mics, floor mics, handheld mics and floating mics (the ones that look like dangling dildos above the stage). The sound engineer also manages the 'foldback' levels, whereby the amplified sound is relayed back to the actors on stage via inward-facing speakers (or monitors) so they can hear the orchestra properly and how good/bad they sound themselves. You'd be surprised how different the orchestra sounds from an actor's point of view.

When actors finish speaking and singing, the sound engineer will turn their mics off. This is very important – as we don't want the sound of actors relieving themselves amplified all around the auditorium. No – what happens backstage, stays backstage, dear.

There is an increasing trend for actors in plays to be amplified as well, which makes some audiences (and classically trained older actors) very angry. In these times, though, when people want shows to be LOUD and hear every word clearly, then sometimes it's the only way to ensure it.

....

Actors – riffing is not singing. It is wanking around the melody.

....

How Actors Get Ready

'Ladies and gentlemen, this is your half-hour call. You have thirty minutes to get dressed, put on your make-up, drink your coffee, digest your food, steam, suck on throat sweets, remember your choreography, tweet fans, learn your lines, put the understudy down, and get into character. Thank you.'

That's (sort of) what it sounds like, but what actually *is* a half-hour call? It is an old theatrical tradition – and theatre, as we all know, is steeped in old traditions (Lionel Blair being one of the oldest). From actors being banned from saying the Scottish play (*Braveheart*), to not being allowed to go through their lines during copulation – traditions are very important. But like anything, some traditions are plain silly and should be forgotten about, just like Michael Barrymore.

The half-hour call (or 'the half') is actually given thirty-*five* minutes before the show is due to start. So, if the show is starting at 7.30 p.m., the half-hour call will be given at 6.55 p.m. – this is simply to make sure that the show starts on time. The half-hour call, and all subsequent calls, are relayed to the dressing rooms by the stage manager, whose godly voice is heard backstage over tannoys. If an actor is not in the theatre by this point then the understudy is prepped and primed (which makes them pant and poo).

Some shows will have a company warm-up long before the half-hour call, and these can last anything between twenty minutes to four hours depending on how pedantic the dance captain is. In a musical there will be a vocal *and* dance call – which are compulsory unless you are famous, in which case you can do whatever the hell you want. The company warm-up is a very important time – as it allows actors to wake up, prepare for the show, and gossip about which actor didn't go home the night before. During these warm-ups, a register will be taken to check that everyone is present, and to make the actors feel like schoolchildren (letters from parents are required if anyone has been off sick). If there are any absences, the guilty party will be contacted and made to feel petrified when the company manager threatens to call their agent.

Just as actors are meant to be in the theatre by the half, they also aren't allowed to leave after it is called. So if you ever see an actor wandering around the streets after 6.55 p.m. you know they are unemployed, uneducated or simply unprofessional.

The 'quarter' is called twenty minutes before the show, the 'five' ten minutes before, and the 'beginners' call' five minutes before the scheduled start time. 'Beginners' is the time when actors are required to go to the stage ready to start. In theatre, everything runs five minutes ahead. Accordingly, you might presume that actors get used to being everywhere early and are never late for castings and social arrangements – but this could not be further from the truth. Most actors are fans of the 'fashionably late' method – which makes me fashionably angry, dear.

'Has he got charisma?' 'No, he's just got a follow spot.'

How Actors Get Attention

Some performers insist on having a follow spot even when the scene isn't about them. This fools the audience into thinking that an actor is particularly charismatic, as they can't take their eyes off them. But in actual fact it's just because they're better lit than everybody else.

I once saw Tommy Steele in *Scrooge* – and whenever he was on stage I couldn't look at anybody else. And then I realised why. Even in scenes when he wasn't talking he had his own follow spot – so no matter what any of the other actors were doing, your eyes were naturally drawn to him. However, these kinds of tricks are only allowed if the actor is a 'name'. It doesn't work if they're playing the second spear carrier on the left and ask to have their own spotlight – then the only thing they'll get is their own P45.

Another trick to get attention is when actors discreetly start clapping as they exit the stage – to start the audience applauding. Many seasoned actors do this to ensure the audience applaud them every time they exit. It usually works, but can be rather dangerous if no one else joins in – because they're just left looking like an arrogant prig.

And the best way of ensuring a personal standing ovation at the curtain call? Actors have been known to ask a friend to sit in the front row and get them to stand at the end – with everyone else in the audience following their lead. Standing ovation guaranteed, dear. If the actor offers their friend money and/or alcohol, they might do it every night.

How to Speak 'Theatre'

Theatre has a vocabulary and a jargon all of its own. It's in English – but not as we know it – and can take years of dedicated study to understand and appreciate this ritualised language of the arts (or 'arse', as it's been known in the business). However, with enough effort and practice, it is possible for people who haven't even heard of Alan Bennett (a rare, organic fruit from Leeds) to learn this ever-popular language.

Begin your bilingual adventure here and now, with some of the most common technical jargon you'll hear backstage in a theatre. Try to use at least one of these words whenever you encounter a professional, and in no time at all you will be conversing freely with the thespiest of thesps and grumpiest of stagehands.

AREAS OF THE STAGE

STAGE RIGHT is the right-hand side of the stage from the point-of-view of the actor. So, if an actor is standing on stage facing the audience, then it is to their right. From the audience's perspective, stage right is on the left-hand side of the stage. And STAGE LEFT is the opposite of stage right. Confusing. Most actors spend their entire careers trying to figure out the difference between stage right and stage left – unless they trained at RADA, where they're taught that the only place is centre stage.

CENTRE STAGE is where all actors crave to be – slap bang in the centre. It is the best position to be seen, and means the whole audience will have a clear view of the actor (unless they're sitting behind a pillar). The main aim of the rehearsal period is to decide which actor is allowed to emote centre stage at which time. UPSTAGE is the back of the stage, furthest away from the audience, and DOWNSTAGE is the front of the stage, closest to them. You can get more specific with areas of the stage – for example, upstage right, downstage centre, centre-stage right. However, some directors just give up and shout, 'Stand over there next to Jacobi, dear.'

APRON   The area of a stage which comes forward of the main curtain – the closest section of the stage to the audience, and where an actor needs to be careful that the first three rows can't see up their skirt.

AUDITION   'They just want me to be myself, be my best, and be right for the role' is the mantra that actors must remember before they enter yet another demeaning, degrading, demoralising round of auditions.

The FIRST-ROUND AUDITION is when an actor is tested and tortured to see if they are right for a role, can hit all the notes and put their legs behind their head. At the RECALL an actor is called back for another session of torture and teasing (there can be up to ten of these for West End shows). And finally, the FINALS are the final stage of the torture process. Lucky actors get the job. Unlucky ones get sacrificed to the gods of profit-share.

BAR   An aluminium pole which is suspended over the stage onto which the lights are hung. Also, a place where you can spot actors sipping cheap ale and bitching after the show (or before the show, if they're doing a particularly long tour).

BARN DOOR   Four metal covers which are placed in front of a stage light to control the shape of light produced. Useful for nice lighting effects, and to help focus light at the good-looking actors.

BLACKOUT   When all the lights are turned off at once, consequently leaving the stage in darkness. A stage manager has to shout 'going to black' before pressing his special blackout button, so that actors can prepare and stand next to the person they want to kiss.

BLOCKING   The setting of actors' positions during rehearsals – when a dominant director will use them like mannequins and tell them where and how to stand.

BOARD   Another name for the lighting or sound desk. Also, something that happens to actors in month two of a year-long tour.

THE BOOK   Or the prompt copy, aka the Backstage Bible, a copy of the script which includes all the cues and notes for a show. It is owned by the stage-management team; touch it at your peril.

CANS   Large headsets with microphones, used by people working backstage so they can talk among themselves about technical matters, and slag off the actors.

CLOTHS   Large pieces of material that have scenery painted on them and form part of the set. These kinds of cloths are often lowered toward the front of the stage so that actors can scramble into dramatic positions behind.

'COME DOWN'   Describing when a show has finished – for example, 'What time does it come down, dear?' The term derives from when the curtain 'comes down' at the end of a show. Also, the feeling of depression experienced by actors when they're unemployed after completing a run in a show.

CREW   The people who work backstage, recognisable by their designer black clothing.

CROSS-FADE   A fade from one light setting to another. Some-times done particularly crossly if the producer has forgotten the lighting operator's Krispy Kremes.

CURTAIN CALL   When the actors jog downstage, blow kisses to the audience, and bow.

CYCLORAMA ('CYC', pronounced 'pysch')   A large piece of white material stretching across the entire back of the stage. It is usually lit to look like part of the set or the sky. You can sometimes see it rustling as late actors run from one side to the other, or stand behind it 'psyching' themselves up for their entrance.

DARK   The term used to describe a theatre where no show is playing. Also, what happens when somebody accidentally flicks a switch and plunges the stage into pitch blackness.

DOUBLING   When an actor plays more than one role. Very common when productions are done on a tight budget (nearly every show). It can either be very effective and show off the skills of an actor, or be very silly and show how bad an actor is – particularly if it's a newly graduated twenty-one-year-old playing a student, an old lord, a fairy, a tree and a toilet seat, all in the same show (the RSC was particularly strapped for cash that year).

DRESSING ROOMS   The place where actors live when they're not at home, and where they apply make-up (hence all the light bulbs round the mirrors), get into costume, and moan about being on Equity minimum. Leading actors get their own palatial dressing rooms; everyone else has to share a couple of cupboards.

DRY   When an actor forgets their line, followed by a dramatic pause and sudden whiff of fart. Particularly frustrating for them when the casting director for *Doctors* is in watching.

ENDEARMENT (TERMS OF)

LOVE – A term overly used by actors.
DEAR – A term overly used by producers.
DARLING – A term overly used by directors to address actors when they can't remember their names.

FIT-UP   The period when the set is built/installed in the theatre. This can take hours, days or weeks depending on how big the set is.

FLATS   Oblong frames of timber covered with canvas, situated around the stage to hide actors, props and scenery. Put a few of these together and, bingo, you've got a set!

FLIES   The area above the stage where the backstage crew hoist in and out parts of scenery – lights, set pieces, curtains, colourful cloths and flying actors. It is operated by a counterweight system which consists of a series of ropes and pulleys – allowing everything to descend and ascend quickly and easily. Men who operate the flies are called 'flymen'. This term is also something on the front of an actor's trousers which can also ascend and descend, allowing easy access when required.

FOLLOW SPOT   A bright spotlight that follows an actor around the stage, usually operated from the balcony area of the auditorium – but occasionally from above the stage itself. Also known as 'limes', as originally limestone was heated to create the light. Actors always have to be nice to the follow-spot operator – otherwise they'll end up acting in the dark.

FOOTLIGHT   Lights on the stage floor running across the front of the stage. Often used in vaudeville shows, or when the director wants the audience to see up actors' nostrils (very popular – well, unavoidable – in more intimate venues). Footlights is also the name of a student comedy troupe at Cambridge University, which everybody important in British comedy belonged to at some point, plus Germaine Greer.

GAUZE   A loosely woven, opaque cloth on which a scene is painted. When lit from the front, only the painted scene can be seen. When lit from behind, it becomes see-through – making the actors posing behind become visible. Very useful, very clever and very popular in pantomimes (to hide Bobby Davro for as long as possible).

GEL   A coloured piece of plastic placed in front of a light to change its colour. Also, something which is liberally applied to actors' hair to make it look nice. More sophisticated, colour-changing LED lighting is being used in most professional productions to replace gels (though not for the actors' hair).

GOBO   A sheet of patterned metal that fits in front of the stage light, so that when the light shines through it, a pattern is projected onto the stage. An easy and cheap way of making a bare stage look interesting.

GREEN ROOM   A small room backstage – rarely green – where actors relax, drink tea, and talk about how quiet/badly behaved/sparse/unattractive the audience are.

HOUSE   A term for both the auditorium and the audience. You will hear it used in expressions such as 'How big is the house tonight?', 'Nice house tonight, love', 'Best seat in the house' and 'Master of the House'. It can also mean the theatre itself – for example, the Royal Opera House (which is often just called 'The House').

IRON   The safety curtain. You will see this dropped onto stage during the interval, where it must be put in place (even momentarily) by law. The role of the safety curtain is to stop a fire from moving backstage to the auditorium, and vice versa. Every theatre will also have a sprinkler system in case of fire. An iron is also something used by the wardrobe department to iron shirts and discipline actors.

JAZZ HANDS   The mating call for actors.

LANTERN   The term for the most common theatre lights used on stage. The bulb is called the lamp.

LEGS   Long curtains which cover the wings so that the audience can't see the actors playing on their iPhones.

MIC BELT   The belt which holds an actor's microphone battery/radio transmitter pack in place. They are also used by actors to store sweets for onstage munching during the boring bits.

MR SANDS   The common code-word used to alert those working in the building that a fire has started, without creating a frenzied panic in the audience: 'Mr Sands is in the green room.' Which is very confusing if Julian Sands ever visits the cast backstage. Because this code is used in most buildings now, West End theatres have cleverly started to use different ones, such as 'Mr Sondheim/Mr Kenwright/Ms Friedman... is in the building' – which is guaranteed to strike instantaneous fear into the heart of everyone backstage.

NOTES   A session after a performance where the director gives notes about the show. In severe cases, actors will be whipped and beaten during these sessions – well, what do you expect if they forget a line? Some actors write down their notes from a director; all actors ignore the ones from the resident director.

PIT   The orchestra pit, traditionally underneath the front of the stage. This is where the conductor beats time, and all the musicians sit and play with each other. Sometimes a director hides the orchestra at the back of the stage – but only when the brass section is particularly ugly.

PRACTICAL   A prop or piece of set that actually has to work – for example, 'We'll need a practical television for that scene.' Sometimes I even ask for practical actors (who can actually act) – regrettably, that's not always possible.

PRESET   How the stage is set before a show starts, with all props, costumes and (occasionally) the actors in their correct positions.

PROMPT CORNER   Traditionally offstage left, this is the place where the deputy stage manager controls the show, calling cues for lights, sound, and ordering Domino's pizza for the interval.

PROSCENIUM ARCH ('PROS ARCH' pronounced 'pross artch') The arch that frames the stage, often very ornate in the West End's Victorian theatres; and very plain and ugly in the Lyttelton. You will sometimes hear actors being told to 'come forward of the pros' – which usually results in them falling into the orchestra pit.

PYROTECHNICS (PYRO)   Explosions, fire and fireworks, smoke, golden showers, and special effects are an invaluable useful way of making a rubbish show better. Is the show shit? Cover it with smoke. Simple.

RADIO MIC   A small microphone that is hidden (sometimes not very well) on an actor's head. They often look like a big mole.

RAKE   When the stage is on a slight angle (usually done so that the audience can see the actors), higher at the back than the front. This can cause trip hazards, and often results in actors flat on their face – especially during hungover matinees, dear.

REPRISE   A musical term, which means to repeat a part of a song that has already been performed. Useful if a show is short and the composers can't think of anything else decent to write.

REVOLVE   A stage, or part of a stage, that moves round in a big circle like a merry-go-round. *Les Mis* has one of the most famous revolves in the world, but it's not so merry. After working on a revolve it can take actors up to two years before they can walk in a straight line again.

ROSTRUM   Moveable platforms which can be used to signify lots of different parts of a set. Crew move them, actors stand on them, and Italia Conti grads fall off them.

ROUND (IN THE)   When the audience is seated 360 degrees all around the actors, it is theatre 'in the round', and makes the actors feel like they're performing in a giant goldfish bowl. Acting in the round demands a technique all of its own, with actors constantly spinning so everyone can see what they're doing. But it's dizzying for both audience and actors, and I find it's only tolerable if you get sloshed in advance. Then all the spinning balances itself out.

SCENE DOCK   Where scenery, set pieces and misbehaving actors are stored.

SET DRESSING   The items on a set which are there for no other reason than to make it look nice. Just like Abi Titmuss.

SIGHTLINES   An invisible line from someone's eyes to what they can see – to reference good or bad visibility. Actors will always try and stand in the place with best sightlines. Unless they feel embarrassed because the show is bad. In which case, they will just hide offstage.

SITZPROBE   The occasion when the orchestra and actors first come together to sing through the whole show. A very exciting moment, which always results in showgasms of the most spectacular kind, particularly if the orchestra play all the right notes.

SMOKE MACHINE   A machine that causes everyone in the auditorium to stop being able to see what's happening and start coughing.

SPECIAL   A lighting effect, where one actor is lit more than the others: 'Can I have a special, please? I want to make sure my mum can see me in this bit.' It helps the audience know who to focus on, and makes the actor act better as they know they are lit.

STAGE DOOR   Where actors and everyone working in a theatre enter and exit the building. The portal to a world of make-believe, magic, music, merriment and mugging.

STATE   A lighting state refers to the levels and number of lights that have been set for a particular scene or cue: 'Can we go back to the state in Scene 2?' Also, can refer to the mental state of an actor – particularly delicate if they've been doing lots of schools' tours.

STRIKE   When a set piece is taken offstage, or the entire set is dismantled and taken out of a theatre. Also, something actors threaten to do each time they hear of someone doing a job for no money.

STROBE   A lighting state where lights flash on and off. Used in chases, comedy routines, and when the director doesn't know what else to do.

TABS   The curtains that close along the proscenium arch – near the front of the stage. These are usually a deep red colour. I also 'keep tabs' on my actors, so I know what they're doing at *all* times, in and out of the theatre.

THRUST   When the audience sit on three sides of the stage. Also, a movement routine that young actors use to get their first job.

TRAP DOOR   A hidden door on stage where actors appear and disappear. Useful when producers want to dispose of actors singing out of tune.

WINGS The areas just offstage where props and sets are in put in place for the show, and where actors loiter before going on stage.

....

'Upstage, downstage, stage right, stage left. Who cares? I just wanna be ON STAGE!' – quote from a six-year-old. He's going to be famous, dear.

....

The Language of Theatre Quiz

And now... a little quiz, dear! Here are some examples of phrases you might hear backstage, using the new theatrical language you've just learnt. Fill in your answers below as accurately as you can, and then check the full translations on page 274. Good luck!

1. 'Alright, love, we're going to put you in a special.'

_____

2. 'Bring the tabs in and go to the state in the scene before.'

_____

3. 'Move stage right and find your light, dear.'

_____

4. 'Walk stage left, turn on the lamp and come forward onto the apron whilst displaying your jazz hands, then we'll cross-fade to the scene stage right.'

_____

_____

_____

5. 'The pyro to the upstage-right corner of the stage will go live at the reprise of the opening number, when the flies will drop down a cloth. This is when you need to stand on the downstage rostra and turn on the TV, which is a practical, before following the conductor. Then watch out for the offstage cue light which will signal cue 45 when the strobe will begin and the lighting state will go to the one prior, before we go to the preset of the next scene. Mind yourself on the rake as the revolve starts, then you'll be joined by the juve who will help you quick change as the smoke machine covers you getting to the front of the pros, by which time the rest of the chorus will be standing behind you doing the splits.'

_____

_____

_____

_____

_____

_____

_____

_____

CHITTY CHITTY BANG BANG

History – It is unusual to think that a flying car called Chitty Chitty Bang Bang and British secret-service agent James Bond are actually siblings. But they were both created in the mind of Ian Fleming, and both films were produced by Albert (Cubby) Broccoli. Daniel Craig is yet to give us his Child Catcher, but it's just a matter of time...

With songs by the *Mary Poppins* tunesmiths, Richard M. Sherman and Robert B. Sherman (also siblings, believe it or not) and a book by Jeremy Sams, *Chitty* flew into the London Palladium in 2002. It was directed by Adrian Noble, then artistic director of the RSC (Shakespearean directors like turning to musicals to forget about iambic pentameter – and make some real money), and choreographed by Gillian Lynne. The £750,000 spent on the fine four-fendered friend made it the most expensive stage prop of all time.

With Michael Ball (Caractacus Potts), Richard O'Brien (the Child Catcher), Brian Blessed (the Baron) and Nichola McAuliffe (the Baroness) in the original cast – the show ran for three-and-a-half years in London, transferred to Broadway, and has toured internationally. That's a lot of toot sweets that have been blown.

Plot – A mad inventor tries to impress a woman by taking her (and his children) for a drive in his car, which magically starts flying. They end up in Bavaria, get caught by a creepy villain, befriend a toy-maker, dress up as dolls, help trapped families, and then fly home just in time for tea. Sponsored by the new Skoda Octavia.

Characters – Caractacus Potts, Truly Scrumptious, Jeremy and Jemima Potts, Baron and Baroness Bomburst, and the Child Catcher.

Best-known actors to have played Caractacus – Dick Van Dyke, Michael Ball, Gary Wilmot, Jason Donovan, Aled Jones and Jason Manford.

Most likely to play Caractacus in the future – Any actor who is good with children, has a full, clean pilot's licence – and can spell Cataract-a-rat-cactus without looking.

Best-known songs – 'Chitty Chitty Bang Bang'; 'Truly Scrumptious'; 'Toot Sweets'; 'Me Ol' Bamboo'; 'Hushabye Mountain'; 'The Roses of Success'; 'Teamwork'.

Rejected songs – 'I Hope That Car is Taxed for Flying'; 'Crazy Inventors Make the Best Lovers'; 'Why Don't You Invent Something Useful Like a Dyson?'; 'Chitty Chitty Gang Bang' (adults-only).

STARLIGHT EXPRESS

History – After the runaway success of *Cats*, Andrew Lloyd Webber sought another story of non-humans to turn into his next global megahit. He originally wanted to adapt the Reverend Awdry's Thomas the Tank Engine stories, but unable to obtain permission, Lloyd Webber confected his own Cinderella story featuring trains. The rock musical, with lyrics by Richard Stilgoe, later revised by Don Black, opened in 1984 at the Apollo Victoria Theatre, dramatically transformed into a playground with ramps and racetracks swirling around the auditorium. Directed by Trevor Nunn and choreographed by Arlene Phillips, all the performers were on roller skates to convey the fast-moving, racing loco-motives. It made for a dizzying, death-defying, somewhat dangerous spectacle, which ran in London until 2002. The production in Bochum, Germany has performed continuously since 1988 in a purpose-built theatre, the Starlighthalle, where a preposterous total of over sixteen million people have seen it. And they say Germans have no sense of humour.

Plot – Some trains race each other to become 'Fastest Engine in the World', and a couple of them fall in love. Yes, that's right. It's a typical love story, with a difference. They are trains. Think about that the next time you're stuck on Southern Rail: trains have feelings too.

Characters – Rusty, Greaseball, Pearl, Poppa, Electra, Dinah and Rocky 1, 2 and 3 (Rocky 4 was added after the release of movie *Rocky IV*).

Best-known performers to have been a train – Thomas, Percy, Gordon, James the Red Engine, Henry the Green Engine, The Orient Express and The Flying Scotsman.

Most likely to play a train in the future – Any actor who can shout in tune whilst skating forwards and backwards. If they can go sideways and do the odd mid-air spin they can play any role they want.

Best-known songs – 'Starlight Express'; 'Only You'; 'U.N.C.O.U.P.L.E.D.'; 'Rolling Stock'; 'AC/DC'; 'Light at the End of the Tunnel'.

Rejected songs – 'Pizza Express'; 'Which Carriage is the Buffet In?'; 'This Performance is Delayed Due to Hazardous Weather Conditions'; 'O.V.E.R.C.R.O.W.D.E.D.'; The Fat Controller's Lost a Lot of Weight'; 'No Train in This Show is a Virgin'.

CHICAGO

History – Set somewhere in Prohibition-era America (Detroit? Las Vegas? Albuquerque? I can never remember, sorry, dear), *Chicago* is based on a 1926 play of the same name by Maurine Dallas Watkins. John Kander (music) and Fred Ebb (book and lyrics) joined forces with Bob Fosse (book and direction) to bring their musicalised version to Broadway, after the success of *Cabaret*, another satirically dark musical by the team, which had made a star of Liza (with a Z) Minnelli (with a double-N and double-L).

The original 1975 production played in New York for 936 performances; and London (in 1979) for 600 performances

– but it was the revival in 1996 which really cemented *Chicago*'s place in musical legend. Today it has been seen in dozens of countries around the world, and in 2002 was made into the first movie musical to win the Best Picture Oscar since 1968's *Oliver!* It is the longest-running musical revival and longest-running American musical in Broadway history, slaying all competition. Some other musicals just can't hold their arsenic.

Plot – A couple of long-legged women who murder men connive to get acquitted for their crimes. They are surrounded by a lot of other murderous women, none of whom wear a lot, and who all like dancing behind high-backed chairs. A sad man believes his wife until the truth finally outs, and a lawyer tries his best to help, but gets distracted by all the stilettos and fishnet stockings. It is recommended that men wear strong pants when watching this production.

Characters – Velma Kelly, Roxie Hart, Billy Flynn, Matron 'Mama' Morton, Mary Sunshine, Amos Hart.

Best-known actresses to have played Roxie or Velma – Chita Rivera, Gwen Verdon, Ann Reinking, Bebe Neuwirth, Ruthie Henshall, Ute Lemper, Renée Zellweger and Catherine Zeta Jones.

Most likely to play Roxie or Velma in the future – Any actress with great vocal range, long legs which she can put over her head, and an virtuosic ability to perform sexy intricate movements. Theresa May is pencilled in to perform both roles once she's ousted from Downing Street.

Best-known songs – 'All That Jazz'; 'Cell Block Tango'; 'We Both Reached for the Gun'; 'Roxie'; 'I Can't Do It Alone'; 'Mr Cellophane'; 'Razzle Dazzle'; 'Nowadays'.

Rejected songs – 'Yes, I Murdered My Lover, But I've Got a Great Butt'; 'These Stilettos Hurt Like Hell'; 'My Jazz Hands are Better Than Yours'; 'It's All in the Position of the Fingers, Dear'.

THE INTERVAL

'But soft! What light through yonder window breaks?
It is the exit, and alcohol is the fun.'

They say, 'Always leave them wanting more' –
which is why I like to cut the second half, dear.

Lush harmonies, copious jazz hands, cymbal crashes, a monsoon of pirouettes, dramatic shouting, a snap blackout, the curtain falls, thunderous applause, and the house lights fade up. Yes, dears, you've survived the first half! And now it's the interval.

Intervals last between fifteen and twenty minutes – depending on how long the queue for the ladies' loos are. This should give you just enough time to leave your seat, eat an ice cream, have a drink, smoke, go to the loo, tweet about how bad the show is, and decide which actor you'd like to take home with you. It's an important part of the whole theatrical experience – particularly if the play is over three hours long. No one likes a long play, especially if it's a version of *The Misanthrope* starring television comics who have never been on stage before. Less theatrical dynamite, more *dire*-mite, dear.

Some modern productions, however, torture their audiences by not giving them their allotted 'break from the drama'. Avant-garde directors like to punish viewers by forcing them to sit and watch the whole play in one sitting, so that the story doesn't get disrupted by all the ice-cream licking. However, this usually has the opposite effect, with the audience wriggling in their seats, coughing constantly, and dying due to this overload of drama (a particular risk at Chichester where the average audience age is eighty-nine).

A Guide to Surviving the Interval

Watching theatre can be tough, particularly if it's a play with lots of long speeches and indulgent overacting, so the need for escape is crucial. Here are my top tips for planning ahead, so that you can take full advantage of your fifteen minutes of freedom.

Split Up

I am assuming you are at the theatre with a friend, partner or someone you met in the local sauna. Having a partner in crime is essential when it comes to planning your interval exercise. As soon as the last word has been uttered and the final jazz hand displayed, jump to your feet and run to the exits. At this point, you and your partner should split up – one of you ball-changing to the toilet, whilst the other pirouettes straight to the bar. It's all about tactics, my dear.

Arrange a Meeting Point

With all the fun and excitement of running around front of house you may get lost. Your friend could end up in the cloakroom wrestling with fake fur, whilst you could find yourself sandwiched between a slow tourist and a confused pensioner. These kinds of theatrical emergencies are common – so it is essential that you have a back-up plan. When you first arrive at the theatre, locate an area that is easy to find – the box office, the back of the auditorium, or just outside the main entrance. This means that when you and your fellow theatregoer get lost, you will know where to find each other. In some theatres there are even areas for lost, upset and confused patrons, generally identifiable by a life-size cut-out of a screaming man clutching his theatre ticket with ice-cream dribbling down his jumper. Obviously you could just phone your friend – but never rely on this, as some cavernous and subterranean theatres swallow up a phone's signal – preventing calling, texting and Grindr-ing during the show.

Carry Your Ticket

Once you've passed the portal between the world of theatre and real life (the exit), you will only be allowed back in if you have your golden ticket. It's very awkward leaving the theatre for fresh air, cheap sweets, and puffs on your gherkin-flavoured e-cigarette, only to be pounced on by an usher before the theatre police lock you up for lack of a ticket. Very harrowing indeed. It's made even worse by the prospect of the Equity president torturing you with Shakespearean recitals all night long. Malcolm loves any opportunity to recite his audition speeches (bless). So be prepared, and have your ticket on your person at all times.

Security and safety has obviously become very important in theatres, so the need for bag checks and re-entry tickets is crucial. If security wasn't as tight, theatres would constantly be invaded by drama students, unwanted critics, and actors who didn't get the job. Jealous actors are a high risk in Theatreland. Not only do they blag their way into shows – losing producers millions of pounds in ticket sales – but they can run on stage, rip costumes off the actors, put them on, and start playing the part themselves. Allegedly, Denise Van Outen tried this during a performance of *Funny Girl* – but Sheridan Smith retaliated with a karate chop to the head and continued singing 'Don't Rain on My Parade' as if nothing had happened. Good on her.

Run Across the Road

If you're attempting to go to the theatre on a budget then the interval is another time when you can save those all-important pennies. Most theatres are situated close to shops – where sweets, ice creams and condoms are substantially cheaper than prices in the theatre. If you head to these shops at the beginning of the interval you will have ample time to purchase your treats, unwrap them to avoid mid-show distractions, and be back in your seat before the second half begins. However, never make your snack smuggling too obvious when re-entering. Plan ahead so that you have somewhere crafty to hide these cheaper sweets. Deep pockets are perfect; large handbags work well; and oversized bras do the job best.

Spot the Actors

Die-hard theatre fans love the interval – it is the perfect time to watch their favourite actors smoking, slouching and slagging each other off outside the stage door. Many people think that the stage door is located at the back of a theatre mainly because it's the quickest route for the actors to get to the stage. But, of course, that's too simple. No – the stage door is at the back so the actors are as far away from the public as possible. Producers all know how naughty actors can be, so we do everything we can to prevent the paying patrons from seeing the actors offstage.

Unfortunately there's not much we can do at the interval – even actors are entitled to some fresh air (Equity has fought hard for it). We always ask the actors to behave themselves at this point, but more often than not they congregate outside stage door, downing vodka whilst shouting down the phone to their agent, begging to be released from the job. If you have a desire to see actors in their natural habitat just pop round to the back of the theatre during the interval. But never get too close, as actors can bite when still in character. They are a particularly dangerous species mid-way through a performance – half in character, half themselves, and half drunk.

Restrain Your Children

In the interval it is imperative that you keep your children with you at all times. This goes without saying. The theatre is not a crèche, and the ushers are not nannies to nurse, entertain and suckle your little bundles of joy. They have a hard enough job looking after the adults.

If you leave your child unattended for even five minutes, the unthinkable could happen. Your little cherub could suddenly realise they want to be an actor and spend their whole life gurning to half-packed houses up and down the country. I recall a tragic incident many years ago when a child was left on her own in the theatre, forgotten about by her parents, and then finally spotted ten years later in the same venue playing little orphan Annie. But then Bonnie Langford was always destined for the stage, dear.

I've decided to offer a dairy-free alternative to ice cream in the intervals. Bacon.

Interval Pees

One of the biggest hurdles during the interval is going to the toilet.

There is – and always has been – a distinct lack of toilets in theatres, resulting in large queues of nicely dressed ladies snaking around, inside and outside of theatres. This is because the old men who designed them didn't think about the necessity of toilets for women – and most eight-hundred-seat theatres have about two.

Here's what you need to do to aid your nice, relieving interval toilet quest. Firstly, ensure that you are fully emptied before the show begins. This hopefully means you can make it through the first half without needing a pee. As soon as the interval starts, do your best Usain Bolt impression, and leg it to the nearest lavatory. The interval is obviously the time when toilets are the busiest – so plan ahead by making sure you know where the nearest ones are. Have a look before the show begins, and calculate your quickest route. Some people are so keen to be the first to the loos that they book their theatre seats based on the proximity of toilets as opposed to their view of the stage. I don't think it necessary to go to this extreme, but if you suffer from a weak bladder I recommend booking an end-of-aisle seat, so you can make a swift exit if ever you need a mid-wee.

If the queue at the start of the interval is too long – and you're desperate – then you can try running round the corner to the nearest pub and surreptitiously using their facilities. If you can hold it in, perhaps you can go to the theatre bar and wait for the loo until just before the second half begins. Wait until the bells ring and the ushers herd everyone back to their seats – when everyone else will have left the toilets for fear of missing the beginning of the second half. Don't worry about this – shows never resume on time anyway, as actors always spend too long nibbling Hobnobs in the green room. You'll have plenty of time to use the loo calmly and wander back to your seat devoid of stress (and urine).

If you suffer from a particularly weak bladder then you could get a special catheter/colostomy bag combo installed from the theatre cloakroom. These are being trialled in certain theatres at present – and proved very popular during the run of the musical *Urinetown* (where the subject matter caused many unscheduled leakages). These devices mean you can sit through an entire show without having to leave your seat once – meaning you won't miss a second of anything happening on stage. However, if the theatre you are visiting doesn't offer this service, just ask for an empty plastic water bottle instead, and be sure to aim well.

....

I'm looking forward to Tim Rice and Lloyd Webber's new show *From Here to Stephen Ward* – a farce about the perils of putting a new musical straight into the West End, dear.

....

Interval Drinks

On top of paying for your ticket, transport, ice cream, programme, souvenir brochure, mug, T-shirt, playscript, CD, DVD, and signed photo of newcomer Lenny Henry – it is imperative you treat yourself to an interval drink. This can be the most important part of watching a show – particularly if it is bad. It allows you to quench your thirst, get through the second half, and forget the fact that you spent £60 on a shit and not a hit.

How to Get Them

Sadly, it is not as simple as just rocking up to the theatre bar and getting a drink. If only. It is a well-known fact that every bar in every theatre in every land has a lack of staff – and this is the most common cause of theatre rage. Usually there will be two energetic drama students situated behind each serving area, smiling and pouring as fast as they can, whilst also trying to flirt with as many casting directors as possible. When you're at the bar, always order two drinks for each person, as you won't have time go back – though be prepared to file for bankruptcy after you've done this.

The huddle of people around a theatre bar can be as intimidating as a rugby scrum – and, unless you are a small person who can crawl between people's legs, it will take an age. Press nights are particularly horrific. Celebs and critics push themselves to the bar in a scrap of self-importance and status, and if Dale Winton gets served before you it is a sure indication that your showbiz career is over.

It is essential you are prepared. The two bar staff will always be looking around like they're at a tennis match, trying to see who is next. Always send the best-looking person in your group, as they will undoubtedly get served first – it also helps if they look primed to purchase by having a fat wad of cash in their hand. You should never be timid – ordering drinks is just like driving around London. You have to be pushy, and prepared to beep your horn whenever necessary. If you don't take every opportunity you'll spend hours going nowhere. As Shakespeare famously wrote, 'Be bloody, bold and resolute' – he'd obviously had the same problem when ordering drinks at the Globe.

Once served, you then have the mission of finding somewhere to drink whatever overpriced liquid is sloshing around your glass. By now, all the seats in the bar will be taken, and just as you find a small patch of wall to lean against, you'll be instructed to go back to the auditorium. When you attempt to get back to your seat you'll be accosted by an usher saying, 'Sorry, you can't take glass in, go back to the bar and put your drink in a plastic cup' – at which point you have two options: return to the bar and join the queue for plastic cups, or down your alcoholic beverage. By this point you'll probably be so infected with theatre rage that all you'll really want to do is pour your drink over the usher – but please avoid doing this. Ushers have feelings too, dear.

Obviously, the way to avoid all this heartache and pain is to pre-order your drinks. This is the smug and professional way of enjoying your interval boozing, and means you won't waste your time or energy fighting to get to the bar. All you need to do is visit your nearest bar before the show, and pay for the drinks you want. Perfect! Then when the interval arrives, you will casually locate your drinks on a little shelf, waltz to a seat and enjoy your tipple whilst everyone queueing stares on enviously.

If you really want to beat the system, then in some theatres you can now have your half-time refreshments delivered to your seat. Available at venues run by ATG, Ordertorium (see what they did there?) offers in-seat delivery of food and drinks, a bit like Deliveroo, or in-flight food on an aeroplane (though hopefully slightly less vomit-inducing). All you have to do is download the ATG app, or wave your menu in the air, and a kindly usher will serve you where you are sitting. However, it's worth pointing out that you can only do this before the show and during the interval; if you find yourself in need of some liquid assistance during a particularly long Shakespeare soliloquy, and start wondering 'Two beers or not two beers?', I'm afraid you'll have to wait. I think in-seat refreshments are a marvellous idea, and one I'm going to insist on for all my future shows. In fact, I'm considering extending this to the curtain call: simply raise your hand, point at the actor on stage who's taken your fancy, and they'll be waiting for you at the exit, bagged and ready to take home.

Another short cut to getting served at the bar is smuggling a small bell into the theatre. At about ten minutes before the show begins, simply ring it. Other audience members will think this is the official bell telling them to go to their seats – and will start leaving the foyer and bar. Ring it again and the whole bar area will clear, leaving you to relax, recline and revel in delight at having the whole bar to yourself. If you are feeling particularly brave you can try this trick in the interval as well. It is a wonderful way of clearing any front-of-house area with a little flick of the wrist.

If all else fails, just go and see a show that isn't selling very well. Yes, the production may be rubbish and make you curse the day that theatre was invented, but at least there won't be any bloody queues, dear.

How to Afford Them

Until Theatreland is owned by Lidl – when you'll get an interval beer for 50p, and also leave with a tin of baked beans, a sleeping bag and a vacuum cleaner – the joy of having a theatrical drink can really burn a hole in your pocket.

A Guide to Buying an Interval Drink Without Breaking the Bank

Here's a couple of budget drinking tips I learnt from Sonia Friedman – she hates paying more than a couple of quid for her Barcadi Breezers. Well, how do you think she got all that money, dear?

Drink Water

Every theatre bar will offer free tap water. Usually you will find a few jugs on the bar, allowing you to help yourself. If you're particularly posh you can even request some ice and a slice at no extra cost. Who said you get nothing in life for free?

Go Elsewhere

There are no laws that forbid you from leaving the theatre – and most theatres, definitely West End ones, are situated close to pubs. (This is mainly so the musicians have easy access – you'd be surprised at the number of musicians who leave the pit mid-show to find beer. That's why there's always lots of bum notes in the second half.) Drinks in a nearby pub will be much cheaper than in a theatre, so it can make sense to take your business elsewhere.

If you're planning this money-saving trip, have a look around before the show begins, decide on a pub, and head straight there at the interval. Before you know it, you'll be in your chosen public house sipping cheap wine and munching on Nobby's Nuts. Obviously you have to keep an eye on the time – you don't want to miss any of the second half. I'd recommend sitting at a window with a view of the theatre, and when you spot everyone disappearing back inside then it's time to drink up.

Take Your Own

You have to be careful when employing this method, as many theatres will search your bags on entry. But you'll be fine if you've only got a couple of small cans of G&T in your pocket (avoid one litre bottles, as this can be quite obvious). Once inside, go to the bar and get yourself a plastic cup of water, and drink this during the first half. Then when it's the interval, open your cans, and pour the contents into your plastic cup – whilst always keeping a beady eye out to make sure an usher doesn't approach you with a stun gun. And hey presto! Not only have you got a marvellously refreshing interval drink – but it cost you a good deal less than it would have done at the bar.

If, however, you don't have the chutzpah to do this alcohol-decanting in public, then take your plastic cup to the lavatory (making sure to put the right liquid in the right receptacle). Of course, if you are desperate for a drink, you can do it during the first half – but it's always harder to judge these things in the dark. You may end up missing your cup entirely and pouring wine all over the lovely lady sitting next to you (in which case just offer her a sip and she'll be quick to forgive). I always use this method in Delfont Mackintosh theatres as Cameron refuses to give me my friend's discount now. It works a treat – and my PA has become a master at smuggling in a crate of Dom under her dress.

These little tricks will save you enough money to go out for another round of drinks after the show. And if you happen to see me out and about, please do pop over and say hello (with a nice glass of something, dear).

Remember: the interval is the perfect time to escape!

BLOOD BROTHERS

History – Liverpudlian playwright Willy Russell originally wrote *Blood Brothers* as a school play in 1982, but later turned it into a musical – writing the book, the music and the lyrics himself, greedy man. This musical version opened at the Liverpool Playhouse in 1983, and after twelve weeks transferred to the West End's Lyric Theatre, where it played for seven months. Sadly, it didn't do good business at first, due to no one understanding the accents, but word of mouth spread and the show ended its run on a high – with packed houses and winning Oliviers for Best Actress (for Barbara Dickson) and Best New Musical.

It didn't take long for fellow Liverpudlian Bill Kenwright to acquire the rights for the show – and, working with Russell, they made improvements to the original production. Willy was initially sceptical about transferring the show back into the West End, but after a particularly good night out with Billy, involving vodka, roulette tables and heated arguments (Everton vs Liverpool FC; nature vs nurture), he quickly changed his mind – and the new version opened at the Albery (now the Noël Coward Theatre) in 1988. It transferred to the Phoenix three years later, and ran there for twenty-one years, won loads of awards, made everyone cry, starred a Spice Girl, and made Willy a milly (millionaire).

Plot – Twin boys are separated at birth, when a working-class mother reluctantly gives one of the boys away to her middle-class employer. One becomes posh and develops floppy hair; the other gets a tattoo saying 'Mam' and does time in prison for ball-changing in public. They both fall in love with the same girl because she sings at them nicely and has the best hair. It's very sad. The whole thing is narrated by one of The Beatles. The moral of the musical: having a twin can be tough, especially if he has a bigger penis than you.

Characters – Narrator, Mrs Johnstone, Mrs Lyons, twins Mickey and Edward, Linda and Sammy.

Best-known actresses to have played Mrs Johnstone – Barbara Dickson, Marti Webb, Kiki Dee, the Nolan Sisters, the Carole King, Lyn Paul, Clodagh Rogers, Petula Clark and Melanie 'Sporty Spice' Chisholm.

Most likely to play Mrs Johnstone in the future – Any actress who has been on *Loose Women* and can sing with a convincing Scouse accent.

Best-known songs – 'Marilyn Monroe'; 'Easy Terms'; 'Shoes Upon the Table'; 'Bright New Day'; 'Long Sunday Afternoon'; 'Marilyn Monroe 2'; 'Marilyn Monroe 3' (this song is reprised a lot); 'Miss Jones'; 'Tell Me It's Not True' (don't worry; it isn't).

Rejected songs – 'I Wish I Wasn't an Only Child' (don't worry; you're not); 'I'm Posh and You're Not'; 'My Liverpool Accent is Real – You're Actually from Epsom, Petula'; 'Me Best Friend is Me Brother'.

JESUS CHRIST SUPERSTAR

History – In 1970, a young Andrew Lloyd Webber and Tim Rice were hiding in a confession box after Sunday school, eating communion wafers, when they had a vision. A man with a long beard and long hair appeared to them singing in a falsetto voice about Jesus Christ becoming a superstar. They were stunned, and thought the man was Jesus telling them to write a musical about Him – but actually it was just a work-experience altar boy who was drunk on sacramental wine. But the experience prompted the dynamic duo to write a rock-opera concept album entitled *Jesus Christ Superstar*.

It was an instant success, topping the US Billboard chart, and in 1971 was transformed into a sung-through show on Broadway. The following year it transferred to the West End's Palace Theatre, where it played (if 'play' isn't an offensive word for a show about a crucifixion) for 3,358 performances. It has been resurrected numerous times – on film, in the West End, in the open air, on tour, and in a stadium version with a company that included a Son of God cast on reality TV (even though Israel in 4 BC had no mass communication), former Spice Girl Mel C as Mary M, an unfunny radio presenter as Herod, and a funny ginger Australian as Judas. The show ends with the immortal words 'I'll be back' – still leaving it open for the sequel, *Jesus Christ Superstar 2: The Resurrection Years*.

Plot – The musical tells the well-known, true-life story of the last seven days of Jesus's life – through the point of view of Judas Iscariot. Judas is worried and jealous about Jesus's popularity, and is concerned that His followers will be perceived as a threat to the Roman Empire. Some priests with silly names agree, and they all state that Jesus and His group must be stopped. However, Jesus's popularity grows, and He is worshipped as though He is Harry Styles. With an onslaught of sandals, long hair and 'Hosannas', the show builds to a climactic ending where Jesus is betrayed, tried, punished and put to death. For all its anthemic rock songs, and regardless of how religious or irreligious you might be, the ending packs a mighty punch. (Warning: nipples are often displayed.)

Characters – Jesus, Mary Magdalene, Judas, eleven other beardy disciples, King Herod, Caiaphas and Pontius Pilate.

Best-known actors to have played Jesus – Ian Gillan, Ted Neeley, Paul Nicholas, Glenn Carter, Ted Neeley, Steve Balsamo, Ben Forster and Declan Bennett.

Most likely to play Jesus in the future – Anyone who has been on a Lloyd Webber reality TV show and has facial hair.

Best-known songs – 'Heaven on Our Minds'; 'Everything's Alright'; 'I Don't Know How to Love Him'; 'Damned for All Time'; 'Gethsemane'; 'King Herod's Song'; 'Superstar'.

Rejected songs – 'This Cross is Bloody Heavy'; 'He's Not the Messiah, He's a Very Naughty Boy'; 'Joseph Got a Colourful Coat and I Got a Crown of Thorns'; 'I Invented the Hipster Beard'.

THE SOUND OF MUSIC

History – With music by Richard Rodgers, lyrics by Oscar Hammerstein II and a book by Howard Lindsay and Russel Crouse, this classic musical is based on Maria von Trapp's memoir *The Story of the Trapp Family Singers*. Originally the producers had envisioned a play with only music from the repertoire of the Trapps. However, after Rodgers and Hammerstein added a couple of original songs to the show it was decided to make it a full-blown 'supercalifragilisticexpealidocious' musical (sorry, wrong show!).

The show opened on Broadway in 1959, starring Mary Martin and Theodore Bikel, and two years later at the Palace Theatre in London. In 1965, Julie Andrews, flying high from her success as Mary Poppins the year before, and Christopher Plummer starred in the film version, and soon *The Sound of Music* became The Sound of Awards – it won five Tonys and five Oscars (one for each Trapp, plus an extra one for the goatherd). Hammerstein never lived to see its success, sadly dying nine months after the Broadway premiere.

The Sound of Music was the first musical awarded the television talent-show treatment, with Andrew Lloyd Webber asking the British public to help him pick the nation's Maria in *How Do You Solve a Problem Like Maria?* After several rounds, various costume changes, and a handful of embarrassing episodes, Connie Fisher was chosen as the answer to the problem, and she starred in the London Palladium revival in 2006. *The Sound of Music* has also been performed live on television in both the US (starring Carrie Underwood) and UK (with Kara Tointon).

Plot – In 1930s Austria, contraception was not widely available – going by retired naval officer Captain von (Clap) Trapp, who is so virile that he has seven children. His wife had died a few years earlier, and he is not very good at looking after the seven darlings on his own – so writes to the local convent to ask if the nuns can provide a governess. The

Captain runs a very tight ship, insisting that his children all dress alike and behave dutifully – but the little cherubs misbehave behind his back, causing all the governesses to quit. However, the nuns at the convent are being driven insane by an all-singing, all-dancing nun called Maria Rainer, and use the Captain's request as the perfect excuse to get rid of her.

When Maria arrives, the children show her no respect – but she quickly wins them round by getting her guitar out, doing an acoustic set of showtunes, and running up some snazzy lederhosen with the curtains. And after the Captain hears Maria strumming, he realises that she's a 'bit of alright' and falls in love with her. Maria is not sure what to do – so runs back to the convent to ask the Mother Abbess for advice. The Reverend Mother cannot bear the idea of the singing nun returning, and famously asks, 'What is it you c*n't face?', which has had audiences giggling inappropriately for decades.

After Maria confesses all, the Reverend Mother tells her not to be so silly by singing a song about mountaineering, instructing her to leave promptly and return to the Captain and his children. This she does, excitedly displaying her jazz hands, rolling back down the hills, singing and finally allowing the Captain to strum her G-string. In a matter of minutes they marry and go off on honeymoon.

Just as they return, the Captain is summoned by the Third Reich to serve in the navy. Using a clever plan, he enters his family into *Austria's Got Talent* – and after their song (which gets a standing ovation from Simon von Cowell), they hide from the Nazis, flee Austria, and head to the Swiss mountains to purchase some big bars of Toblerone.

Characters – Captain Georg von Trapp, Maria von Trapp (née Rainer), Baroness Else von Schräder, Max Detweiler, the Mother Abbess, lots of nuns, Liesl von Trapp, Friedrich von Trapp, Louisa von Trapp, Kurt von Trapp, Brigitta von Trapp, Marta von Trapp, Gretl von Trapp, Rolfe.

Best-known actresses to have played Maria – Julie Andrews, Carrie Underwood, Connie Fisher, Mary Martin, Jean Bayless, Kara Tointon, Charlotte Wakefield and Danielle Hope.

Most likely to play Maria in the future – Any young actor who has been on a Lloyd Webber TV talent show and looks nice in a blonde wig.

Best-known songs – 'The Sound of Music'; 'I am Sixteen Going on Seventeen'; 'My Favourite Things'; 'Do-Re-Mi'; 'The Lonely Goatherd'; 'Climb Ev'ry Mountain'; 'Edelweiss'.

Rejected songs – 'The Sound of Munich'; 'I am Sixteen... You Are a Nazi'; 'I Wonder What Nuns Wear Under Their Habits'; 'Do-Re-He-Is-Cute'; 'I Bet Those Kids Went to Sylvia Young'; 'Climb Ev'ry Nunnery'; 'Egg-fried-reiss'.

ACT FOUR: GONE!

'Tomorrow, and tomorrow, and tomorrow,
Creeps in this petty pace from play to play...'

Just been for a run. Oh sorry. Bloody autocorrect. I meant a drink, dear.

As the show comes to its conclusion, the actors start bowing, and the people around you start waking up – it's time for you to applaud, pack up your things, and get the hell out of the theatre as quickly as possible. This chapter will help you prepare for everything that happens after the show – from leaving the theatre, talking to actors, and going home with them. But firstly – you need to think about showing your appreciation... or not.

How to Clap

Where my first book (for actors) explained how to bow, this book (for muggles) will explain how to respond to that bowing. The fact is: it's not hard. Even young babies instinctively know how to bang their hands together, making a clapping sound that registers their approval and delight. It's exactly the same for audiences at the theatre (without the gurgling and squealing – though you can do that too if you want). It's part of the age-old contract between audiences and actors, and is a liberating release at the end of any performance.

What's less natural is judging whether to give a standing ovation. If you've seen a show and all the people around you jump to their feet, you have a dilemma. You may not be as enthusiastic as everyone else about the show, so do you stand to be polite, or stay firmly rooted to your seat?

A standing ovation is something that should be awarded sparingly. Just because some actors managed to say all their lines in the right order doesn't mean they're deserving of an ovation. No, you have to be more careful in your rewarding of this gift. A standing ovation should be held in reserve for when you've seen something truly extraordinary. It is important to remember that when you stand, you are not just standing for the actors – but for the whole team. You are showing appreciation to the crew, the director, the designer, the writer, the actors, the casting director's boyfriend, and the cleaner who removed all that old acting juice from your seat.

However, if you do choose to stand, don't be embarrassed. You will usually be standing with lots of others – and that's a good thing, as there's always safety in numbers. However, if you feel particularly confident, and really fancy someone in the cast then go for it! Stand on your own for the world to see! It will certainly ensure the actors will notice you, and maybe even give you a little wink (which is theatrical code for 'Pop by stage door, dear, and I'll show you my cufflink collection').

When ovating, always stand on two feet, and, whenever possible, try not to be overly drunk. It can be very embarrassing leaping to your feet only to wobble sideways and fall on top of the old dear sitting to your right – especially if it's the director's mum. The best stance is to have your legs hip-width apart and slightly bent, with your bottom perching out at a 45-degree angle (perfect in case you fall back into your seat). Your arms should reach out just in front of your nipples to applaud, and the odd fist pump is encouraged during moments of particular excitement. If you have difficulty standing, just put your hands on the head of the person sitting in front – and use them as an anchor from which to lift up. They won't mind – and if they do, just say you're related to the leading actor and all will be forgiven.

The way in which you stand signifies how much you enjoyed the show. If you take a half-standing stance with your knees bent then you thought the show was very good, but not as good as *Wicked*. If you stand straight upright then you loved the show so much it made you forget all about Donald Trump. And if you stand on your seat, jump up and down, whoop and cheer, and swing off the chandelier then you thought the show was even better than Barry Manilow's coming-out tour. And of course, if you do the opposite and lay on the floor, it means you didn't like the show at all. Either that or you're dead.

When you don't want to give a standing ovation, simply stay in your seat, applaud in a desultory fashion, and stare at the person's bum in front of you. Which can be a much better view than the view of the actors getting an undeserved ovation anyway, dear.

Some shows want you to do even more than stand – and literally force you to start dancing. And I'm not talking about a little bit of shoulder shaking – no, these shows want to see tightly rehearsed choreography. Shows like *Sunny Afternoon*, *Jersey Boys*, *Million Dollar Quartet*, *Mamma Mia!* – all rely on the audience getting up at the end and having a good bop in the aisles. It's very obvious when the performers are manipulating the audience to their feet – they'll do one lot of bows, then sing a song, then run off, then run on again, then shout 'Get up and join in!', then run off, then run back on again, then bow again, then run off, then run back on again – and by this time you'll be so worried that they're going to keep running off and on forever that you quickly jump to your feet. This will be followed by a cheesy megamix – which is designed to fool your brain into thinking that you actually enjoyed the show.

From time to time, you may even get to go on stage. The musical *Once*, based on the delightful Irish film of the same name, was set in a bar – and during the interval the audience were invited to go on stage and have a drink. An excellent idea, making everyone experience what it felt like to be in the show. Some people liked it so much that they hid on stage and gate-crashed the curtain call. Well, you can't blame those Italia Conti kids – they need to get on stage somehow, dear.

Actors – want the biggest applause? Bow with a child.

A Guide to Applauding

Here is a list of the different types of response you can choose at the end of a performance. Decide on the appropriate action, commit to it, take a deep breath and then...

Whoop, cheer and stand on your seat – You loved the show.

Shout 'Bravo!' – You really liked it. The use of this word also confirms that you're rather theatrical, dear.

Shout 'Encore!' – You liked the performance so much that you'd like to see even more. In the theatre, if enough people shout 'encore' and clap for long enough, the performers may come on for another bow – and occasionally another song. (If you're going to see *Joseph and the Amazing Technicolor Dreamcoat* you should avoid crying 'encore' at all costs. Otherwise you'll be forced to endure an extra-long megamix that lasts as long as the show itself.) I've always thought it a shame that the same doesn't happen at the end of plays. If the clapping and 'encores' are loud enough, then actors should come back on and give another dramatic monologue, or just stand centre stage and display their crying technique.

Clap energetically but *no* vocals – You liked it.

Clap politely – You thought it was okay, but wished you'd stayed at home to watch *Corrie*.

Clap slowly – You didn't like the show at all and now have a desperate desire to get drunk.

Sit on your hands and not clap – You hated the show and wish that theatre came with a money-back guarantee.

Throw something at the actors – You feel so passionate in your disliking of the show that you have the urge to do something about it. In olden times the tradition was to throw rotten tomatoes and other putrid vegetables at performers. You don't often see this tradition utilised in theatre any more – but perhaps now is the time for a comeback. If you decide to throw something, make sure it's nice and squishy – because even if the show was terrible you should avoid killing an actor, as they may not have an understudy. Actors today are all very health-conscious – gone are the days of drunken hellraisers like Rod Hull and Emu. Any rotting fruit and veg you hurl should be organic, so the actors can pick them up and use them in their NutriBullet the following morning.

'There's no business like showbusiness
Like no business I know.
Everything about it is misleading,
Everything the casting will allow,
Nowhere will you get that sinking feeling
When they're leaving, during your bow…'

How to Leave

Leaving a theatre can be just as stressful as entering one. Not only is everyone racing to be the first one out, but you can also get stuck behind a slowcoach, a drunk, or someone who is actually asleep. So be prepared and plan your exit before the end. Usually in each area of the theatre there will be fire exits, or different exits which lead straight to the street – which are entirely different doors to the ones you will have entered through. These are the ones to head towards.

Often at the theatre, I find people in the row where I've been sitting start to queue patiently to leave – so I divert into another row. If you're particularly spritely you can just jump over some seats to get to the row that is leaving quickest. Next, everyone usually heads straight to the back of the auditorium, retracing their steps from when they entered. This is an amateur mistake – but you'd be surprised at how many people join these time-wasters in another pointless queue. It takes an age! As we all know, the British love a queue, and we'll take advantage of any opportunity to get involved in one. It makes us feel secure and safe in the knowledge that we're following the rules. But break the rules, dear! It will save you valuable minutes you could be using for drinking.

When you see a queue developing, look around for an exit that fewer people are using, or one that isn't open. These smaller, secret, not-so-glamorous exits will lead you to the side of the theatre. 'But I've got my cloak, bag and umbrella in the cloakroom!' I hear you scream. No problem, just go round to the front and re-enter to get your belongings. It'll still be quicker, I promise, dear.

Things get even more complicated when audience members decide to veer off to the toilet as they are leaving. Another error. Everyone suddenly decides to do this at the end of the show – and another vexatious queue forms. Which starts interrupting the queue of people leaving. How frustrating. No! If you desperately feel the need to go to the WC, then you've only yourself to blame for downing that bottle of wine in the interval. In such an emergency you should quickly leave the theatre and go to the cocktail bar next door. Not only will they have more toilets – some small bars have more loos than an eight-hundred-seat theatre – they will be infinitely nicer. You may even meet some of the cast supplementing their acting wage by handing out perfume in there.

If you are extra-determined to make a speedy getaway you could be one of those annoying individuals who stand up before the end, pack their things up, and ruin the final few minutes for everyone else. Now I know some people have buses to catch, and I understand that you may have a cab waiting – but if you've paid £65 for a ticket, you may as well wait until the very end, and watch every last second of entertainment you've paid for. At least some people have the consideration to wait until the curtain call, but even then the whole thing is rude. This is where an audience should show their appreciation to the talent on stage. Even if the production was average, and the acting as exciting as balsa wood, it's only polite to reward the actors for the time they've spent shouting at you. If you really must leave during the curtain call, then at least ask people to let you past politely by explaining that you're the director and you've got to get backstage to slap the actors.

Here are some final tips for getting out of the theatre and into the bar next door (or onto the last train home) as speedily as you can:

- Plan in advance and put your programme, leftover sweets and stolen binoculars into your bag.

- Find out what the last musical number is by checking the list in the programme, then you'll know when the show is nearly finished. If you're watching a play, check the running time and keep a beady eye on your watch. Or, if it's Shakespeare, it's when everyone starts dying/getting married.

- Refrain from stopping for any unnecessary purchases of ice cream, souvenir brochures or branded show condoms – the *Mary Poppins* ones are 99% safe, they're 'practically perfect'.

- Open the exit, inhale the London smog, and glory in the fact that you're the first one out of the building.

A Guide to Leaving Before the End

There are a few excuses when I will accept your early departure, and these are:

- You are going into labour mid-show.

- You have to avoid an emergency leakage in the stalls. Not nice for anyone, particularly those sitting in front of you.

- The bows are going on for ever. (Very common at the RSC and the Royal Opera House. The curtain call for one production of *Hamlet* lasted longer than the play itself.)

- You are stocking up on Maltesers (the lighter way to enjoy chocolate).

- You suddenly realise you're in the wrong theatre. (Only recently a bus group were meant to be watching *Miss Saigon*, but were actually watching *Chitty Chitty Bang Bang*. They only realised their mistake when the car started flying – they'd been expecting a helicopter. Bless.)

- The show you're watching is *Dirty Dancing*. (See below for how to cope with a rubbish show.)

If you find yourself in one of these unfortunate situations and are forced to leave before the end, here are some suggestions on how you can do it:

- Wait until a scene change.
- Wait until the audience is applauding a musical number, causing as little distraction possible.
- If it's a particularly long and boring show, just leave – as everyone will be glad of the distraction.
- Sit at the end of a row – and leave whenever you wish.
- Hide in the toilets in the interval.
- Don't go back for the second half.
- Alternatively, stay at home in the first place. Simple.

Overheard at a drama school.
Teacher: Name a Shakespearean play.
Student: *Shakespeare in Love*.

How to Cope with a Shrubbish

We've all been there. Bought an expensive suit from Debenhams, invested in a tub of Jelly Babies, and remortgaged our house for a ticket to the coolest show in the West End. Only to discover that the show is rubbish (a shrubbish), that the sexy celeb you went to see has left to film a guest lead on *Emmerdale*, and that David Essex is taking their place. That's enough to put anyone off theatre for life, dear.

At the theatre we never offer refunds, unless the show is stopped due to reasons beyond our control. And if you simply want a refund because the play was 'boring', 'long' and 'had no tap numbers', then I'm afraid there's nothing we can do apart from suggest you avoid watching Greek tragedy in future.

When watching a shrubbish you have three options to choose: either snooze, booze or excuse (yourself and leave). If you've paid for your seat then you are entitled to use it for the entirety of the show, so if you're feeling tired after a particularly long day you could close your eyes and get some sleep. Theatres can be the perfect places to catch forty winks. They are dark, comfortable, warm – and sometimes they even offer a willing partner in the next seat along. As an added sleeping aid, the dialogue in some shows is so tedious that it will naturally help you fall asleep (the libretto for *We Will Rock You* is a personal favourite at bedtime).

Of course, it all depends on the specific seats in a theatre and how loud the show is. If you're going to the theatre simply to sleep you should go to a show that has famous screen actors in it – as you can never hear what they're saying anyway. If you want to be extra comfortable, take earplugs, an eye-mask, blanket and hot water bottle along. You may even want a teddy bear – I often take my Jean Valjean teddy with me, cuddling him always helps me nod off in the overture.

If you go for the 'booze' option, glide to the dress-circle bar, down a few vodkas, and fill several plastic cups with as much house wine as possible. By the end of Act One you will be so sloshed that anything happening on stage will be brilliant (wine was the only thing that got me through *Dreamboats and Petticoats*). I shamefacedly recall watching a dire production of *Macbeth*, which ended up being frightfully funny because I was so sloshed. I laughed at all the long speeches, giggled during the fighting, and danced excitedly when Macbeth died. I then blacked out and got sent to hospital to have my stomach pumped. It certainly wasn't a dagger Macbeth saw before him that night, it was me passed out in the aisle, dear.

These days, my own preferred method of survival during a shrubbish is to invest money in a good bottle of Dom and stick it out. But if the theatre only offers bad prosecco, I retreat to The Ivy, where I sip from my flute and throw salty nuts at Serena McKellen.

If you've been particularly badly affected by your shrubbish and find yourself waking up in the middle of the night in a cold sweat screaming, 'Oh God no, the interval can't be over already!', then you may be suffering from PTSD, or Post-Terrible-Show Disorder. Symptoms can include non-stop crying, involuntary triple-time steps, and jumping out of your skin at the sight of anyone who looks even a little bit like Sarah Harding. If you find yourself afflicted by this debilitating condition, then consider joining a Shrubbish Survivor Support Group. These are held on weekday mornings in the Grand Saloon at Theatre Royal Drury Lane, and give you and fellow sufferers the chance to swap stories and coping mechanisms, and plot your revenge against the sadistic creative teams who did this to you. The groups are safe, non-judgemental places, full of people just like you – and usually led by a shell-shocked, dead-eyed former cast member of *Viva Forever!* Those people are so brave, dear.

What to Say About the Show

The thrill of seeing a great show doesn't stop when you leave the theatre – it can stay with you for days, weeks, even years. It is thrilling to leave a theatre feeling elated and inspired (sadly this doesn't happen all the time). One of my favourite things to do after a show is to listen to the comments people make as they leave. You should try it yourself. Loiter in the lobby, or hang around in the toilets, and overhear the wonderful words of wisdom. Things like 'Where did they hide the orchestra?', 'The singing was too high', and 'They weren't real horses – they were made of wood.'

A Guide to What to Say About the Show

Here is a selection of some of the best comments overheard after a show. I promise they are all genuine. Well, most of them, dear.

The Phantom of the Opera

'I admire that actor with all those facial injuries. Good on him.'

'So was it an opera, or a musical? I dunno. I'll call it a "mopera".'

'That actress playing Sarah Brightman was good.'

'He's basically just an ugly stalker.'

'You can't have a healthy relationship with someone who wears a mask. Fact.'

The Lion King

'The best bit was the beginning, it was all downhill from there.'

'"The Circle of Life"? More like "The £80 Circle Ticket of Life".'

'I bet Simba works out.'

'I couldn't see any of the actors – they all had those bloody masks on.'

'Simba was walking so slow I told him to Mufasa.'

'What was Scar's name before he got his scar?'

Miss Saigon

'The helicopter was great. That must be a nightmare to fly in every night.'

'What on earth was "a song played on a solo saxophone" about? It wasn't romantic at all. It reminded me of Lisa Simpson.'

'I don't see how this musical was based on a butterfly.'

'When a person is dying in a musical, they sing. And then die. I wish they'd just die. Then I wouldn't miss my last train home.'

Wicked

'Gosh, that green girl was great. She sang, danced, acted *and* flew in the air. Now *that's* talent.'

'That blonde one got on my nerves. She reminded me of your mum.'

'I wonder if she paints her bits green?'

'Well, if that's theatre, it comes at much too high a cost...'

'Was Elphaba meant to sound like Tarzan at the end of "Defying Gravity"?'

'They named that show after my mother-in-law.'

Les Misérables

'It was a bit long, wasn't it?'

'Javert spent his life hunting down Jean Valjean because he stole a loaf of bread? Jeez. Must have been an expensive loaf.'

'They've totally nicked everything from the film.'

'Where was Susan Boyle?'

'I liked the set. Especially those two big ships that kept moving together.'

'Do you hear the people sing? No. They're all dead.'

War Horse

'My favourite was the goose. He stole it for me. Give him his own show – *War Goose*.'

'Jesus, I need a drink after that. It was so emotional. And so moving. And the accents were so bad.'

'When you've seen one horse you've seen them all.'

'I can't understand why they didn't just use real horses. I mean they're intelligent animals, aren't they? Just look at *Free Willy*. And he was a whale.'

'What were those "half horses" about? They must have run out of budget, or maybe they were meant to be seahorses.'

'A real horse would have shat on the stage – that's the kind of detail I expect from a National Theatre production.'

Matilda

'Tim Minchin didn't write that, Roald Dahl did.'

'Miss Trunchbull reminded me of that tall blonde one off *Game of Thrones*. You wouldn't want to get in a fight with her.'

'I hope the kid that Trunchbull threw off stage is alright. If I was her mum I'd be fuming.'

'Were they real children?'

Kinky Boots

'I think I just fancied a lot of men.'

'How can they walk in those heels?'

'They missed out on a trick. They should sell those boots front of house.'

'That wasn't based on Cyndi Lauper's life at all.'

Charlie and the Chocolate Factory

'I preferred *Matilda*.'

'Why did they get rid of the good songs from the film?'

'That glass elevator was plastic.'

'The Oompa-Loompas looked good. But it was obvious they weren't real Oompa-Loompas.'

'The chocolate river looked shit. Literally.'

Mamma Mia!

'Thank God they could all sing better than Pierce Brosnan.'

'It's basically theatre for hen parties.'

'The woman in front of me kept waving a giant inflatable penis around. It was my favourite bit.'

'Do you think ABBA actually like this?'

The Curious Incident of the Dog in the Night-Time

'That was proper good acting. I mean proper good. I mean Sally Webster good.'

'So was he meant to be stuck in a big computer game or summat?'

'The dog was the best. Didn't he win *Britain's Got Talent*?'

'Not sure about all that "movement" stuff.'

The Woman in Black

'I screamed so loud I peed myself.'

'It was good, but too expensive for a two-hander. My ticket was £60 – so I basically paid £30 per actor.'

'There wasn't one black woman in it. Racists.'

The Play That Goes Wrong

'If the play was rehearsed to go wrong, then it was supposed to go wrong – so actually it didn't go wrong at all. It went very right. So it's not *The Play That Goes Wrong* at all. It's *The Play That is Meant to Look Like It's Gone Wrong, But Hasn't*.'

Macbeth

'Last time it was a lot funnier.'

'Those witches are right bitches, aren't they?'

'The actor playing Macbeth looked nothing like Macbeth.'

'I'm really disappointed that they cut the "To be or not to be" speech.'

One...
...Day More?
...Singular Sensation?
...Last Time?
...Direction?
So many choices, dear.

What to Say to Actors

It can be very hard knowing the correct things to say to actors – particularly if they are close friends or family members. Actors, more than anyone, are sensitive beings – and if you accidentally compare them to The Chuckle Brothers, or suggest that their true talent lies in children's theatre, you might as well slap them with a crusty pair of show-pants.

The best tactic is always to be prepared, knowing exactly the right thing to say. If an actor is out of work, never ask them if they are resting or suggest they write to the director of *Holby City*. Of course, everyone knows you're saying these things with the best of intentions, but it can have the opposite effect on the damaged wings of a frustrated actor.

A Guide to What to Say to Actors

Here is a list of things to say to actors that won't cause lasting hatred and deep depression. Memorise your favourites – and say them loudly and confidently when complimenting actors. You will quickly become their favourite person to invite to opening nights.

I've also included a list of things that must never, ever pass your lips. Do so at your peril – and only if you know how to cope with an actor sobbing in front of you.

What to Say to Actors After a Show

'You were brilliant.'

'Oh my God, I can't stop crying.'

'You're going to be famous one day.'

'That was proper drama.'

'You acted that really well.'

'Wow. I didn't know you could sing.'

'You're the next Olivier.'

'Those ball changes were something else.'

'You redefined the art of jazz hands with that performance.'

'You're better than Kenneth Branagh. And he can do Shakespeare *and* modern.'

'Bravo!'

'Encore!'

'May I touch you?'

'You looked really sexy on stage.'

'Let me get you a drink.'

'Here's some wine.'

'Here's a bottle of champagne.'

'Here's a lager.'

'Fancy a tipple?'

'Drinks at The Ivy?'

'I'm coming again.'

'Can you sign my programme/plaster cast?'

What *Not* to Say to Actors After a Show

'That was a really *energetic* performance.'

'You *are* brave.'

'Oh, you must be tired.'

'Were you meant to do it like that?'

'You looked like you were enjoying yourself.'

'It could do with a bit of editing.'

'I didn't understand it.'

'God, it was long.'

'I loved the lighting.'

'I prefer something with more songs.'

'Were there lots of understudies on?'

'Where was Shane Ritchie? I thought he was supposed to be in it?'

'You didn't have as much to do as I thought you would.'

'Not to worry... I'm sure it'll lead to something better.'

'Didn't you get long to rehearse?'

'I preferred the film.'

'I think you should have done it like this...'

'It was badly written. You had no chance.'

'Aunt Sally left and went to the pub.'

'You were very funny. Were you meant to be funny? Oh. Sorry.'

'Did you get paid?'

What Not to Say to Actors *Ever*

'What would I have seen you in?'

'Are you resting?'

'Can't you get a better agent?'

'You must have made loads of money being in a show like that.'

'When are you going to get a proper job?'

'Keep going – one day you'll make it.'

'Maybe if you had a couple of singing lessons you could be in *Phantom*?'

'You've really improved since that production of *Grease* at school.'

'So you're an AC-TOR.' (in a posh, deep voice)

'You done any telly?'

'Who's the most famous person you've met?'

'Your turn to do some karaoke. You're an actor. You must be good at it.'

'Do you do kids' parties?'

'Can you get me comps?' (Do you ever ask your plumber to work for free?)

'How do you remember all those lines?'

Take your finger and draw ' −2 −2 + = ' on your pillow and it sounds like 'Chim Chim Cher-ee', dear.

How to Be a Fan

Some shows become cult hits, developing huge fanbases that can propel them to global success, film adaptations, and runs that last decades. *The Rocky Horror Show*, *Les Mis*, *Phantom* and *Wicked*, for instance, all have an army of followers who dedicate their lives to seeing, supporting and stalking these shows up and down the country with an unwavering passion and devotion that is truly remarkable. They save their money, Theatre Tokens and Nectar points to invest in the same show, the same seat, wearing the same outfit numerous times a year. It's about time there was a theatre loyalty card for these people – for every six shows you get the next one free.

Every night at stage doors across the West End (and regional theatres if the show stars Linda Lusardi), there will be a sea of excitable fans waiting for their favourite actors – hoping for a little glance, cheeky wink, and even a lingering hug. Fans are a vital part of the theatre world – discussing productions online, arranging meet-ups, running fan sites, writing questionable fan fiction, getting even more questionable tattoos, and most importantly spending lots of money. Bravo and thank you, dears! Their continued energy helps publicise shows and add a much-needed ebullience to the theatre world – particularly amongst younger audiences.

There's no initiation ceremony required to become a fan – you simply say that you're one and you are. Those who enjoy it a little bit more, and invest time, energy and enough money to buy a three-bedroom semi in Surbiton can award themselves the title of 'super fan'. Super fans, just like Superman (or Gran), have two identities. They have their normal life, where they go to work, mingle with friends, and discuss every tiny detail of *Breaking Bad* – and then they have their theatre life, where they have another network of friends, with whom they share their love of shows and taste for showbusiness.

The theatre community is wonderfully diverse, and welcomes everyone with open arms, even those who like *Love Never Dies*. That's the marvellous thing about being a fan – theatre wouldn't exist without them, so they become an important part of the theatrical ecology, like a member of the extended family. And like anything else that makes you feel good, it can become addictive – once you've experienced Kenneth Branagh up close it's very hard not to want to experience him again (unless you're Emma Thompson, of course). The only problem comes when fans become a little too obsessed. Now obviously this can happen to supporters of anything – but theatre fans can become a little more obsessed than others, purely because they know where their idols will be every night (and two afternoons a week). Fans and admirers should always be careful not to cross the line. In the theatre world it's a big, pink, sequinned line – and if you step over it without permission the god of theatre (Sir Benedict Cabbagepatch) will hit you with his acting rod.

Most actors are very nice, and will be only too happy to give you their autograph. After all, your support and enthusiasm makes them feel successful (actors and artists rely on the kindness of strangers). If you want to be a particularly nice fan and cause of lots of backstage excitement you should ask everyone *except* the actors for their autographs: the stage management, the front-of-house staff, the cleaners, the band, the casting director, the sound engineer... These people won't have their photos in the programme (though they should!), so you have to identify who they are by asking at stage door. Their response will usually be: 'Autograph? Me? Really? But I wasn't in the show!' – but after gentle persuasion they'll be more than happy to put pen to paper. And in fact, they will be *delighted*. These hidden stars of Theatreland deserve just as much recognition as the performers – because without them, the actors would simply be naked mutes wandering around in the dark.

A Guide to Being a Good Fan

Choose the Right Moment

The best place to speak to actors, ask for selfies and beg for autographs is at the stage door, directly after a show. Avoid asking in restaurants, during school runs, and in the local swimming baths (you don't want a soggy signature, dear).

Stay Calm

Although you may be meeting one of your idols, always remember to breathe. It is rather off-putting having someone breaking down in front of you. Actors and celebrities are just normal people — no different to you — apart from the fact that they work in the entertainment industry. If at any point you think you may start crying, take two steps back, breathe, and imagine the person in front of you is Dean Gaffney. Crisis averted, dear.

Be Polite

Actors will sometimes be in a rush after a show, desperately trying to catch their last train home, or attempting to make last orders at the nearest pub. You can always spot such actors, doing their utmost to make a speedy exit from the theatre, often whilst they're still on stage. Watch actors during the curtain call – most will stride downstage confidently taking great pride in their bow, offering a wink, a wave, a kiss.

But sometimes you will notice actors running downstage with contempt and disapproval. They'll nod their head slightly, smile through a grimace, and walk to their designated 'stand and wait' spot impatiently. These actors will have taken some of their costume off, and be under-dressed in normal attire. Look out for jeans, T-shirts and polo necks popping out from beneath an actor's seventeenth-century garb. You may even see the occasional wig flapping about – as it will already have been unsecured and quickly popped back on to save time later. If the actor you are waiting for bursts out of stage door sprinting for their life, you can guarantee the last thing they want is to be stopped for a chat. It is far more sensible to give chase and secretly follow them until they're just outside their front door. Then they won't be in a hurry to get home at all, as they're already there. Simple.

Don't Touch (without permission)

Actors are not animals in a zoo. They don't always want to be hugged and touched – it is essential you ask prior permission before cupping Michael's Balls. However, saying that, some actors *adore* being touched, and can't get enough of it – even offering fans a 'backstage tour'. If an actor offers you one of these, you can expect a swift walk around the stage followed by something called a 'touch tour' in their dressing room. Touch tours are excellent as they allow fans to see and touch actors in their natural habitat.

Give Presents

Who doesn't like receiving a gift? Everyone loves it! Especially actors. If you want to impress and leave a lasting impression on your favourite actor, do some detective work and find out what things they adore. Most performers love receiving flowers, alcohol, chocolate and John Lewis giftcards. The best way of giving an actor a gift is at stage door – it's a definite way of making even the most famous of performers stop and say hello. However, never leave home-baked goods of any kind, since edible gifts are treated with severe suspicion. Who knows what special ingredients have been added for extra flavour (like the time Mr Mistoffelees received a chocolate cake with a special fan-furball filling)?

Buy Drinks

Refrain from following actors to the pub, sitting at a nearby table, and staring. This can be rather unnerving. I've known grown actors gobble down nuts at inhuman speeds when they notice a table of fans watching their every move in the local Wetherspoons. Actors and celebs will always treat you with respect if you do the same to them. However, the one way to guarantee a warm welcome by a group of performers is by getting them a round of drinks. The only thing actors love more than a drink is a free drink. Buy shots as well and you'll find yourself pole dancing with your new friends until 4 a.m. Especially if you're cute.

In bed with an actor or director? Not sure which it is? One will always hit their mark, the other will tell you which mark to hit.

MISS SAIGON

History – Flicking through *Heat* magazine one day, Claude-Michel Schönberg came across a heart-breaking photograph of a Vietnamese mother making the ultimate sacrifice – leaving her child at Tan Son Nhut Air Base, so that the child could have a better life in the United States with her ex-GI father. With the other members of the *Les Mis* dream team – Alain Boublil on lyrics, and Cameron Mackintosh on producing – they used this photo (and a Puccini opera) as inspiration for their new musical set in Saigon at the end of the Vietnam War.

After polishing off the songs in a holiday villa in Skegness, the next stage was finding an actress to play the leading lady, a Vietnamese bargirl called Kim. After months of searching and numerous cocktails around the world, the creative team finally discovered Lea Salonga – and a star was born. Next on the agenda was finding a leading man, but after the exhaustion of discovering Salonga they couldn't be bothered to do any more travelling, so just cast Jonathan Pryce instead. The original production, directed by Nicholas Hytner, opened at the Theatre Royal Drury Lane in 1989, was an enormous success, and played for 4,264 performances. The production transferred to Broadway in 1991 (after some controversy over Pryce playing a Eurasian character), before also topping four thousand performances. In 2014, a new, fresh production (basically the same but with a different helicopter) opened at the Prince Edward Theatre, before another Broadway transfer, a tour, and another cast recording. Loosely based on a butterfly.

Plot – It is April 1975, near the end of the Vietnam War, in Saigon (now Ho Chi Minh City). A seventeen-year-old Vietnamese girl, Kim, works in Dreamland (not the one in Margate), and is crowned Miss Saigon. Kim meets Chris, an American marine, who gets all hot and bothered when he sees her (the heat was on in Saigon). They're both a bit shy, but with some money and a bit of gentle persuasion it doesn't take long until Kim plays a solo on Chris's saxophone. After experiencing Kim's sax skills, Chris quickly falls in love with her and buys her from a pimp called the Engineer. The Engineer is desperate to be American, and offers women, men and ping-pong balls to anyone he believes will give him a US passport. In the morning, Chris promises to take Kim back home – 'Hey mom, look what I bought from Vietnam!' However, that plan doesn't work out.

Three years pass. Chris is back in the US of A and married to Ellen (who isn't very good on the sax). Meanwhile, Kim has been waiting in Vietnam for Chris to return – with a surprise – his child, a boy called Tam. After some shouting about Bui Doi there is a flashback sequence, showing how Chris tried to rescue Kim three years earlier. Cue lots of emoting, some camp GIs, and the biggest chopper in showbiz. Back in 1978, Chris, his wife, and their live-in-lover John go over to Bangkok to see Kim and Tam. After some confusion, Kim meets Ellen first, making Ellen so upset that she sings a dreary song. Chris and John arrive, they all tell Ellen to stop singing, and go to find Kim. Kim is in her hotel waiting for room service, but they leave her waiting so long that she shoots herself. Chris enters – they embrace, and she dies in his arms. Everyone cries. And the Engineer has another wet dream about being American.

Characters – Kim, Chris, Ellen, the Engineer, Tam, Gigi, John Thomas (yes, really).

Best-known actresses to have played Kim – Lea Salonga, Joanna Ampil and Eva Noblezada.

Most likely to play Kim in the future – A genetically engineered baby growing in a lab underneath one of Cameron Mackintosh's theatres. I'm sure that's how he finds these remarkable young talents.

Best-known songs – 'The Heat is On in Saigon'; 'The Movie in My Mind'; 'Why, God, Why?'; 'Sun and Moon'; 'Last Night of the World'; 'This is the Hour'; 'If You Want to Die in Bed'; 'Bui Doi'; 'The American Dream'.

Rejected songs – 'I Want to Visit Universal Studios, So Give Me a Passport, Please'; 'Sleep with My Whore and You'll Want More'; 'Excuse Me, Jonathan, But You're Not Asian'.

JOSEPH AND THE AMAZING TECHNICOLOR DREAMCOAT

History – Way, way back many centuries ago, a young Andrew Lloyd Webber (20) and a slightly-older-but-still-young Tim Rice (23), collaborated on a twenty-minute 'pop cantata' based on the story of Joseph from Genesis (an anti-quated pop group). It was first performed at Colet Court School in London in 1968, and not long after, Decca released a recording with Tim Rice starring as the Pharaoh (worth buying just to listen to that). After adding some more songs and a few more brothers, the show went to Edinburgh presented by the Young Vic Theatre Company, and finally found its way into the West End at the Albery Theatre (now the Noël Coward), when Robert Stigwood and Michael White gave them the budget to afford a better coat.

The show was tweaked over the following years, until the current, sung-through version was performed at Leicester's Haymarket Theatre in 1974. Since then, the show has toured constantly, going in and out of the West End every few years, with various celebs – Jason Donovan, Phillip 'The Schofe' Schofield and Stephen Gateley, amongst them – donning the colourful jacket to help push tickets. The show also became another one of Lloyd Webber's to undergo the casting-by-reality-TV method, with Lee Mead winning the coveted title of 'Most Likely to Marry Denise Van Outen'.

Plot – An annoying narrator squeaks in a high octave for a bit about how we should all live our life, and eventually starts reading from a book called the Bible. The story features Jacob and his twelve sons – his favourite being Joseph, whom Jacob presents with a dazzling coat of many colours, which makes him look lovely and multi-coloured. All the other brothers turn plain green with envy, living in denial about their sexuality (just watch the current tour to see how camp the brothers actually are), and they hatch a plan to kill him. But by chance they meet a group of theatre owners and sell him as a front-of-house slave instead. The brothers stain the coat with fake stage blood, which they show to their father who breaks down, whilst the brothers take it in turns to pose and pout.

Meanwhile, Joseph is sold to a front-of-house manager where his duties include tearing tickets, selling merchandise, and working behind the bar. After a rich producer tries to seduce him, and Joseph declines her advances, he is punished by being sent on a Theatre-in-Education tour. There, Joseph meets some other performers who have been enslaved to the world of TIE, all of whom have been eating too much cheese before bedtime and consequently having dreams about working for more than Equity minimum. Joseph interprets their dreams, correctly predicting their future of understudying in the regions.

News spreads of Joseph's dream-interpreting talent, and a wealthy impresario (who looks like Elvis) calls on his services. Joseph interprets his dreams, and tells the impresario that jukebox musicals are the future of theatre. Thrilled by this, the impresario gives Joseph a wad of cash and lets him go. Joseph eventually finds his family and, being the forgiving type, saves them from ruin – and they all do a megamix to make the show last a bit longer.

Characters – Joseph, Jacob, Narrator, Potiphar, Mrs Potiphar, Baker, Butler, Pharaoh, Joseph's eleven brothers, some sheep, lots of children.

Best-known actors to have played Joseph – Jason Donovan, Phillip Schofield, Donny Osmond, Stephen Gately, Ian 'H' Watkins, Joe McElderry and Lee Mead.

Most likely to play Joseph in the future – Any young actor who has sung on a reality-TV show.

Best-known songs – 'Any Dream Will Do'; 'Joseph's Coat'; 'Joseph's Dreams'; 'Poor, Poor Joseph'; 'One More Angel in Heaven'; 'Close Every Door'; 'Go, Go, Go Joseph'; 'Song of the King'; 'Benjamin Calypso'; that bloody 'Megamix'.

Rejected songs – 'This Coat is a Bit Loud for My Taste – Can I Have a Parka Instead?'; 'My Brothers Are Brutes'; 'That's Called a Wet Dream, Sir'; 'Benjamin Dubstep'; 'But Dad, I Said I Wanted a Multi-coloured *Goat*'.

MATILDA

History – After leaving a meeting at the Royal Shakespeare Company, director Matthew Warchus overheard a hairy ginger man singing on the streets. He presumed the man was homeless and gave him a tenner to get his hair cut, before realising the man wasn't homeless at all – but an Australian! It wasn't long before the ginger Australian got his didgeridoo out and played Matthew the theme tune to *Neighbours*. Matthew was so impressed that he asked the Aussie to write the music and lyrics to *Matilda*, a new musical based on Roald Dahl's family favourite – and their beautiful theatrical relationship was born. With Dennis Kelly writing the book, and Peter Darling (by name and nature) as choreographer, *Matilda the Musical* opened for a limited run in the temporary Courtyard Theatre in Stratford-upon-Avon. It was universally acclaimed, transferred to London's Cambridge Theatre in 2011, where it won seven Olivier Awards, to Broadway in 2013, where it won five Tonys, and has toured around the world. A film version is planned.

Plot – *Matilda* is the story of young girl who reads a lot, dreams of a happy family, and moves things with her mind. It's basically a blonde Annie, but with a scarier Miss Hannigan.

Characters – Matilda, Miss Trunchbull, Mr Wormwood, Mrs Wormwood, Miss Honey, Mrs Phelps, Bruce Bogtrotter, and lots of children.

Best-known actors to have played Miss Trunchbull – Bertie Carvel, Craig Els, David Shannon, Alex Gaumond, Craig Bierko and Christopher Sieber.

Most likely to play Miss Trunchbull in the future – Any actor who is tall, physically intimidating, and can carry off a pair of false boobs convincingly. Or Fatima Whitbread.

Best-known songs – 'Miracle'; 'Naughty'; 'Pathetic'; 'Telly'; 'When I Grow Up'; 'Quiet'; 'My House'; 'Revolting Children'; 'This Little Girl'.

Rejected songs – 'I'm Small, But I Can Move Things with My Mind'; 'I've Eaten All the Haribo and I Feel *Violent*!'; 'My Accent is Easier to Understand Than Billy Elliot's'; 'I'm Moving In with My Teacher. Laters, Mum and Dad'; 'Are You DBS Checked?'

ACT FIVE: GOING AGAIN

'Friends, Romans, audience-men – lend me your ears.
And your eyes, your focus, your applause, and your money.'

I hate it when actors confuse their Grindr photo with their Spotlight photo. There are enough dicks in Spotlight already, dear.

If you've followed every chapter in my book, you'll have successfully made it to the correct theatre, watched the right show, and dealt with any mild attacks of theatre rage. You applauded in the optimum style, kissed your favourite actor, and negotiated the ladies' loo. Bravo! Hopefully, you will have watched something that enlightened and entertained, moved and inspired you.

Once you've been bitten by the bug, your theatrical cherry has been popped, and you know how good a showgasm feels, I hope you'll be coming back, again and again, dear! Join me in embracing a lifetime of warm white wine and a severely depleted bank balance, by making Theatreland your favourite destination.

In this chapter, like the best tour guide, I'll hold my pink umbrella aloft, and take you on a tour of the weird and wonderful place that is the West End, unveiling some secrets about each of the theatres and their histories, and how not to be a hot mess on the streets of Soho in the early hours. That's not where you want to be at 5 a.m., unless of course you are Hugh Grant.

A Walking Tour of Theatreland

Start by putting on your nicest pair of shoes, and going for a wander. Don't use the Underground for now (or 'the Tube' if you want to sound savvy), walking is better for your waistline – and allows you to take in the sights, sounds and dubious smells that London has to offer.

Let's start our tour at that renowned London landmark, the statue of Eros (actually, it's Anteros, his twin brother) who stands in Piccadilly Circus. Also located on this pedestrianised patch is the **Criterion Theatre** (opened 1874, capacity 588), which was home to a comic adaptation of *The 39 Steps* for nine years (that's one step per 84.2 days), and before that the Reduced Shakespeare Company. It's also where lots of drama schools hold their end-of-year showcases – in which student actors begin their professional careers as slaves to the entertainment business.

Walk eastwards down Shaftesbury Avenue, deftly avoiding portrait artists and RADA graduates dressed as floating Yodas, and you will spot a murky little road to your left called Denman Street – at the end of which is hidden the **Piccadilly Theatre** (opened 1928, capacity 1,232). It looks like a dump from the outside, but thankfully is a lot more inviting once you get in, with its lovely art-deco interior. Early on in its history it was used as a cinema – and was the first place in Britain to show a talking picture – *The Singing Fool* starring Al Jolson. Recently, it has been the home of *Ghost the Musical*, *Jersey Boys* and The Spice Girls' jukebox show *Viva Forever!* (which wasn't forever – it was seven months, dear).

Moving on and back up Shaftesbury Avenue you will walk past Great Windmill Street – which is where you can find **The Windmill Theatre** (opened 1931), now Windmill International, and not really a theatre but a strip club. When it first opened, naked showgirls would stand still in tableaux to circumvent nudity laws – as long as they didn't move they weren't doing anything illegal, so the scenery would be moved around them instead. Clever. The Windmill and particularly this time in its history is the subject of the film and stage musical *Mrs Henderson Presents*. In fact, if you get bored at any point walking along Shaftesbury Avenue you can simply veer off to the left and treat yourself to a more revealing form of entertainment.

The next theatre along Shaftesbury Avenue is the **Lyric Theatre** (opened 1888, capacity 915). Originally a venue for operettas, this theatre has been the home of performances by Alec Guinness, Leonard Rossiter, John Malkovich, Judi Dench and Mrs RSC herself – Antony Sher. It is currently home to *Thriller Live* – a tribute to the phenomenon that was Michael Jackson. Nice singing, nice band, no story. If you are forced to go, take earplugs.

Literally about five strides up from the Lyric is the **Apollo Theatre** (opened 1901, capacity 775). Because of its size and history, it mostly hosts plays and comedies. It was the theatre where Peter O'Toole first bought *Jeffrey Bernard is Unwell* to London (1990), where John Gielgud appeared in *Forty Years On* (1968), and where Jez Butterworth's *Jerusalem* transferred from the Royal Court (2010) – causing mild-mannered theatrical rioting as people camped outside for days to see Mark Rylance being rather bloody good. In 2013, part of the Apollo's ceiling fell into the stalls, though thankfully no one was seriously injured and the theatre has reopened.

Just up from the Apollo, past a few Chinese restaurants on either side of the road (where you can treat yourself to an 'All You Can Eat Fried Onion and Rice' meal for £8.95) is the **Gielgud Theatre** (opened 1906, capacity 986) on the corner of Rupert Street. The theatre was originally called the Hicks Theatre – named after Sir Seymour Hicks, a famous actor, producer and playwright who made his money producing musical comedies – the original Cameron Mackintosh. It was renamed the Globe shortly after in 1909 (poor old Hicks), and the Gielgud in 1994, in honour of the great honey-voiced Sir John Gielgud.

The longest-running show at this theatre was the comedy *Daisy Pulls It Off* – which ran for 1,180 performances. However, the most famous resident was Beerbohm the theatre cat, named after the actor Herbert Beerbohm Tree. Apparently, Beerbohm appeared on stage during every production whilst he lived there – resulting in the actors doing some rather brilliant pussy-based improvisations – but he died in 1995, and had an obituary on the front page of *The Stage*. These days, theatres aren't allowed resident cats – due to health and safety regulations, and fragile actors moaning about furballs and allergies (let's be honest – you're much more likely to catch something from the boys in the chorus). It really is a shame – cats do a wonderful job of clearing theatres of rats and mice, and have marvellous intuition in telling which actors are good and which ones are bloody awful. It's always very telling when cats take a disliking to somebody – in fact I think they would be quite brilliant at casting shows (catsting). *The Curious Incident of the Dog in the Night-Time* played a long West End stint at the Gielgud, so perhaps it's a good job Beerbohm wasn't around. Cats and dogs in the same theatre? It would be like Jonathan Pryce and Martine McCutcheon working together again.

Another few paces down Shaftesbury Avenue brings you to the **Queen's Theatre** (opened 1907, capacity 1,074), which was designed by the architect W.G.R. Sprague as a pair with the theatre (now the Gielgud) next door. In 1913, instead of getting sloshed and vomiting in Soho, the craze was for Tango Teas, where people sipped tea and nibbled cakes whilst watching dancers perform tango – and consequently the stalls seats were replaced with tables and chairs. What an excellent idea! If *Les Misérables*, the current occupant, ever closes, we'll have to reintroduce it. I'm sure we could convince Bruno Tonioli and Darcy Bussell to do a nice Argentine cross for us – they're generally willing to do anything for a bit of extra cash.

Les Mis moved to the Queen's in 2004, after centuries at the Palace down the road – and has the accolade of being the world's longest-running musical. It also used to be the world's *longest* musical until they trimmed about four hours off it. Now it's the perfect length of about three hours (depending on the mood of the conductor), leaving just enough time to get to the local public house before last orders, where you can sing 'One pint more' at the top of your voice.

A five-minute walk (or two-minute run) down Shaftesbury Avenue takes you to the **Palace Theatre** (opened 1891, capacity 1,400). Its gorgeous and grand red-brick façade was commissioned by Richard D'Oyly Carte to make it the home of English opera. Recently, there hasn't been much opera in it (though *Priscilla Queen of the Desert* had lots of loud singing and big frocks, so that's pretty close, I suppose). Over the years the Palace has been the home of numerous big musicals – many of them long-runners: *Jesus Christ Superstar* ran from 1972 until 1980, and then *Les Misérables* ran for nineteen years from 1985 until 2004 when it moved down the road. A new piece of experimental low-tech theatre called *Harry Potter and the Cursed Child* is the current resident – but will probably be there for the next few decades...

Turning left outside the Palace, you'll soon find the **Prince Edward Theatre** (opened 1930, capacity 1,716). Named after Prince Edward (later Edward VIII and then Mr Wallis Simpson), it was renamed the London Casino in 1935 and converted into a dance hall. After getting bombed in 1941, it closed for a year and reopened as the Queensbury All Service Club for servicemen, and the shows performed there were all broadcast on the BBC. It was here in 1978 that Elaine Paige first exhorted Argentina not to cry for her as Eva Perón in *Evita*. The stage size was increased in 1993 (for the Gershwin hit *Crazy for You*), and since then the theatre has housed the premiere of *Mamma Mia!* (which transferred to the Prince of Wales after five years), *Mary Poppins* (which really was practically perfect), *Jersey Boys*, a revival of *Miss Saigon*, and Disney's *Aladdin*. It's conveniently located next to many of the homosexual watering holes of Old Compton Street – where you can often find Aladdin and the genie rubbing their lamps until the early hours of the morning. Sadly, a lot of old Soho has been sanitised recently, as rents have gone up by astronomical amounts – forcing many of the older and more characterful establishments to close. Which has infuriated my casting director – he enjoyed nothing more than a happy ending after a long day of casting.

Nip out of Old Compton Street and up Charing Cross Road and you will arrive outside the **Phoenix Theatre** (opened 1930, capacity 1,012). This venue got off to a starry start with the premiere of Noël Coward's *Private Lives*, featuring the writer himself, alongside Gertrude Lawrence and Laurence Olivier (Lawrence of Arabia wasn't available). Coward later returned to the Phoenix in his plays *Tonight at 8.30* (1936) and *Quadrille* (1952), and Paul Scofield's Hamlet played here in 1955, directed by Peter Brook. Since then the theatre has primarily housed musicals, including Stephen Schwartz's *The Baker's Wife* (1989), Stephen Sondheim's *Into the Woods* (1990), and Willy 'I'm not called Stephen but I'm still good' Russell's *Blood Brothers* (1991) – which ran for twenty-one years, making it the longest-running show at the Phoenix. More recently, the theatre has been home to *Once: The Musical* (I didn't go once, I went three times); *Bend It Like Beckham* (which didn't star a bent Beckham), *The Girls* by Gary Barlow and Tim Firth, and a stage version of *The Exorcist* – which was used to exorcise theatrical demons left behind by *Dirty Dancing* (which played there in December 2016).

Heading out of Soho and walking all the way to the end of Shaftesbury Avenue you will reach the **Shaftesbury Theatre** (opened 1911, capacity 1,400), originally called the New Prince's Theatre, and now the largest independently owned theatre in the West End. In its early days, the theatre housed mainly Gilbert and Sullivan operas (where people sing fast and in a pompous way) – most of which were presented by the D'Oyly Carte Opera Company. In 1962, EMI bought the theatre and renamed it the Shaftesbury, transferring Broadway hits such as *Gentlemen Prefer Blondes* and

How to Succeed in Business Without Really Trying, both in the early sixties. The hippy-trippy, love-rock musical *Hair* played there for 1,998 performances until the ceiling fell in, which wasn't quite so happy-clappy. The theatre was nearly closed permanently – until those lovely people at Equity ran a campaign and got it listed as a Grade II building in 1974.

Perhaps they'd rather not have bothered, since the Shaftesbury has become known as the cursed theatre of the West End because it has housed a number of notable flops. Saying that, *Hairspray* lasted there a while (because it featured a cross-dressing Michael Ball), but *Flashdance* closed quickly (because it didn't). Other cursedly short runs include *Bat Boy* (a musical about a young Ian Botham), *Thoroughly Modern Millie*, *Peggy Sue Got Married*, *The Far Pavilions*, *Daddy Cool* and *From Here to Eternity* (which seemed to go on for an eternity, but still closed early).

Heading north of the Shaftesbury and turning left along New Oxford Street you'll find the enormous, art-deco **Dominion Theatre** (opened 1929, capacity 2,163) on the corner of Tottenham Court Road. During the record-breaking twelve-year run of *We Will Rock You*, the theatre had a giant statue of Freddie Mercury standing outside. I've no idea where it is now, which makes me rather grumpy as I wanted it for a water feature in my garden. Musicals seen at the Dominion in recent years include *Beauty and the Beast*, *Grease*, *Notre Dame de Paris*, *Scrooge the Musical* and *An American in Paris*. The Dominion has also been a popular venue for concerts including performances by Dolly Parton, U2 and Van Morrison, and a very well-attended church, which takes up residency for four performances (or services) every Sunday. If you want to sound like a pro, then always shorten the name of a theatre: hence 'the Nash' (the National); 'the Lane' (Theatre Royal Drury Lane); and why the Dominion is my favourite – 'the Dom'.

Walking westwards down Oxford Street, just before it meets Regent Street, is Argyll Street – and the home of the **London Palladium** (opened 1910, capacity 2,286). Perhaps the most famous theatre in the West End, it was designed by the great theatre architect Frank Matcham, and was a big venue for pantomime and music-hall – though before that there had also been a circus arena and a skating rink on the same site. The beautiful theatre was almost destroyed by a German parachute mine in May 1941, which fell through the roof and became lodged over the state. A Royal Navy bomb-disposal team successfully defused the bomb, lowered it to the stage, and removed it.

By the 1950s, the theatre was known as the home of variety, mainly because of the television show *Sunday Night at the London Palladium*, famously hosted by Bruce 'Nice to See You...' Forsyth. It has been the venue for the Royal Variety Performance over forty times, which is a special show involving a parade of unfunny comedians trying to make the Queen laugh. In 2000, a hugely successful production of *The King and I* played here with Elaine Paige and Jason Scott Lee, taking over £7 million before it had even opened – Elaine's still got it (in fact she never lost it, apart from occasionally on her weekly radio show). Other notable musicals include *A Chorus Line*, *Sister Act*, *Chitty Chitty Bang Bang*, *The Sound of Music*, a recent revival of *Cats*, and Simon Cowell's ill-fated foray into the theatre world, *I Can't Sing!: The X Factor Musical* (some people should stick to wearing high-waisted trousers, dear).

Head down Regent Street, back towards Piccadilly Circus, but now take a right turn after Eros, down Haymarket. A minute or two later you'll reach the splendour of **Her Majesty's Theatre** (opened 1897, capacity 1,216). The theatre is the closest to Buckingham Palace, and always takes the monarch's pronoun: so it has generally been known as His Majesty's, until Queen Elizabeth succeeded the throne in 1952.

There have been several theatres on this site, but the current one was erected by the actor-manager Sir Herbert Beerbohm Tree (who also wins the prize for the Best Name in Theatre History). Herb Beer Tree (for short) loved this theatre so much that he lived inside it, in his own flat, and had a banqueting hall and living room installed in the dome. In 1904, he started a drama school at the theatre, called the Academy of Dramatic Art (with an acronym, ADA, that sounds like a little old lady); later moving to Gower Street, getting royal status and a rather better acronym (RADA). The theatre housed the original production of Bernard Shaw's *Pygmalion* (which became *My Fair Lady*), and many successful musicals including *West Side Story* (which came from *Romeo and Juliet*) in 1958, *Bye Bye Birdie* (1961), *Fiddler on the Roof* (1967), and, since 1986, *The Phantom of the Opera*.

Just over the road is the **Theatre Royal Haymarket** (opened 1821, capacity 893). This is one of the easiest theatres in London to find as it is located exactly where you would imagine – on the Haymarket. Life would be much easier for the wandering tourist if every theatre was named exactly where it was located. The Criterion would be called the 'Piccadilly Circus Theatre'; the Cambridge, the 'Seven Dials Theatre'; and the Prince Edward, the 'Theatre next to G-A-Y Bar'. Originally called 'The Little Theatre in the Hay', the theatre first opened in 1720 and was located a little further north, before moving to the current site in the 1820s. It is the third-oldest London playhouse still in use, and the first ever to have a matinee performance, in 1873. So it is entirely the Haymarket's fault that actors now have to undergo the tortuous pain of two-show days, whilst making more money for us ever-thankful producers.

Theatre Royal Haymarket Productions was established in 2007, with an artistic director helming each season in its early years, such as Jonathan Kent, Sean Mathias and Trevor 'Double Denim' Nunn, and between them directing numerous hits with actors such as Patrick Stewart, Ralph Fiennes, Joanna Lumley, Anna Friel, Robert Lindsay and Ian McKellen. The theatre also offers a season of masterclasses, where established performers give advice to young actors about which directors to give their phone numbers to.

Around the corner from the Haymarket, on Panton Street, is the **Harold Pinter Theatre** (opened 1881, capacity 796).

This theatre was originally called the Royal Comedy Theatre, but after realising that the monarchy wasn't funny, the 'Royal' bit was taken off. After this, it was known simply as the Comedy Theatre, but after a spate of unfunny comedies, it was changed to the Harold Pinter – though not all productions there are required to be menacing plays with lots of swearing and overextended pauses.

This theatre played an important role in overturning stage censorship by the Lord Chamberlain, who had the right to ban or edit any play if it was 'fitting for the preservation of good manners' (or if he didn't like it). By forming the Watergate Club based at the theatre, it meant that banned plays could be performed in 'club' conditions without being censored. Using this little ploy, productions of Arthur Miller's *A View from the Bridge*, Tennessee Williams's *Cat on a Hot Tin Roof* and others were shown. Thankfully, the law was revoked in 1968, and productions could once again use naughty words and gratuitous nudity.

Heading up back towards Leicester Square, you'll find the lovely **Prince of Wales Theatre** (opened 1884, capacity 1,160) on the corner of Coventry Street. The first hit production at the theatre was a comic opera called *Dorothy* – which became the longest-running musical of that time (musicals about Dorothys are always popular). After the theatre was rebuilt in 1937, it was well known for French-style revue shows and the theatre was nicknamed 'London's Folies Bergère'. Some of these shows ran non-stop from 2 p.m. to 11 p.m. – and actors moan about long hours these days... Notable performances here have included a young Barbara Streisand in *Funny Girl*, James Stewart in *Harvey*, Vanessa Redgrave in *The Threepenny Opera*, and Danny La Rue being the first man to play Dolly in *Hello, Dolly!* in 1984. After further refurbishments in 2004, the theatre housed *Mamma Mia!* (the longest-running show in this theatre) and currently the family favourite *The Book of Mormon*. Legend has it that every few months the actual Prince of Wales can be spotted on the turret waving a big Union Jack around – so always keep your eyes out, dear.

It was the actor-manager Charles Wyndham's dream to open his own theatre and, if you can dodge the hordes marauding across Leicester Square, you'll be rewarded with **Wyndham's Theatre** (opened 1899, capacity 759) on Charing Cross Road. Celebrated shows here include Graham Greene's first stage play *The Living Room* (1953), Sandy Wilson's musical *The Boyfriend* (1954) – and productions of *A Taste of Honey* and *Oh What a Lovely War* (1959), both from Joan Littlewood's catalogue. Cameron Mackintosh's first international hit, *Side by Side by Sondheim*, opened here in 1976, and introduced British audiences to the genius of Stephen Sondheim. Prior to this, *Godspell* had played for almost three years at the venue, introducing British audiences to the geniuses of Marti Webb, David Essex and Jeremy Irons. More recent productions include two thousand performances of Yasmina Reza's play *Art*, with its revolving star casts; the National Theatre's transfer of *The History Boys*; and a Donmar Warehouse season, which culminated in Jude Law getting his Hamlet out eight times a week.

Just up from Wyndham's, on Great Newport Street, is the **Arts Theatre** (opened 1927, capacity 350), the smallest commercial receiving house in the West End, but, as the well-known prophet Alfie Boe said, size isn't everything, it's what you do with it that counts. The theatre opened as a members-only club – to avoid censorship from those po-faced lieutenant-colonels and brigadiers in the Lord Chamberlain's office – and was run by the late, great Peter Hall from 1956 to 1959, after his landmark production of Beckett's *Waiting for Godot* played there. Recent productions include *Ushers: The Front of House Musical*, *American Idiot: The Donald Trump Musical*, and the petrifying *Ghost Stories*, which always resulted in a rather damp auditorium.

Theatreland Hauntings

London can be a terrifying place, steeped in murderous history and bloody audition stories. Many of the capital's most haunted buildings are theatres – and it's easy to understand why. Some theatres are built on sacred sites (like ancient pubs), and others have the trapped energy of deceased actors wandering the corridors. In fact, many times I've encountered terrifying spectres myself – but that serves me right for hanging out with casting directors.

If you watch a show in a haunted theatre, you should always be on the lookout during the curtain call for spooky silhouettes in the auditorium – no, it's not a dusty director leaving to give notes; it's a ghost, dear. To arm you in your ghost-hunting, here are a few of Theatreland's most notorious ghouls.

Arthur Bourchier – A former manager of the Garrick Theatre, Bourchier frequently haunts an eerie staircase there, patting actors on the back before they go on stage. A notorious hater of theatre critics, in 1903, he once famously refused to admit *The Times*' reviewer into the building, which every producer has fantasised about doing since.

John Baldwin Buckstone – Many a famous actor, including Donald Sinden, Judi Dench and Patrick Stewart, has witnessed this ghost of the nineteenth-century actor-manager of the Theatre Royal Haymarket. Stewart was on stage in *Waiting for Godot* at the time, so no one can be quite sure that it wasn't his co-star Ian McKellen.

Eleanor Cooper – The Dominion is built on the site of an old brewery, which exploded in 1814, drowning eight people in a tidal wave of beer, including fourteen-year-old Eleanor Cooper who worked there. She now haunts the theatre on the site, with staff reporting mysterious bangs, crashes and the giggle of an invisible child.

Joseph Grimaldi – The Theatre Royal Drury Lane is so big it's got plenty of room for its numerous ghosts. The last request of nineteenth-century clown Joseph Grimaldi was to be decapitated before burial. His disembodied head, complete with white clown make-up, has been seen watching shows at Drury Lane.

Dan Leno –Dan Leno, the Victorian panto star, also haunts Drury Lane – and can be heard rehearsing his clog-dancing routine in his former dressing room. The theatre smells of lilac whenever his ghost has been on the stage, since this was Leno's perfume of choice to hide his incontinence.

The Man in Grey – Drury Lane's most seen ghost, however, walks across the upper circle wearing an eighteenth-century wig, tricorn hat, cloak – and then disappears through a wall. In 1939, most of the cast of Ivor Novello's *The Dancing Years* were on stage for a photo call and witnessed him. During renovations in the nineteenth century, builders found a bricked-up room behind the wall through which the Man in Grey disappears. Inside was a skeleton with a dagger through its ribcage. Some understudies go to extreme lengths to ensure they play the role, dear.

Mrs Shireburn – The Old Crimson Staircase in the London Palladium's royal circle is believed to have been part of Argyll House. The lady seen climbing the stairs in a crinoline dress is thought to be Mrs Shireburn, the mistress of the eighteenth-century Duke of Argyll. Or it could be Elaine Paige.

William Terriss – In 1897, the leading Shakespearean actor William Terriss was murdered by a jealous bit-part actor outside the Adelphi Theatre. He now haunts Covent Garden Tube station, built on the site of his favourite bakery, and the theatre – where he knocks on the dressing-room door that belonged to his lover, in whose arms he died and whom he promised to visit from the other side...

Strolling back down Charing Cross Road, a few yards further on from Wyndham's, is the **Garrick Theatre** (opened 1889, capacity 718). Named after legendary actor-manager David Garrick (the Kenneth Branagh of his generation), the theatre was financed by W.S. Gilbert, famous for those little operas he wrote with Sir Arthur Sullivan, such as *The Pirates of Penzance*, *The Mikado* and *HMS Pinafore*. The Garrick has mainly been associated with comedies, one of the most well known being *No Sex Please, We're British*, which ran for four long, sexless years from 1982 before transferring to the Duchess. Other notable shows included Lionel Bart's *Fings Ain't Wot They Used T'Be*, the National Theatre's production of *An Inspector Calls*, *Chicago* (moving from longer runs at the Adelphi and the Cambridge, and from good casts to Darius Danesh), and the recent Kenneth Branagh season, where darling Ken got to say as much iambic pentameter as his little heart desired.

Around the corner from the Garrick on St Martin's Lane is the **London Coliseum** (opened 1904, capacity 2,558). Designed by Frank Matcham and originally called the London Coliseum Theatre for Varieties, it is still the largest theatre venue in London (if you don't count *Disney on Ice* at the O2). In many ways, the London Coliseum is just like a Roman coliseum – only a lot smaller, with a roof, and in London. For a period, the theatre was used to show films, particularly when the 'talkies' arrived – apparently, *King Kong* played here to an audience of ten thousand people every single day. It was also one of the first theatres to have electric lighting, and one of the first two places in Britain to sell Coca Cola (the other being Selfridges). In 1968 it became the home of Sadler's Wells Opera, which in 1974 changed its name to English National Opera. As well as long and expensive operas, always translated into English, the ENO also produces high-quality musicals, such as *Bat Out of Hell* (the Meatloaf musical) and a revival of *Sunset Boulevard* starring Ria Jones as Glenn Close.

On the other side of St Martin's Lane is the **Duke of York's Theatre** (opened 1892, capacity 640), originally called the

Trafalgar Square Theatre, but assuming its current name in 1895 to honour the future King George V. It was here where the composer Puccini saw David Belasco's play of *Madame Butterfly* in 1900, and was so impressed he wrote a rather well-known opera about it, which in turn inspired the musical *Miss Saigon*, David Henry Hwang's play *M. Butterfly*, and Mariah Carey's album *Butterfly*. J.M. Barrie's *Peter Pan* premiered here in 1904, which in turn inspired Michael Jackson. More recent productions include *Goodnight Mister Tom* (a poignant love story about Tom Jones's bedroom ritual), *Doctor Faustus* (starring Jon Snow and his bum) and *Hay Fever* (sponsored by Piriton).

The **Noël Coward Theatre** (opened 1903, capacity 872), a short distance further up St Martin's Lane, is another of W.G.R. Sprague's finely designed West End playhouses. It was originally called the New Theatre, but when it got old, was renamed the Albery Theatre in 1973, after Sir Bronson Albery, the theatre manager for many years; and yet again, after a substantial refurbishment, to the Noël Coward, in tribute to the Master himself, whose first West End play, *I'll Leave It to You*, premiered here in 1920. *Oliver!* ran for 2,618 performances here; Olivier starred in three productions with his wife, Vivien Leigh; and several puppets had full-on, full-frontal sex in the musical *Avenue Q*. *Mrs Henderson Presents*, another musical with nudity, also played at the Coward for musical-lovers and men in long coats.

Carrying on up St Martin's Lane and onto Monmouth Street, you'll see an eye-catching fluorescent sign to your left screaming 'Agatha Christie's *The Mousetrap*'. This neon warning is outside the **St Martin's Theatre** (opened 1916, capacity 550), instructing visitors to enter at their own risk and – if they do – never, ever to reveal the secret twist in the tale – or they'll be sending a police inspector round to arrest you. It's a bit of a ropey whodunit to be honest, but it's the longest-running play in the world – currently in its sixty-fifth year, with over 27,000 performances under its belt (which is even more performances than Cher, but not quite as old). I doubt it will be closing any time soon because, as everyone knows, you can never really get rid of a mouse infestation. Two buildings down from the St Martin's is the head office of Equity, the actors' union – conveniently sited so you can run there afterwards to complain about the bad acting.

Next door is the **Ambassadors Theatre** (opened 1913, capacity 444), formerly the New Ambassadors, which was designed and built alongside the St Martin's. It's one of the smallest theatres in the West End, where *The Mousetrap* premiered before moving next door in 1973, and it also witnessed the stage debut of a twenty-two-year-old Vivien Leigh in *The Mask of Virtue* in 1935. Its many other productions have included *Sweeney Todd*, *Stones in His Pockets*, *The Vagina Monologues*, and most recently *Stomp* – a musical about some dustbin men who form a pop group called 'Take Trash'. The theatre has been purchased by Delfont Mackintosh who intend to redevelop it and open it as the Sondheim Theatre to house 'exciting and innovative productions emerging from the subsidised theatre sector... that would otherwise vanish following their closure in their originating theatres'. A marvellous, much-needed venture.

Returning back to Monmouth Street and walking north, you reach the district called Seven Dials, a lovely little area designed and laid out by Thomas Neale MP in the early 1690s, possibly the last time an MP did something useful. Opposite the Sundial Pillar at the centre of the seven interlocking streets is the **Cambridge Theatre** (opened 1930, capacity 1,231). Built in steel and concrete and on an irregular triangular site, the theatre is one of the more modern in the West End – though there's still been time to refurbish it, twice, in 1950 and 1987. Notable productions at the Cambridge have included Tommy Steele in *Half a Sixpence* (1963), Bruce '...to See You Nice' Forsyth in *Little Me* (1964), *Chicago*, which played here in the early seventies and again when it was revived in the noughties, *Jerry Springer: The Opera* (2003) and the marvellous musical *Matilda* since 2011. It was also the home of *Return to the Forbidden Planet*, a retelling of *The Tempest* with rock-and-roll songs, which won the Olivier Award for Best New Musical in 1990, beating *Miss Saigon* – which caused Cameron Mackintosh to go on a theatrical rampage for several years. The Cambridge Theatre is also very close to Pineapple Dance Studios – which is (in)famous for giving Louie Spence a job.

A little further down Earlham Street is the **Donmar Warehouse** (opened 1977, capacity 251). The producer Donald Albery created Donmar Productions in 1953, the name 'Donmar' formed using the first three letters of his name followed by the first three letters of his wife's second name, Margaret (good job she wasn't called Keyla). In 1961, he bought the warehouse – which originally stored hops for a local brewery – and converted it into a rehearsal studio. In 1977, the RSC bought the space and turned it into a theatre extremely quickly. Apparently the electricity for the theatre was only turned on thirty minutes before the first production and the concrete steps outside were still drying. The RSC had much success here – with landmark productions including *Macbeth* with Judi Dench and Ian McKellen, which transferred to the Young Vic and beyond.

In 1992, the Donmar Warehouse was converted into its current form as an independent producing house. Wunderkind Sam Mendes became the artistic director at the tender age of twenty-five, and reopened the theatre with the British premiere of Sondheim's *Assassins*. Michael Grandage took over in 2002, and current incumbent Josie Rourke succeeded him in 2012. It's a wonderfully intimate venue – if you sit in the front row and stretch your legs out, you actually appear in the production (I've known actors to do this and then put it on their CV). The roll call who have legitimately performed at the venue is quite something – recognisable from just their surnames: Kidman, McGregor, Law, Paltrow, Redmayne, Hiddleston… Maybe it's because the runs are comparatively short, or because it's so small they could act as if they were still on film.

Theatreland Haunts

In central London apparently you're never further than six feet away from a rat. Which may be true – especially if you're watching a production in The Vaults underneath Waterloo Station. But even more common than rats are places to eat or drink, given the number of bars and restaurants strewn across Theatreland. It's impossible to put together an exhaustive list, but here are some of my favourite haunts for a pre/mid/post-show nibble/tipple/nipple.

Brasserie Zédel – Just near the Piccadilly Theatre, down several flights of stairs, you enter this opulent art-deco basement brasserie. It's also home to one of London's finest cabaret venues, Live at Zédel, where many a West End star has showed off their range.

The Ivy – This famous celeb favourite is opposite *The Mousetrap* on West Street, and has been around even longer. Blag your way in after your show and you could find yourself sipping wine and eating steak next to an obscure celebrity. A marvellous way to finish your theatrical evening. I'm there every Friday night to celebrate the end of another week. If you ever see me, wave, and send a bottle my way, dear.

Joe Allen – This restaurant, just behind the Lyceum Theatre, is modelled on its sister restaurant in New York, and is often known as the 'West End's Canteen'. The walls are strewn with memorabilia, including a 'Wall of Flops', featuring posters of shows which I had no involvement with.

The Nell Gwynne Tavern – This small, traditional pub is named after the famous actress and mistress of Charles II. Tucked away up an alley next to the Adelphi on the Strand, it's near enough for audiences to escape for an interval drink, and is where you can find all the actors from the Adelphi in a drunken haze at midnight.

Nell of Old Drury – Also named after Nell Gwynn, this cosy pub is directly opposite the Theatre Royal Drury Lane. It's rumoured that there's a secret passage connecting the theatre to the pub cellar, making it convenient for cast and crew to escape for *their* interval drinks. This pub is the best place to go before watching a show at the Lane, as you can see everyone piling inside, allowing you to sip your drink until you spot the foyer is less busy. Perfect, dear.

Phoenix Artist Club – Underneath the Phoenix Theatre, this private members' club is open to the great, unwashed public before 9 p.m. – and to the tired, make-up-laden actors after their show until 2.30 a.m. Pretend you're an actor by shouting 'darling' repeatedly and you'll easily blag your way in.

Rules – Opened in Covent Garden in 1798, Rules is the oldest restaurant in London and remains unapologetically old-fashioned. It is where Dickens came to write, so perhaps got the idea for *Oliver Twist* after a serving of Rules' Gruel.

The Savoy Hotel – Located on the Strand, the Savoy is one of the most famous hotels in the world, with plenty of bars and eateries. Many legendary stars have stayed there – including the actor Richard Harris, who lived there for the last few years of his life until his death in 2002. As he was being taken to an ambulance on a stretcher, he called out to fellow guests: 'It was the food! Don't touch the food!'

J. Sheekey – On a pedestrianised street between the Wyndham's and Noël Coward Theatres, this famous fish restaurant is a favourite of theatrefolk. Thesps love fancy fish. Fact.

Theatre Café – On the opposite side of Shaftesbury Avenue from the Queen's is this newcomer, which opened in 2015. It is decorated with photos of performers and genuine props, plays back-to-back showtunes, overflows with theatre gossip, and serves enough caffeine to keep you awake through *Les Mis*.

Down Earlham Street and crossing over onto Drury Lane and you'll be outside what appears to be a rather unprepossessing and ugly office block, but is actually the **New London Theatre** (opened 1973, capacity 1,118). There have been theatre venues on the site for much longer – the Mogul Music Hall in 1847; the Middlesex Music Hall in 1851; and the Winter Garden Theatre in 1919. Legends have been born at the New London: Richard Gere gave us his Danny Zuko in the 1973 London premiere of *Grease*; Elaine Paige her Grizabella in the 1981 world premiere of *Cats* (which was finally put to sleep on its twenty-first birthday), but I think its most exciting feature is the escalator taking audiences up to the theatre. Underneath, the building also houses an underground car park, cabaret venue and nightclub (so if the show is boring you can simply go to the club and have a pole-dancing session with Lloyd Webber in his amazing Technicolor dream-pants). The National Theatre's mighty equestrian epic *War Horse* – otherwise known as *War Whores* by its cast – played for over three thousand performances here before cantering off into the sunset – otherwise known as multiple international tours.

South down Drury Lane, and then turning onto Russell Street, is the **Fortune Theatre** (opened 1924, capacity 432), the first theatre to be built after the First World War. It stands on the site of the old Albion Tavern, a pub that was always full of drunken actors (some traditions never change). It was originally called the Fortune Thriller Theatre which is appropriate because, since 1989, it has been home to the scream-inducing *The Woman in Black*, which is indeed thrilling, not to be confused with the musical *The Woman in White*, which is not.

Over the road from one of the smallest theatres in the West End is one of the biggest: the **Theatre Royal Drury Lane** (opened 1821, capacity 2,196). There have been four theatres on this site since 1663, making it the oldest theatre site in London that is still used as such. The current building is where many of Rodgers and Hammerstein's musicals made their debut (including *Oklahoma!*, *Carousel*, *South Pacific* and

The King and I), where the careers of Edmund Kean and Ivor Novello began – and where, after *My Fair Lady*, the stage career of Martine McCutcheon ended. It's an awful lot of tickets for a producer to sell each week, and the stage is correspondingly large, so the venue is usually used to house musicals on a spectacular scale, including *Miss Saigon* (which premiered and ran here for ten years), Mel Brooks's *The Producers*, *Shrek* (aka *Dreck*), *Charlie and the Chocolate Factory*, *The Lord of the Rings* and *42nd Street*.

On the opposite side of the road, and a little further down Catherine Street is the **Duchess Theatre** (opened 1929, capacity 494). The stalls level of the auditorium here is below street level – as this was the only way it was allowed to be built, so as not to block out the natural light for neighbours. As a fairly small space, it's a good venue for plays: plays that go right, plays that go left, and *The Play That Goes Wrong* which has gone very right for its producers, playing here since 2014.

The Novello Theatre (opened 1905, capacity 1,105) is just opposite the Duchess. It was built as one of a pair with the Aldwych Theatre, on opposite sides of the Waldorf Hotel, and was originally called the Waldorf Theatre, later the Strand Theatre. Since 2005 it has commemorated the popular composer and entertainer Ivor Novello, who lived in a flat above the theatre from 1913 to 1951. After several years of being the London base of the Royal Shakespeare Company, the theatre has seen a few unfortunate flops: audiences fell asleep for *The Drowsy Chaperone*, and *Desperately Seeking Susan* desperately sought an audience. Currently the theatre is home to a tragedy set on a Greek island called *Mamma Mia!*

Walking past the Waldorf, and stopping off for a quick salad (you must be a bit peckish by now), is the **Aldwych Theatre** (opened 1905, capacity 1,200). Like its twin, the Novello, it was also designed by W.G.R. Sprague, and financed by Sir Seymour Hicks, and also housed the Royal Shakespeare Company for twenty years before they 'consciously uncoupled' and moved to the Barbican for a bit. The theatre also saw the London premiere of *A Streetcar Named Desire* in 1949, starring Vivien Leigh as Blanche DuBois, and directed by her husband, Laurence Olivier. In recent years, the Aldwych has housed some rather well-known musicals including Lloyd Webber's *Whistle Down the Wind*, *Fame: The Musical* and *Dirty Dancing* – where nobody put baby in a corner for over five years. Lloyd Webber also opened his ill-fated *Stephen Ward* here (I did tell him he should have written *Stephen Hendry* instead – all those ensemble dancers dressed as snooker balls would have been marvellous fun).

Let's all go down the Strand now, and you will come to the **Lyceum Theatre** (opened 1904, capacity 2,100), where there has been a venue on the same site since 1765, including a circus, a chapel and the first place where Madame Tussaud exhibited her waxworks (sadly no Leonardo DiCaprio back then). From 1816 to 1830 it served as the English Opera House, and between 1871 and 1902, Henry Irving and Ellen Terry performed at the theatre in many Shakespearean plays. It was set to be demolished in 1939, but was saved and converted into the Lyceum Ballroom, where many well-known bands played, including Led Zeppelin, Queen, U2 (sadly no Girls Aloud back then). It was converted back into a theatre in 1996, and since 1999 has been the Serengeti of the Strand – and the home of *The Lion King*, which I imagine will be there until at least 2099 judging by its continued success.

On the other side of the Strand, located beneath the Savoy Hotel is the **Savoy Theatre** (opened 1881, capacity 1,150), a beautiful venue, built by Richard D'Oyly Carte, who wanted somewhere to premiere many of Gilbert and Sullivan's operettas. Oscar Wilde's *Salome* (1931) and Noël Coward's *Blithe Spirit* (1941) were also premiered at the Savoy. Like so many others over the years, the theatre was gutted by fire in 1990, later rebuilt using the 1929 designs. It was the first public building in the world to be lit entirely by electricity and has lovely multi-coloured, patterned seating, from which you can now watch transfers and revivals of many American musicals like *Dreamgirls, Dirty Rotten Scoundrels, Gypsy, Legally Blonde* (with Sheridan Smith) and *Funny Girl* (sometimes with Sheridan Smith).

Moving westwards down the Strand towards Trafalgar Square, the next theatre along is the **Vaudeville Theatre** (opened 1870, capacity 690). The theatre often hosts shorter runs of plays and comedies, including the puppet play *Hand to God* (so bad that God wanted his name removed from the title) and an *Importance of Being Earnest* starring Poirot in drag. The longest-running production at the Vaudeville remains *Stomp* – which ran for five years from 2002, before going and clogging up the Ambassadors.

A few paces on is the magnificent art-deco **Adelphi Theatre** (opened 1930, capacity 1,500). There have been three other theatres on this site prior to the current building, the first being the Sans Pareil (i.e. 'Without Compare') which was built in 1806 by a businessman with the purpose of putting his daughter in all the shows (an excellent way of ensuring you have an illustrious career – get Daddy to build you a theatre). In 1819, the theatre reopened with its present name, taken from the Adelphi Buildings opposite on the Strand. The theatre has housed many large musicals – including the revival of *Chicago* in 1997 which holds the record as the longest West End run of an American musical (and the record for the most number of celebs who could be fitted into tight Lycra® and heels). Several Lloyd Webber productions have played there, including *Sunset Boulevard* (1993), a revival of *Evita* (2006), the reality-TV-cast production of *Joseph* (2007), and *Love Never Dies* (it did; every night). Now, movie-to-musical adaptations are the norm (some good, some not), including *The Bodyguard, Made in Dagenham* and the inspirational footwear musical *Kinky Boots* – sponsored by Clarks.

At the bottom of the Strand you reach Trafalgar Square – home of Admiral Nelson on a big pole, some lions, the National Gallery and, very nearby on Whitehall, the **Trafalgar Studios** (opened 1930). Originally the Whitehall

Theatre, it opened with *The Way to Treat a Woman* by Walter Hackett, surely and sorely due for a revival in the current climate. During the Second World War, it housed mainly revue shows, with *The Whitehall Follies* opening there to great success in 1942 with Phyllis Dixey, the first stripper to perform in Theatreland. The theatre became known for the 'Whitehall farces', long-running comic stage plays, produced by actor-manager Brian Rix, which ran for decades from the 1950s, as well as a nude revue called *Pyjama Tops* which titillated audiences for five years from 1969. Performing in the buff has obviously been popular at this theatre, since *Puppetry of the Penis* also played here, so to speak: truly the most remarkable piece of physical theatre I've ever seen. Their helicopter trick was very different from the one in *Miss Saigon*. The current building comprises two theatres – Studio 1 (capacity 380), which has housed seasons by the RSC, Jamie Lloyd Productions, and the sensational *End of the Rainbow* starring Tracie Bennett as Judy Garland; and Studio 2 (capacity 100), where fringe plays often transfer (finally allowing the performers to act without the distracting scent of wee and pork scratchings).

Northumberland Avenue runs down from Trafalgar Square to the Thames, with the **Playhouse Theatre** (opened 1907, capacity 786) just before you get to the river. It was first built in 1882 and originally called the Royal Avenue Theatre, though the 'Royal' bit was dropped because it didn't have a separate entrance for corgis. Florence Farr, appearing in an unsuccessful series of plays there, pleaded with her friend George Bernard Shaw to hurry up and finish his play – which he did, even though his plays are full of long words and last for days. *Arms and the Man*, his West End debut, subsequently premiered there in 1894, and was such a hit he gave up music criticism and became a full-time playwright. Lucky us.

When the theatre was being rebuilt in 1905, part of neighbouring Charing Cross railway station collapsed and fell through the roof and wall of the theatre, tragically killing six people. The venue reopened as the Playhouse in 1907, and between 1951 and 1976, the BBC used the theatre for recordings of, amongst others, *The Goon Show*, *Hancock's Half Hour* and *Steptoe and Son*. The theatre's owners have included the novelist, playwright and modest all-rounder Jeffrey Archer (who bought it for £1 million), and Ray Cooney (who bought it off him for £2 million, allowing him to produce several of his own farces there). Long-running productions have included a 2008 revival of *La Cage aux Folles* which starred Douglas Hodge, Graham Norton, John Barrowman, Roger Allam, Philip Quast and Denis Lawson, but not all at once. 'I Am What I Am' doesn't work as a company number, dear.

Cross the Thames here and you will be rewarded with the delights of the cultural strip of London's South Bank – from the museums and galleries of County Hall, past the London Eye, the temporary Underbelly Festival during the summer months, the Royal Festival Hall and Hayward Gallery, and the British Film Institute – to a 'nuclear power station in the heart of London', which is how Prince Charles described our **National Theatre** (opened 1976). The LED screen across the front of the building, which is visible from the riverside, will tell you what is playing at the theatre currently – or what the actors think about their directors if they've hijacked the screen.

The National Theatre company was established in 1963 by artistic director Laurence Olivier, originally performing at the Old Vic nearby, and down in Chichester. In 1976, the company moved to its current South Bank HQ which houses three theatres: the Olivier (capacity 1,160) with a large, open stage and fan-style auditorium; the Lyttleton (capacity 890), a more conventional proscenium-arch theatre; and the Dorfman (capacity 400) which is smaller and more flexible, like Wayne Sleep. The Dorfman was called the Cottesloe until 2014, and was renamed after a large donation of £10 million from philanthropist Lloyd Dorfman. I am finding out what naming rights to the Olivier would cost me, as a theatre named after Julie Andrews is long overdue. After Olivier, subsequent artistic directors have been Sir Peter Hall, Sir Richard Eyre, Sir Trevor Nunn, Sir Nicholas Hytner, and currently Rufus Norris. (One of the perks of being artistic director of the Nash is that you get knighted. Rufus is waiting patiently, Ma'am. Who knows – one day let's hope there may even be a Dame?)

Each of the three theatres at the National tends to run shows in repertoire – where more than one production is played on each stage during a season, but not on the same night. That would get confusing. It is hard to overestimate the contribution that the National has made to the theatrical life of the UK, not just in London, as productions often tour the UK and worldwide – with many transferring to the West End and Broadway. Recent successful shows have included *War Horse, London Road, Jerry Springer: The Opera, The Curious Incident of the Dog in the Night-Time, One Man, Two Guvnors, The History Boys, People, Places and Things, This House* and numerous productions from the classical canon. The National also has many other public facilities – toilets, bars, restaurants, shops, exhibition space – and is a wonderful place to hang out, meet friends, buy books, read books, write books, and play Spot the Actor.

The National is also situated very close to the Thames – making it ideal for watery stage productions like *Free Willy, Jaws* and *The Little Mermaid* (I do hope Rufus puts on one of these wet adaptations soon – it's what we've all been waiting for).

Walking away from the river and past Waterloo Station, you will reach the **Old Vic Theatre** (opened 1871, capacity 1,067). A theatre first opened here called the Royal Coburg Theatre (after Prince Leopold of Saxe-Coburg) in 1818, and has gone through various name changes and rebuilding programmes since then, especially after being badly damaged in the Blitz. It had some of the first female artistic directors in British theatrical history (Emma Cons from 1880, and her niece Lilian Baylis from 1898), and several actors in the role (John Gielgud from 1929, Laurence Olivier from 1963, and Kevin Spacey from 2003). Famous performances have included Derek Jacobi and Ben Whishaw's Hamlets, Sir Ben

Kingsley in *Waiting for Godot*, Alan Bates in *The Master Builder*, Glenda Jackson as King Lear, and lots of actors with their hands up puppet's bottoms in *Dr Seuss's The Lorax*.

The Old Vic also does lots of valuable work with young people, offering various opportunities throughout the year. These include summer schools, staring masterclasses, gurning workshops, and most famously the Old Vic New Voices scheme. In Matthew Warchus's first year as artistic director he established the Old Vic 12 – which offers twelve emerging artists the chance to have a year-long mentorship. Competition is very fierce, and the panel look for people who show exceptional promise, have unique experience, and look nice in group photos.

After the Old Vic had a one-night stand with the Sylvia Young Theatre School, the **Young Vic Theatre** (opened 1970, capacity 420) was born. What a happy mistake, though, because the Young Vic is a younger, cooler version of the Old Vic, but further down The Cut, on the site of an old butcher's and adjacent bombsite, and with lots of tattoos and body piercings. Built for a relatively modest £60,000, the theatre was only intended to last for five years. Happily, it's still there with its entirely flexible main space, and two smaller studios: The Maria (capacity 150), named after Maria von Trapp, and The Clare (capacity 70), named after Clare Balding.

The aim of the Young Vic was to develop plays and work for younger audiences. Frank Dunlop was the first artistic director, followed by Michael Bogdanov (who got the job because of his theatrical surname), David Thacker, Julia Bardsley, Tim Supple and David Lan, who has been an enormously popular and successful artistic director since 2000. In 2018, Kwame Kwei-Armah (director, playwright and *Casualty* actor-extraordinaire) takes the helm. Recent acclaimed productions include *A Streetcar Named Desire* starring Gillian Anderson, *A View from the Bridge* directed by 'I've a Van in Hove', *Yerma* with a rather brilliant Billie Piper, and *Happy Days* – the Samuel Beckett one, not the American sitcom.

Back on the South Bank – past ITV (Studios), OXO (Tower) and TAT (Modern) – is **Shakespeare's Globe** (opened 1997, capacity 1,400), a reconstruction of the original Globe Theatre, only a few hundred yards from its original site. The original Globe was built in 1599, rebuilt after a fire in 1613, and demolished in 1644 – and many of Shakespeare's plays premiered there. His Globe had a capacity of 3,000 because they didn't believe in health and safety regulations back then. They didn't believe in washing more than once a year either, so I imagine it was all rather stinky.

The new Globe was the dream of American actor and director Sam Wanamaker, who set about raising the money and the support required to build it, and the theatre is an astonishing achievement. An indoor, candle-lit theatre has been built next door, and named the **Sam Wanamaker Playhouse** (opened 2014, capacity 340). The Globe has a thrust stage that projects into a circular yard where the groundlings stand to watch (for the incredibly good value of £5 each), with three tiers of seating on wooden benches. You can hire cushions if you can't face three hours on a hard plank, or take a thick jumper you can roll up and sit on. Choose the back row if you want something to lean back against. Stage and seating areas are covered, but the rest of the theatre is open to the elements, so it's a good idea to take a waterproof or your best poncho – or simply hide under the armpit of the person next to you. The summer season at the Globe runs between May and October – though it offers educational tours and workshops throughout the year. Mark Rylance was the first artistic director from 1995, with Dominic Dromgoole taking over in 2006, and Emma Rice in 2016, though she left because she was using actors who weren't alive in Shakespeare's time, which apparently made the whole experience inauthentic. Actress Michelle Terry is artistic director from 2018.

Also on the bank of the Thames, further down near Tower Bridge, is the brand-spanking-new **Bridge Theatre** (opened 2017, capacity 900). After leaving the National Theatre, Nick Hytner and Nick Starr (two Nicks are better than one) got a bit bored, and so established the London Theatre Company (I hope no one was paid to think of that name), and built the first commercial theatre of significant scale in London for over eighty years. It was designed by Haworth Tompkins Architects, who have worked on refits, redesigns and refurbishments of numerous theatrical institutions, such as the Royal Court, the Young Vic and several actors' faces. Work started in 2015, took just over two years to complete, and cost £12 million. However, the money was well spent – with a flexible space where the auditorium can be moved around to create different stage layouts, but best of all – lots of ladies' loos! Yes, ladies, finally someone has listened – and a London theatre has a decent number of rooms in which you can rest. Bravo to the Nicks! The Bridge is going to focus principally on new writing, which is why its opening season featured *Julius Caesar* by a promising new playwright called Will.

A little distance away from the West End, near Victoria Station in the Slightly South-West End, live two other theatres: the Victoria Palace and the Apollo Victoria. Both, very handily, have the word 'Victoria' in them to help confused tourists.

The first venue on the site of the Victoria Palace was a small concert hall above the Royal Standard Hotel built in 1832. In 1850, it was enlarged and became Moy's Music Hall and later, in 1863, refurbished and renamed the Royal Standard Music Hall. In 1886, the theatre was demolished after Victoria Street and Station were built; until finally, the current Frank Matcham-designed **Victoria Palace** (opened 1911, capacity 1,550) was built. Costing £12,000 to build (which barely buys you a souvenir brochure these days), it was primarily known as a music-hall venue, but in 1934 staged a play called *Young England* by an eighty-three-year-old vicar about the 'virtues' of the Boy Scout Movement, which received such bad reviews that it became a cult hit. Audiences would turn up and join in with all the lines. Reportedly, 'the scoutmistress rarely said the line, "I must go and attend to my girls' water" without at least fifty voices in good-humoured support joining in'.

The original production of the musical *Me and My Girl* played here in 1937, a huge success which resulted in hordes of happy locals singing 'The Lambeth Walk' on their way home from work for years. In 1982, Dame Elizabeth Taylor also made her London stage debut here in *The Little Foxes* by Lillian Hellman (written when she wasn't making batches of mayonnaise). The theatre also housed many long-running shows, including *The Black and White Minstrel Show* (throughout the 1960s to 1972) which was decidedly dubious; *Buddy: The Buddy Holly Story* (1989) which was 'Buddy brilliant' and ran for thirteen years in London; and *Billy Elliot* (2005) which ran for eleven years and set new theatrical standards by being the only West End show ever to have decent-sounding North East accents. In 2017, the theatre had a multi-million-pound refurbishment by its owner Cameron Mackintosh to make it the new home for an obscure little American piece called *Hamilton*.

Just across the road is the **Apollo Victoria** (opened 1930, capacity 2,328), which was originally a cinema called the New Victoria Cinema. It opened by screening a film called *Old English* and a variety show called *Hoop-la* (I like to imagine this was a two-hour spectacle of performers doing the hula-hoop, but I can't be sure, dear). The venue, with its art-deco underwater theme, decorated all about with scallop shells, reopened as the Apollo Victoria in 1981 with that Welsh pearl Shirley Bassey. Subsequent productions have included *Fiddler on the Roof* (with Topol), *Camelot* (with Richard Harris), *The Sound of Music* (with Petula Clark), *Starlight Express* (with actors on roller skates pretending to be trains) and *Bombay Dreams* (with some fountains). In 2006, *Wicked* took up residence, sponsored by the colour green, starring an American (Idina Menzel), some Australians (Helen Dallimore and Adam Garcia), a talking goat (Doctor Dillamond), and a little English woman who likes to talk about farting (Miriam Margolyes). Clearly a winning combination; eight million audience members can't be wrong.

Tips on watching Shakespeare: Laugh when
everyone laughs. Cry when everyone cries. And
drink. Lots.

Beyond the West End

Although this walking tour – and this book – are focused on
the marvels (and very occasional miseries) of the West End,
we are blessed to have so many theatres throughout the UK
where the work is often equally as brilliant, and just as
rewarding to watch. So, here are a handful of other London
venues that are also well worth a visit.

The **Royal Court Theatre** (opened 1888) can be found on
Sloane Square, in the posh bit of Kensington and Chelsea. The
theatre is famous worldwide for being the 'Writers' Theatre' –
finding, cultivating and supporting new playwrights as they
search for bolder stories, braver voices and bigger words.
Earlier theatres were situated near the site, but the present
red-brick building was built in 1888 as the New Court
Theatre, with a capacity of 841, managed by Harley
Granville-Barker. Second World War damage forced the
building to close, and it was reopened with a refurbished
interior in 1952, under the artistic leadership of George
Devine, who sought 'hard-hitting, uncompromising writers'
and to follow his maxim that new plays be treated like
classics, and classics like new plays. In 1956, the English
Stage Company was established and their third production
– John Osborne's *Look Back in Anger* – blew out the post-war
cobwebs and revolutionised British theatre by showing a
woman ironing on stage. The shockwaves caused by this
ironing – and other plays at the Royal Court – were
instrumental in the abolition of theatre censorship by the
Lord Chamberlain in 1968.

Since then, the extensive list of well-known plays and playwrights discovered by the Royal Court include Richard
O'Brien (*The Rocky Horror Show*), Caryl Churchill (who has

written seventeen – and counting – structurally inventive plays for the theatre), Peter Gill, Christopher Hampton, David Hare, Joe Orton, David Edgar, Howard Brenton, E.L. James, Edward Bond, Jim Cartwright, Terry Johnson, Timberlake Wertenbaker, Sarah Kane and Jez Butterworth. Recent artistic directors include Stephen Daldry (before he buggered off with *Billy Elliot*), Ian Rickson, Dominic Cooke and Vicky Featherstone.

By the early 1990s, the building had pretty poor facilities, with flooding a frequent occurrence underneath the stage, and dressing rooms which Olivier had described as 'slightly worse than Blackpool's were in 1932'. A hefty Arts Council grant of £16.2 million allowed the theatre to be redeveloped in 1995, opening with the Jerwood Theatre Downstairs (capacity 380) and the flexible Jerwood Theatre Upstairs (capacity 85). If only they had been awarded another few million, the venue would also have a 200-seat Jerwood Theatre in the Middle, a 40-seat Jerwood Theatre in the Basement, and a single-seat Jerwood Theatre in the Loos.

The **Almeida Theatre** (opened 1980, capacity 325) is conveniently located on Almeida Street – just off Upper Street in Islington – so it's very easy to find when putting it into your Google Maps. Originally built as the Islington Literary and Scientific Society in 1837, it featured reading rooms, library, laboratory and a lecture theatre. In 1972, a campaign was launched to turn the derelict building into a working (non-lecture) theatre, and it opened in 1980, quickly growing a reputation for its annual summer International Festival of Contemporary Music and Performance. Later, with actor Ian 'Palpatine' McDiarmid and director Jonathan Kent as artistic directors, the venue became renowned as a producing company – of European plays, of Pinter plays, and of plays in a converted bus station in King's Cross during renovation work. After a successful stint by Michael (son of Dickie) Attenborough, Rupert Goold assumed the artistic directorship in 2013 – and his productions have included a musicalised *American Psycho* (starring Doctor Who), Mike Bartlett's brilliant *King Charles III* (set in an imagined future where Charles becomes king, Harry marries an American actress, and William and Kate have eleven children), and *Hamlet* starring Andrew Scott and directed by Robert Icke ('Icky' to his friends).

Also known for creating new work and supporting emerging playwrights, **Hampstead Theatre** (opened 1959, capacity 325) is another of London's off West End treasures. James Roose-Evans was the first artistic director of the Hampstead Theatre Club, situated in a school hall in Hampstead village, and one of the early producers of Harold Pinter, including *The Dumb Waiter* (an absurdist comedy about an idiotic waiter in Pizza Express) and *The Room* (about a room). The theatre moved to a portacabin in Swiss Cottage in 1962, where it showcased work by Michael Frayn, Terry Johnson and Mike Leigh, before its purpose-built home opened in 2003. This new venue, also with a downstairs studio (capacity 100), has been run by Anthony Clark and Edward Hall (son of Sir Peter, sister of Rebecca, and second-cousin twice-removed of the Royal Albert).

Venture back into the sadly sanitised streets of Soho and you'll find **Soho Theatre** (opened 1969) on Dean Street. The Soho Theatre Company was originally based at a venue on Old Compton Street, after which it moved to Soho Poly for eighteen years, before moving to its current building in 2000. Now led by artistic director Steve Marmion, it programmes comedy, cabaret and new writing, and comprises three venues – Soho Upstairs/Soho Theatre/Soho Downstairs (capacities 90/182/150) – and a lovely big bar for pre- and post-show boozing and for actors to bitch about their agents. Over the years, the theatre has supported and developed the careers of playwrights including Diane Samuels, Laura Wade, Barrie Keefe and Sue Townsend amongst many others. Soho Theatre is where the live heats and final of my Search for a Twitter Composer contest were held – so it has a special place in my heart (yes, I do have one, dear).

Fringe venues are another, even smaller and even less air-conditioned breed of theatre, and London has more than its share. There is always something going on – new plays, reinventions of classics, revivals of musicals – which, in all honesty, can be more challenging and exciting than work in the West End, where we producers can only mount safer, mainstream projects that will get bums on seats. On the fringe, the stakes are still high – but the budgets are lower – and, as such, more risks can be taken. Audiences are rewarded with seeing the birth of something – or someone – really special, plus a close-up view of the performers gurning and gyrating.

The following off West End and fringe theatres are particularly good for challenging, contemporary plays: the **Finborough** (closest station: Earl's Court), **Battersea Arts Centre** and **Theatre503** (both Clapham Junction), the **Arcola** (Dalston Kingsland or Dalston Junction – take your pick), the **Bush** (Shepherd's Bush), the **Gate** (Notting Hill Gate), **Park Theatre** (Finsbury Park), the **Tricycle** (Kilburn), the **King's Head** (Highbury and Islington/Angel), the **Old Red Lion** (Angel)… Literally every time I finish this list, I think of some others that are worthy of mention. Ah yes, **The Yard** (Hackney Wick), and the **Orange Tree** (Richmond). See what I mean? Oh, and **Jermyn Street Theatre** (Piccadilly). I'll stop now.

Musicals at **The Other Palace** (Victoria), **Southwark Playhouse** (Elephant and Castle), **Charing Cross Theatre** (Charing Cross), the **Union** (Southwark) and the **Menier Chocolate Factory** (London Bridge) are particularly strong, often with big bands, spectacular sets and well-known performers with big fan bases (so book early). And the musicals produced at the stunning **Regent's Park Open Air Theatre** (Baker Street/Regent's Park) rival the best West End shows, and come with added pigeons.

Some fringe productions have grown from their humble beginnings to take over the world. For instance, the wonderful Mischief Theatre Company were a group of unemployed LAMDA graduates who decided to put their own show on at the Old Red Lion. That show was *The Play*

That Goes Wrong. It was an instant success and has since been seen in the West End, on tour, and on Broadway – and the company have had numerous follow-up works, with more in development – but it all began in a little fringe venue that smelt of stale ale.

Another bonus about fringe venues is that – unlike in West End theatres – the bar will stay open *after* the show. The booze is cheaper, the playwright gets sloshed with you, and last orders is called only when the producer is vomiting in the loos. And this is something I adore. Nowadays, theatre can be far too healthy. Gone are the days when actors were hellraisers – drinking to extreme, smoking until their lungs gave in, staying out all night, getting in fights with critics... Not that I condone any of this, but there was a passion and urgency in it all which is now somewhat lacking. Today all you get are actors drinking water, posting photos on Instagram, and spending their days doing sit-ups in an attempt to get the perfect six-pack. How very boring, dear.

This lost passion of yesteryear can still be found on the fringe. A lot of the actors and people involved in these venues are younger – and have a thirst and desire to do well in the business – and with that comes a courage and bravery that I find inspiring. They dare to do more, and are not sanitised by a resident director who is instructing them how to say the lines, filling their performances with insecurities. They are allowed to be bold, and are often pushed to be.

This fire can often be lost in some commercial shows – where it's simply harder to take those kinds of risks. Obviously we get some that break through – like Mark Rylance in pretty much anything he does – but they can be few and far between. I like how rough fringe theatre can be, how raw and bad-smelling it is. So broaden your horizons, stretch your mind, and get off the beaten track to some really exciting places. Please don't just stick to the West End (but do come back, dear).

HAMILTON*

History – The most exciting musical to have been written in years, looking at a very important time in political history. Everyone says this show has changed the theatrical landscape, and I'm inclined to agree.

Plot – A sung and rapped musical about the tumultuous life of Neil Hamilton – the founding father of fame-hungry politicians – and his indomitable wife Christine. The show starts when Neil is elected the Conservative MP for Tatton, and a Tory whip in the 1980s ('The Room Where It Happens'), under Prime Minister Margaret Thatcher ('Helpless'), whom he supports during her doomed leadership battle ('Cabinet Battle'). He later becomes Minister of Deregulation and Corporate Affairs for John Major ('My Shot'). Hamilton was an advocate of such policies as shutting down coalmines ('History Has Its Eyes on You') and he opposed the removal of lead in petrol ('Burn'). The musical then follows Hamilton's political downfall in 1996 ('Stay Alive') in the 'cash for questions' scandal ('We Know'), where he asked questions in the House of Commons in return for brown envelopes stuffed with cash from Mohamed Al-Fayed ('Hurricane'). Act One ends as Neil loses his Tatton seat to journalist Martin Bell ('The Election of 1997').

Act Two follows the Hamiltons' quest for Z-list celebrity ('You'll Be Back') – as they appear on a Louis Theroux documentary ('Dear Theroux'), where Christine famously flirts with Louis ('The Erection of 2001'), and they make numerous awkward PR appearances ('Say No to This'), including Christine's appearance on *I'm A Celebrity... Get Me Out of Here!* ('Wait for It'). Neil joins UKIP ('Blow Us All Away'), and then gets voted the leader of their Welsh Assembly group ('Meet Me Inside'), before the rousing final number: 'Who Lives, Who Dies, Who Wants to Buy a Question?'

* It may be worth mentioning that there's another musical with the same name about the American Founding Father, Alexander Hamilton – but I don't really know much about that one, dear.

SIX TWENTY-FIRST-CENTURY FLOPS

For every show that offers theatrical Viagra, many more musicals have dismally flopped. Theatre is a difficult beast to tame – there is no definite way to know whether you have a hit or a shit on your hands, though naturally we producers always work hard to achieve the former. Sometimes even with the biggest budgets, productions can fail to ignite the public's interest – and it is often the shows that seem unlikely that become the biggest sensations. Everyone knows that *Les Mis* was branded a miss by the critics, but public word of mouth proved that was a mistake, and made it one of the most successful musicals of all time.

I am full of admiration for our theatre community, taking risks and mounting new work – it's a tricky business, and no one likes to see a show fail. It is difficult not only for the producers, investors and creative teams – but also for the actors who suddenly find they no longer have a job. But as ever in showbusiness, the show continues until the bitter end – with the actors giving their all until the final curtain falls. Here are half-a-dozen shows of recent years which failed to set the West End alight.

Gone with the Wind – It's a difficult task to adapt a 1,000-page novel into a stage musical – and on the back of this £4 million 2008 musical, I might advise others not to bother. In previews the show lasted four hours twenty minutes – but by press night it was reduced down to a spritely three hours forty. There were cancelled shows, audience members missing their last trains home, and people yearning to leave due to 'show fatigue'. Not even Trevor Nunn directing Darius Campbell (née Danesh) as Rhett Butler could save this production. The production at the New London Theatre had a short run of 79 long performances. Frankly, my dear, nobody gave a damn.

Imagine This – Imagine this: a show within a show telling the story of a ghetto theatre company putting on a musical about Masada, where almost one thousand Jewish zealots defied the Romans in a mass suicide around 70 AD – which ran in parallel with the violence in the ghetto. A tough watch. It lasted for a month at the New London Theatre in 2008, after one reviewer said, '*Imagine This* is a Holocaust musical that makes *Springtime for Hitler* look like *The Sound of Music*.'

I Can't Sing! *The X Factor* **Musical** – Simon Cowell's foray into musical theatre cost £6 million and closed after only six weeks in 2014, despite largely warm reviews. Written by Harry Hill and Steve Brown – and with a marvellous cast – it had the ingredients of a hit. The problem was that the show had been put straight into the Palladium, one of the biggest theatres in the West End, a challenge for any show to fill. It also suffered a confusion of target and tone – and wasn't really sure which audience it was aiming at: people who love *The X Factor*, or who hate it (or who love to hate it). The show portrayed Simon Cowell (played by Nigel Harman) as a crazy megalomaniac – which the real-life Simon found hysterical – who was revealed as an alien at the end, and took off in a UFO. The show also starred the brilliant Cynthia Erivo, before she conquered Broadway in *The Color Purple*. I suppose the musical was really a theatrical version of *Harry Hill's TV Burp* (which is not a bad thing) – and I must admit, I really enjoyed it.

Oscar Wilde – DJ Mike Read's musical about Oscar Wilde closed after just one night (press night) at the Shaw Theatre in 2004. This one performance was hindered with big sound problems – radio mics not working properly, and actors' backstage conversations being amplified to the audience. The production was labelled in one review as 'the worst musical in the world, ever', and was awarded no stars in the *Guardian*. Truly, a musical that dare not speak its name.

Stephen Ward – A musical about an osteopath, sex, spies, a '60s society scandal, and the Conservative government. Obvious subjects for a sure-fire hit! Alas not. Andrew Lloyd Webber, Don Black and Christopher Hampton's musical was based on the true story of Stephen Ward, a socialite who was instrumental in the Profumo sex scandal, which nearly toppled the Tory government in 1963. The musical opened to some good reviews in 2013, but closed after less than just four months. However, the show had a Mayfair orgy scene with a leather-masked slave and a whip-wielding dominatrix (so it had its good points, dear).

Viva Forever! – A Spice Girls jukebox musical seemed to have all the right ingredients for a bona-fide smash hit. Jennifer Saunders wrote the book, *Mamma Mia!*'s Judy Cramer was producing, and the songs were provided by Baby, Posh, Sporty, Scary and Ginger (well, their songwriters). The 2012 show satirised *The X Factor*, and told the story of an aspiring singer called Viva (yes, really) who gets swept up and lost in a TV talent show. After dismal reviews, the show had a revamp to try and make it 'lighter, brighter, and funnier'. It didn't work and closed after seven months, losing £5 million. Some audience members were disappointed that The Spice Girls weren't characters in the show.

Although it's hard to predict what will and won't be a hit, the six shows receiving their post-mortem here have convinced me not to move forward with any of the following ideas, for fear of the floppiest flop of all time on my hands:

- **Middlemarch: The Musical** – A five-hour version of this lengthy literary classic.
- **TitandNic** – The sequel to *Titanic*, looking at the shipwreck of the relationship between David Cameron and Nick Clegg (playing at the King's Head Theatre as part of their gay-drama season).

- **I Can't Do Anything!** – The *Britain's Got Talent* musical.

- **Franz!** – A musical chronicling the life and works of Kafka.

- **Theresa and Boris** – A story of love and lust in Number 10.

- **Love Machine!** – The Girls Aloud musical. Scripted by a famous comedienne, produced by Judy Cramer, with songs by the Girls (and a cameo role for Louis Walsh).

THE EPILOGUE

OR
THE BIT WHERE YOU WAKE UP AND REALISE YOU MISSED EVERYTHING

'If it be true that good wine needs no bush, 'tis true that a good book needs no epilogue. Yet to good wine they do use good bushes, and good books prove the better by the help of good epilogues.'

'A horse, a horse! My kingdom for another *War Horse*!' – overheard in the offices at the National Theatre.

Heading home from a show, you'll be reading your programme, humming the songs, planning what to see next (and how to save up for it), and may even feel the urge to try the splits when you get there. (Just don't attempt this on your own – as you may never get back up again.)

But doing the splits is just the start of your own burgeoning theatrical career – and my little epilogue now looks at some ways in which you can bring a daily dose of drama into your life.

How to Be an Amateur

Amateur theatre is a wonderful community that exists up and down the country. In church halls, Cub Scout huts, the Edinburgh Fringe, even in local playing fields – am-dram productions offer the perfect way of practising the craft of acting without the necessity of paying nine grand a term for the privilege.

Most cities, towns and villages will have at least one amateur dramatic society of their own – with the aim of putting on a show at the local theatre. Admittedly, most shows are usually musical-theatre classics like *Grease*, *Little Shop of Horrors* and *Oliver!* – but that doesn't matter – the thrill of performing on stage with eighty-four-year old Bertha from across the road is wonderful. And that's the joy of am-dram groups – it's as much about the socialising as it is about the actual show.

Amateur shows are also frequently the biggest-selling productions in local theatres. If the acting company is made up of thirty people, each one of those will bring along at least five to ten friends and family members to support them – which is why theatres love their local amateur productions. People love paying a few quid to see their friends and family look silly on stage. And just like professional theatre – they can be very competitive to become a part of.

Amateur theatre can offer excellent ways for people to work on their confidence, performing and dating skills. The circuit is very much like the professional theatre world – and is a community that welcomes all. There will, of course, be some people who have been involved from the start – these are the people that think they *are* the society. They'll be the ones who treat you with an air of suspicion when you first arrive, feigning friendship in fear that you may be better at singing than them. And this is a fact – the only time it can be problematic for new members is if they are actually really rather good. Regulars despair at the 'new blood' who quickly establish themself as a Strallen of the company – so I would suggest you begin by auditioning for smaller roles, leaving it at least a year before aiming higher and auditioning to play Annie in your little ginger wig.

However, when you get your dancing feet firmly established in your local society, there will be no looking back. Amateur companies are very important in the theatre world, and I know many former professional actors who have joined these societies upon leaving the acting business. Acting is a bug, and it's very hard just to stop doing it.

For many, amateur shows will be the first productions they will see at a theatre. Whether supporting their neighbour or going to dribble over all the locals performing in *Brigadoon* – it can be the way into a life of theatre for many.

I adore supporting local amateur shows, and indeed sometimes the standard is as good as professional productions – some will even have a paid director who will put the show together – with budgets for sets and costumes that can be higher than professional companies. A principal difference between an amateur and professional performer is that professionals can do it eight times a week for long periods of time, whereas an amateur tends not to have the capacity to get it up that frequently. But that is why professionals go to drama schools – to build and train their voice and body to withstand long and exhausting runs. That is not to take anything away from the amateurs – their energy and commitment is second to none – and indeed some amateur actors quickly take the leap to drama schools themselves to become professionals. Many of our most celebrated actors started in am-dram – so you'll be following in the footsteps of such legends as Glenda Jackson, Judi Dench, Sir Ben Kingsley and Sheridan Smith.

So, to all of you thinking about popping over to your local amateur club, I say go for it! It will be an experience that will uplift and inspire you – and as a bonus you'll get a whole new bunch of theatre-loving friends. You will perform in local theatres and arts centres – and have an exciting, important goal to strive towards. Your confidence will be challenged, and you'll find yourself wearing things on stage that people in your office can only dream of. You may even learn how to sing decently too.

Generally, you can tell how good an amateur company is by how long their name is. The more words in their name – the more respected they are on the amateur circuit. Most of them are about four or five words long, containing words like 'dramatic' and 'operatic' to make them more impressive. In fact, some societies add as many similar-sounding words as possible to make them even longer and even grander. Here's just a few I've heard of (I think I've remembered them right):

• Chichester Amateur Operatic Society (ChAOS)

- Bolton Amateur Dramatic Sapphic Society
- Bognor Regis Amateur Operatic and Dynamic Dramatic Society
- Edinburgh Amateur Acrobatic Dramatic and Biodynamic Society
- Devon Amateur Charismatic Dramatic and Alcoholic Operatic Society
- Dartford Amateur Pedantic Operatic and Overenthusiastic Dramatic Fanatic Society
- Weston-super-Mare Amateur Homeopathic Operatic Oceanographic Pornographic Dramatic Society

Because most areas have a number of amateur societies, there is always a sense of competition, with each group trying to outdo the others. This is a very serious sport – with companies fighting over the big shows, the best actors, the well-equipped venues and popular performance dates. In some of the bigger cities, am-dram groups have even formed gangs, fighting over rehearsal turf. It can be very intimidating for locals – there's nothing more frightening than gangs of amateurs shouting showtunes at each other in the middle of a public car park (but that's perfect practice for *West Side Story*, dear).

Of course, if you're not keen on actually being on stage then there are always opportunities for people behind the scenes – whether this involves making costumes, moving scenery, or cleaning the director's cravat. A number of regional theatres also rely on the goodwill of volunteers, who work front of house, tearing tickets and showing people to their seats. With theatres suffering financially, the support offered by local volunteers becomes fundamental in allowing them to continue operating. In return, these volunteers get free tickets, invites to socials, and the chance to meet lots of well-known (and not-so-well-known) actors.

For younger, aspiring actors, there are further opportunities to get involved in school productions, drama classes and youth theatres. I realise I write this at a time when the importance of arts in our education system is being questioned, and the cuts in resources always seem to hit the arts first. Which is infuriating. Children need art, drama, music and dance – simply to allow them to explore who they are, and to create and express themselves in a way that algebra doesn't allow. By educating a generation of children that doesn't have the capacity of creativity, we are blocking any chance of a fully rounded society. Art expresses what we are – it is a reflection of our humanity.

To be a truly great actor you must be able to cry on demand. Do it *now*. Whatever you're doing – stop and show the world you can act. *CRY!*

How to Voice Your Opinion

Another way to become involved in theatre is by picking up your metaphorical pen or figurative loudhailer, and voicing your opinions to the world. Whether you want to start a fan site for an actor with the best hair in the business, or just want to get your thoughts out there and review shows – there are many ways to get started. The simplest is to start your own blog, where you can upload your opinions, reviews, photos and gossip.

Tweeters and bloggers now play an important part in the theatre world. With many newspapers getting rid of resident critics, and less frequently giving space for theatre reviews, the online community provides another way for people to review, research and read about productions on both the professional and amateur stage.

The secret to running a successful site is to keep it live, fresh and up-to-date. Whether that means posting a new review every week, or uploading another photo to your 'Stalking Famous Actors' album, by regularly adding content, readers will return to see what's changed.

However, when writing reviews, do try and be as professional as possible – and don't post your reviews until the show has officially opened. You don't want to upset me – or anyone else – so don't write anything rude or offensive. Include information about the show, the venue, the date you watched it, if any understudies were on, and what you thought about the piece. It may take a little while, but before you know it, you'll find your own writing style – and your thoughts and ideas will flow freely.

One thing you should particularly avoid is including any spoilers – especially if a show is still in previews. Spoilers give away major plot points – and can ruin the whole thing for people who haven't watched it yet. Never presume that everyone knows how the story ends. Some people don't know if Godot turns up, if Lear lives happily ever after, or if everyone dies at the end of *42nd Street*.

Always remember that reviews are an individual's thoughts – there is no right or wrong (unless you're saying that *Thriller Live* is good). So don't be shy – let your voice be heard.

Actors – for Mother's Day, give her the gift she really wants: tell her you're retraining to be a doctor.

How to Be an Addict

You know you're addicted to the theatre when:

- The soundtrack to your life is a constant stream of musical-theatre showtunes.

- You spend all of your hard-earned money on theatre tickets – prioritising the musical *Rent* over your actual rent.

- You name your teddy/pet/firstborn child after your favourite musical character: 'This is my new baby. We're calling her Frank N. Furter.'

- 'Love', 'darling', and 'dear' are the most common words used in your vocabulary.

- You check *The Stage* and WhatsOnStage websites over fifty times a day.

- Your response to someone criticising your favourite musical or performer is a swift butt to the head.

- At home you have a 'theatre room' – full of programmes, posters, CD soundtracks, and stuffed actors.

- You get excited whenever a new cast is announced for a show and spend the next two hours Googling photos of the actors.

- You go to the same show more than once every two weeks.

- You refer to half-time in a football match as 'the interval'.

- You don't feel the need to apologise for any of the above. And quite right too, dear!

The Curtain Call

My dear readers.

I hope that theatre in this country continues to flourish. We are lucky to have the best theatre companies, creatives, actors, technicians and (ahem) producers in the world – and the chance to see the work produced by them should be grabbed with your fingers whenever you can afford it – and then celebrated.

But by celebrating them, we also celebrate *you* – the audiences who watch enraptured, with your fizzy pop and crisp packets opened in advance in your lap. When we gather in the rehearsal room on day one to make some magic (we hope), we do it all for you, dear audience – and it is *your* support that keeps Theatreland thriving.

So I want to say thank you. Because *you* are the audience for whom we create theatre. And without you, it simply would not exist. You are as vital as the director, the actors, the wardrobe mistress, and the ArtsEd graduates selling ice cream during the interval.

Theatre is a way of life. I've been changed by a lifetime of quick changes, scene changes, step-ball changes and 'Love Changes Everything', ever since I was a bonny boy enjoying all those lithe, young dancers in their body stockings. I hope it has this effect on you too.

In these troubled, uncertain times, when the chance to come together is even more vital, the theatre should be prescribed on the NHS. We need to come together to celebrate – to share the joy of a good belly-laugh, the catharsis of a good weep, the release of the clap – it is something our society desperately needs. And I pray you get to experience this magic, and it allows you to escape, to embrace, and most importantly – to turn off your bloody phone.

As Shakespeare almost said:

'If we darlings have offended,
Think but this, and all is mended –
That you have but slumber'd here
While this fair book did appear.
And this weak and idle theme,
No more yielding than a dream.
Gentles, do not reprehend:
If you pardon, we will mend.
And, as I am an honest schmuck,
If we have unearnèd luck
Now to 'scape the critic's tongue,
We will make amends ere long.
Else the WEP a liar call;
So, good night unto you all.
Give me jazz hands, if we be friends,
And theatre shall restore amends.'

With much love to you all,
WEP
x

They say I'm fat. I say I'm successful, dear.

Answers to the Language of Theatre Quiz (page 158)

1. 'Alright, love, we're going to put you in a special.'

   'Alright, darling, stop moaning, we're going to give you your own light.'

2. 'Bring the tabs in and go to the state in the scene before.'

   'Close the front curtains and set the lighting to how it was for the previous scene.'

3. 'Move stage right and find your light, dear.'

   'Sigh. Stop acting in the dark and walk to your right where the stage is lit, you fool.'

4. 'Walk stage left, turn on the lamp and come forward onto the apron whilst displaying your jazz hands, then we'll cross-fade to the scene stage right.'

   'Walk to the left of the stage, turn on the lamp, then walk downstage in front of the area of the main curtain whilst displaying the actors' mating call, and we'll fade the lights to the scene that's happening on the right of the stage.'

5. 'The pyro to the upstage-right corner of the stage will go live at the reprise of the opening number, when the flies will drop down a cloth. This is when you need to stand on the downstage rostra and turn on the TV, which is a practical, before following the conductor. Then watch out for the offstage cue light which will signal cue 45 when the strobe will begin and the lighting state will go to the one prior, before we go to the preset of the next scene. Mind yourself on the rake as the revolve starts, then you'll be joined by the juve who will help you quick change as the smoke machine covers you getting to the front of the pros, by which time the rest of the chorus will be standing behind you doing the splits.'

   Sorry. No idea, dear.

The Cut-Out-and-Keep Guide to Going to the Theatre

Here's a handy 'how to' guide to help you conquer the most essential tasks you will be faced with as an audience member, in case you need it for easy reference (or didn't have time to read the whole book – tut tut). Cut it out, and keep it in your wallet or down your padded bra.

How to book your ticket

Ring the box office or click on a website. Select show, choose seat, enter debit- or credit-card details, buy ticket. Also, be sure to print off your booking confirmation if you've booked your ticket online, as not doing this confuses the grumpy box-office staff.

How to avoid being late

Plan ahead, make sure it's the right day and you know the fastest journey to the Theatre, and aim to arrive at least half an hour early. Theatre waits for no man (or woman), particularly a late one.

How to get into the theatre

Present your ticket to the people standing at the entrance – the bouncers, ushers, security guards or Nica Burns. They will tear your ticket, sneer (or smile if it's lovely Nica), and grant you access inside.

How to buy a programme

Go to a merchandise kiosk in the foyer with some money, and ask for a programme. You can also buy programmes from ushers who are skulking about in the auditorium (under the seats, etc.).

How to order interval drinks

Go to the bar closest to where you will be sitting, choose your desired beverage, and pay. During the first half, your drink will be lovingly crafted by a member of bar staff and left in a designated area with your receipt underneath. The best way to avoid the interval-bar stampede.

How to turn off your phone

Locate the off button, hold it down, and wait until the phone turns completely off. Failing that, just drop it into your alcoholic beverage and it will shut down of its own accord.

How to find your seat

Look on your theatre ticket, which will have your seat number printed on it. This usually takes the form of a letter followed by a number (for example, G15 if it's a good one; YY84 if it's not). Walk down the theatre aisle until you find your row, then walk along the row to your allocated seat. If at any time you feel lost, confused or frustrated shout, 'Help! I can't find my seat!' – and a qualified usher should race to your aid.

How to stop coughing

Put something in your mouth, suck, and then swallow. Repeat as necessary, and until you and the person sitting next to you feel satisfied.

How to locate the toilets

Look for signs, ask ushers, or follow the smell of wee.

How to get to the toilets quickly

Run, shout, push, shove, rugby tackle, yell 'Fire in the second row!'

How to find your ice-cream spoon

Lift the lid, look underneath, and – hey presto! – your plastic spoon will be there waiting, ready to be licked.

How to applaud

Pull your hands apart, then push them together in a swift, consecutive motion – resulting in a slapping sound. This is known in the business as a 'clap' (or 'applause' for those on the Advanced Audience Course).

How to show your appreciation

Shout 'Bravo', 'Encore', stamp your feet, and throw flowers and lingerie onto the stage.

How to meet your favourite actor

Go to the stage door after the show and wait patiently. When your acting idol exits, kindly ask them to sign your programme and/or take a selfie, but only after you've given them at least twelve compliments about their performance.

Now you're ready, get set... SHOW!